# YOUR GUIDE TO
# *Cemetery Research*

## Sharon DeBartolo Carmack

Photographs on pages 120, 121, 123, and 124 © 2001 by Susan Rust.

Photograph on page 164 courtesy of the New England Historic Genealogical Society. All rights reserved.

Illustration on page 214 © 2001 by Johnny Titmus.

Appendix B: "Historical Time Line of Deadly Diseases, Epidemics, and Disasters in America 1516–1981," © 2001 Sharon DeBartolo Carmack and Katherine Scott Sturdevant.

Appendix C: "Historical Medical Glossary for Causes of Death," © 1988 James Byars Carter, M.D. Reprinted with permission of Dr. Carter's heirs. Originally published as "Disease and Death in the Nineteenth Century: A Genealogical Perspective," *National Genealogical Society Quarterly* 76 (December 1988): 289–301. Supplemented by Sharon DeBartolo Carmack.

Appendix D: "A Case Study Using Obituaries as Family Histories," © 2001 Katherine Scott Sturdevant, adapted from her forthcoming book, *Organizing and Preserving Your Heirloom Documents* (Cincinnati: Betterway Books, 2002).

Other fine Betterway books are available from your local bookstore or on our Web site at www.familytreemagazine.com. To subscribe to Family Tree Magazine Update, a free e-mail newsletter with helpful tips and resources for genealogists, go to http://newsletters.fwpublications.com.

07  06  05  04  03      6  5  4  3  2

**Library of Congress Cataloging-in-Publication Data**

Carmack, Sharon DeBartolo.
    Your guide to cemetery research / Sharon DeBartolo Carmack.
        p.   cm.
    Includes bibliographical references and index.
    ISBN 1-55870-589-9 (alk. paper)
        1. Cemeteries—United States. 2. United States—Genealogy—Handbooks, manuals, etc.
    I. Title.
    CS21  .C36  2002

                                                                        2002022871
                                                                        CIP

Editor: Roger D. Joslyn, CG, FASG
Production editor: Brad Crawford
Production coordinator: John Peavler
Cover designer: Wendy Dunning
Interior designer: Sandy Conopeotis Kent
Icon designer: Cindy Beckmeyer

# DEDICATION

*This book is dedicated to Jerry and Jane (Nethercott) McGraw,*
*who took me to a cemetery for the first time when I was about nine or ten*
*and who, unknowingly, sparked in me a lifelong interest in things dead.*

## About the Author
Sharon DeBartolo Carmack is a Certified Genealogist, the author of twelve books, and the editor of Betterway Genealogy Books. She is also a contributing editor for *Family Tree Magazine* and has taught personal and family memoir writing for WritersOnlineWorkshops.com. Look for Sharon's video demonstrating tombstone photographic and rubbing techniques, *Cryptic Clues in the Bone Yard*, on her Web site: <www.sharoncarmack.com>.

## Other books by Sharon DeBartolo Carmack
### GENEALOGICAL GUIDEBOOKS
*A Genealogist's Guide to Discovering Your Immigrant & Ethnic Ancestors*
*Organizing Your Family History Search*
*A Genealogist's Guide to Discovering Your Female Ancestors*
*The Genealogy Sourcebook*
*Italian-American Family History: A Guide to Researching and Writing About Your Heritage*

### FAMILY HISTORY NARRATIVES/COMPILED GENEALOGIES
*A Sense of Duty: The Life and Times of Jay Roscoe Rhoads and his wife, Mary Grace Rudolph*
*My Wild Irish Rose: The Life of Rose (Norris) (O'Connor) Fitzhugh and her mother Delia (Gordon) Norris*
*David and Charlotte Hawes (Buckner) Stuart of King George County, Virginia, Including Three Generations of Their Descendants*
*American Lives and Lines*, co-authored with Roger D. Joslyn
*The Ebetino and Vallarelli Family History: Italian Immigrants to Westchester County, New York*

### PUBLISHED ABSTRACTS
*Communities at Rest: An Inventory and Field Study of Five Eastern Colorado Cemeteries*

# Table of Contents

*There are many records associated with a person's death. This chapter explains what they are and what they will tell you and shows you how to access the records. Covered are autopsy and coroners' records, death certificates, obituaries, death notices, wills and probate, prayer and memorial cards and funeral home records, mortality schedules, and more.*

*Some of the records in chapter one should give the name of the cemetery where an ancestor was buried, but that doesn't mean it's a hop, a skip, and a jump to the actual burial ground. Inactive cemeteries, those on private property, and ones that have been "moved" are difficult to locate. And what if the records do not tell where the ancestor was buried? This chapter gives advice and suggestions for finding elusive graveyards as well as the records a cemetery generates. It also covers published cemetery transcriptions and accessing information when you can't visit the cemetery yourself.*

*Once they learn their ancestor's final resting place, many genealogists eagerly rush to find the ancestor's tombstone and forget that there are other aspects to cemetery research. In this chapter, learn how to survey the cemetery for overlooked clues (such as how knowing the composition of a tombstone can date it), the best time of year to go graveyard hopping, and the importance of noting who's buried around an ancestor.*

*Learn the best methods for recording and photographing tombstones, as well as how to make tombstone rubbings and cast replicas of your ancestors' headstones.*

*Explore overlooked aspects of a tombstone: the artwork and epitaph. Symbols and verses on headstones were not randomly chosen, and one might be able to tell whether the deceased was an adult or child, male or female, was serious or had a sense of humor, membership affiliations, and more.*

# *This is a Cemetery...*

Lives are commemorated
Deaths are recorded
Families are reunited
Memories are made tangible
and
Love is undisguised.
This is a cemetery.

Communities accord respect
Families bestow reverence
Historians seek information
and
Our heritage is thereby enriched

Testimonies of devotion, pride and warmth are carved in stone to pay
warm tribute to accomplishments and to the life—not the death—of a loved one.
The cemetery is homeland for memorials that are a sustaining source
of comfort to the living.

A cemetery is a history of a people—a perpetual record of yesterday
and a sanctuary of peace and quiet today.
A cemetery exists because every life is worth loving and remembering—always.

*—Author unknown. The Lutheran All Faiths Cemetery brochure,*
*Middle Village, New York*

# Foreword

*by Marsha Hoffman Rising, CG, CGL, FASG*

My first genealogical research experience occurred in a cemetery. In 1978, in the summer heat of central Kansas, I dragged the eldest member of the family, my mother's sister, Aunt Margaret, up and down the rows of the Highland Cemetery in Harvey County. My great-grandfather had donated the land for the cemetery, and it was filled with ancestors, in-laws, and cousins, all of whom my aunt remembered vividly.

I quickly learned that for genealogists, cemeteries are not frightening or gruesome places. In fact, we often hope ghosts or spirits will appear while we are searching. We would love to ask them some well-placed questions about those missing wives and parents. In my hundreds of cemetery research trips, I never considered the graves beneath my feet to hold decaying bodies. For me, they held people, people with personalities and pasts. They were just covered by a veil I needed to sweep away. I learned about all sorts of records connected with death that would help me recreate the character of those individuals.

It was not, however, until I read Sharon DeBartolo Carmack's *Your Guide to Cemetery Research* that I realized how many records and data I may have overlooked. I knew about death certificates and obituaries, but records created when moving bodies? I had never looked for an autopsy report or a coroner's report for any of my ancestors. I knew Aunt Abigail had died in 1918 of something called "swine flu," but it was only later I realized her death was one of millions in a disastrous pandemic.

Sharon has researched historical medical texts and many kinds of death records, and she has discovered sources for information about death and cemeteries that most people never consider. She describes the funeral practices of the past, including those of various religions and ethnic groups, and reveals customs you may have noticed in your family but not really understood. She also details the meanings of tombstone art and verse. She may even give you some ideas of your own!

This reference is full of anecdotes and abstracts of fascinating data that Sharon found during her research. You won't want to put it down unless it's to follow some of her suggestions for uncovering your *own* ancestors.

# Introduction

*The fence around a cemetery is foolish, for those inside can't come out, and those outside don't want to get in.*

—*Arthur Brisbane*

This quote isn't entirely true. There is one group of people that wants to get into cemeteries: genealogists. Some of them have been known to climb fences and scale walls in order to get in and locate an ancestor's grave.

Did you know that scientists have isolated the gene that makes certain people predisposed to an interest in genealogy and cemeteries? It's true. It's called the cemetery gene. That's the one that makes you unconsciously turn your head and slow down when you drive by a cemetery. Non-genealogists don't do that. And you don't even realize that you've begun doing it. Just one day, after you've become addicted to climbing your family tree, you start to look at cemeteries in a new light. All of a sudden, the cemetery is your favorite place to be outside of a research repository or in front of the computer. Pretty spooky, huh?

My interest in genealogy began in a cemetery. As a child, I had a fascination with the macabre. My favorite TV show was *Dark Shadows*, and my favorite novel was *The Haunting of Hill House* by Shirley Jackson. Relatives and close family friends knew of my gothic side, so one summer when we were visiting our friends Jane and Jerry McGraw in New York, they took me to an old cemetery. I was about ten, and this was the greatest adventure I had ever experienced. We were not alone in the cemetery, though. An elderly gentleman was there copying down tombstone inscriptions. He turned out to be a genealogist. The McGraws invited him back to the house for dessert—this was in the days when you could invite a stranger you had met in the cemetery back to your home—and he gave me my first lesson in genealogy, providing me with a pedigree chart and a family group sheet.

**Quotes**

Martha Brewster: *"Well, Elaine must be the happiest girl in the world."*

Mortimer Brewster: *"Happy! Just look at her leaping over those gravestones."*
——Joseph Kesselring
*Arsenic and Old Lace*

1

Today, I still have a fascination with cemeteries. Police officers have eyed me warily because I spend a lot of time hanging out in cemeteries, wearing jeans and a black T-shirt emblazoned with a bright white skull with wings. Although the police may be skeptical, what I'm wearing is actually a seventeenth-century winged death head, a popular piece of art carved on gravestones then; but I just know that one of these days, I'm going to be "hauled downtown" for questioning.

Cemeteries are the one place where you can be the closest to your ancestors, both physically and spiritually. While it is always a thrill to find your ancestors' names in historical documents, nothing can beat finding their names carved on tombstones and knowing that your ancestors' remains are just six feet below. You are likely treading on the same ground where they and their families once walked, looking at the same headstones they looked at. Here you have physical evidence that your ancestors existed. But there's much more to visiting your ancestors' grave sites than meets the eye. As you locate your ancestors' final resting places, you'll find on headstones folk history in the form of art and literature, as well as evidence of America's changing attitudes toward death. In these pages, you'll learn the meanings behind those mysterious symbols that are carved on your ancestors' headstones. You'll also discover what happened to your ancestor's body between death and burial and how your ancestor's loved ones dealt with their grief.

Quotes

To the truly dedicated genealogist, nothing can beat traipsing around an old cemetery looking for a dead ancestor's tombstone. . . . No family historians worth their salt would let a few minor inconveniences (such as knee-high clumps of thistles, or swarms of attacking bugs) deter them from copying down a crucial date or making a good rubbing off the deteriorating surface of an old marker.

—Henry Z Jones Jr., *Psychic Roots: Serendipity and Intuition in Genealogy*

Despite its title, this book covers far more than cemetery research. Some researchers may not even know when and where their ancestors died, let alone where they're buried. So this book begins with a look at American records surrounding death, followed by sources and information for cemetery research and a discussion of different burial customs. The literature on American cemeteries alone is massive; the goal here is to synthesize those sources, as well as to offer you insights and advice from my own years of researching in cemeteries. (If you are interested in cemeteries beyond the United States, there's plenty of information out there on that, too. Check libraries and the Internet for your country of interest.)

Alas, a writer's debts are many. My undying appreciation extends to the following:

- Marsha Hoffman Rising, CG, CGL, FASG, who shares my morbid fascination for things dead, for lending me some of her books on cemeteries and gravestones. Marsha also kindly read and offered comments on a draft of this manuscript, agreed to write the foreword, and contributed several items to the book.

- Roger D. Joslyn, CG, FASG, for passing along cemetery tips he found online and off, for serving as the content editor for this book, and for finding the great passage "This is a Cemetery."
- Brad Crawford, editor at F&W Publications, for also reading and commenting on the manuscript and for taking photographs for me at Spring Grove Cemetery in Cincinnati. Brad also attempted to track down the marker for William Gallager, discussed on page 43, but the cemetery office had no record of what might have happened to the headstone.
- Katherine Scott Sturdevant for adapting and granting me permission to use the obituaries case study from her forthcoming book as Appendix D, and for helping me compile the time line of diseases, epidemics, and disasters in Appendix B, which originated as a handout for the course we teach in family history research. Kathy also provided information and reviewed the section on Quaker burial customs.
- Jean F.C. (Mrs. James Byars) Carter for granting me permission to reprint her husband's nineteenth-century medical glossary.
- Betty Ring for generously providing me with a photograph of a mourning sampler.
- Johnny Titmus for sketching my headstone.
- Anita Lustenberger, CG, for acting as my personal clipping service for *The New York Times*. Anita always kindly remembers me when she finds an article or a book review on the topics that fascinate me: abortion and contraception history and cemeteries.
- Detective Thomas P. McVetty of the Nassau County Police Department for providing me with a copy of New York State's Consolidated Laws pertaining to cadavers, graves, and stealing bodies.
- Drs. Lanny Moore and Jerry Oldshue, my professors at The University of Alabama, for a valuable course I took in 1993 called Cemeteries and Local History.
- Barbara and Roger Joslyn for taking photographs of Ruth Sprague's headstone in Hoosick Falls, New York.
- Eileen Polakoff and Gary Mokotoff for information on Jewish burial practices and for reviewing that section.
- Dwight Radford for information on Latter-day Saints' burial practices and for reviewing that section.
- Kyle Betit for information on Roman Catholic burial practices and for reviewing that section.
- Dwight Radford, Kyle Betit, and Suzanne McVetty for reviewing the Irish burial customs section.
- And to all of those who generously contributed cemetery photographs, stories, and tips. I've noted their names with their contributions.

Now let's journey to your ancestors' final resting places.

# ONE

# Records of Death

*The topic of death, insofar as it has been studied by historians at all, has proven interesting mainly to cultural historians, who have been far more drawn to cemeteries, novels, letters, and works of art . . . than to the pedestrian affairs of business.*

—David Burrell, "Origins of Undertaking"

B efore you can locate an ancestor's grave, you first need to know when and where that person died. If your ancestor died since the early twentieth century, when statewide vital registration became common, you will probably find a death certificate, which will likely give you the place of burial. But if your ancestor died prior to statewide vital registration, there are other types of records you can seek to establish the date—or approximate date—your ancestor died. Following are different types of sources, discussed in alphabetical order, for death-related information. You won't find every type of record for all of your ancestors, and not all of the records will give the exact date of death or the place of burial. But each will help you get one step closer, and some records may reveal information about your ancestors that you never dreamed existed. Even if you already know where all of your ancestors were buried (boy, are you lucky!), you still might want to consider checking some of these records.

## AUTOPSY RECORDS

Modern death certificates might tell you whether an autopsy was done. You can find autopsy reports among coroner's records (see page 13) or in hospital records. If the autopsy report is in the coroner's records, you'll have a better chance of obtaining the record. Hospital records are considered private, and unless you can prove you are the next of kin, you may not be able to access the autopsy report—if it still exists. Each hospital has its own policy as to how long it keeps records.

An autopsy is usually performed when the cause of death is uncertain, questionable, or suspicious. If the medical examiner suspects foul play, then she does not need consent from the family for an autopsy. While the details of an autopsy are incredibly fascinating and will give the date and possibly the time of death, rarely, if ever, will it list the place of burial. (See figure 1-1 on page 6 for an example of an autopsy record.)

## BIBLE RECORDS

Family Bible records won't typically tell you where someone was buried, and maybe not even the place of death, but they should give the person's date of death. If you are researching a slave family, you may find slave deaths recorded in the plantation owner's family Bible. **Because family Bibles can be tricky to find, even assuming one was kept and still exists, I have listed some places and sources below to check.** Remember also as you are searching to look for allied family lines: those who married into your family. Perhaps none of your ancestors kept a Bible, but a relative who married into the family did and recorded some of your family's events in it. You'll find a sample Bible page in figure 1-2 on page 10.

Tip

1. **Ask your relatives—all of 'em.** Even though you may have already bugged Aunt Martha and cousin Joey for all the family information to the point that they try to avoid you when you call or visit, go back to them and ask specifically if there is a family Bible somewhere. A relative may be harboring this treasure in an attic without realizing it's the pot of gold at the end of the rainbow for you. Non-genealogy folks don't immediately think of the family Bible as a source of information.

2. **Place queries in genealogy magazines and on Internet sites.** After you've checked with your known relatives, look for that fifth cousin, twice removed who may have inherited the family Bible. When you place or post a query saying that you are seeking the Bible for the Mulligan family (or whatever), make sure you put enough identifying information to help others help you, such as the locality and time period, as well as some family names.

3. **Check the Internet.** In the sidebar on page 7, there are several Web sites to check for family Bibles and links to Bible records; or, merely type "family bible" into a search engine and see what you come up with. **The Bible Records Web site <www.biblerecords.com> is perhaps one of the best sites to check routinely.** It is run by Tracy St. Claire, a "Bible hunter" who purchases family Bibles on eBay and at antique stores. She not only transcribes the pages, including the title page and publication date of the Bible, but she also digitizes the family pages and makes those available on her site. "Transcription errors are a fact of the genealogy business," St. Claire says, and that's why she decided to post the actual pages. Some of the Bibles date to the seventeenth century. Tracy will also reunite family Bibles with their rightful descendants for whatever her cost was to obtain it. Since she started her Web site in March 2001, St. Claire has had

Internet Source

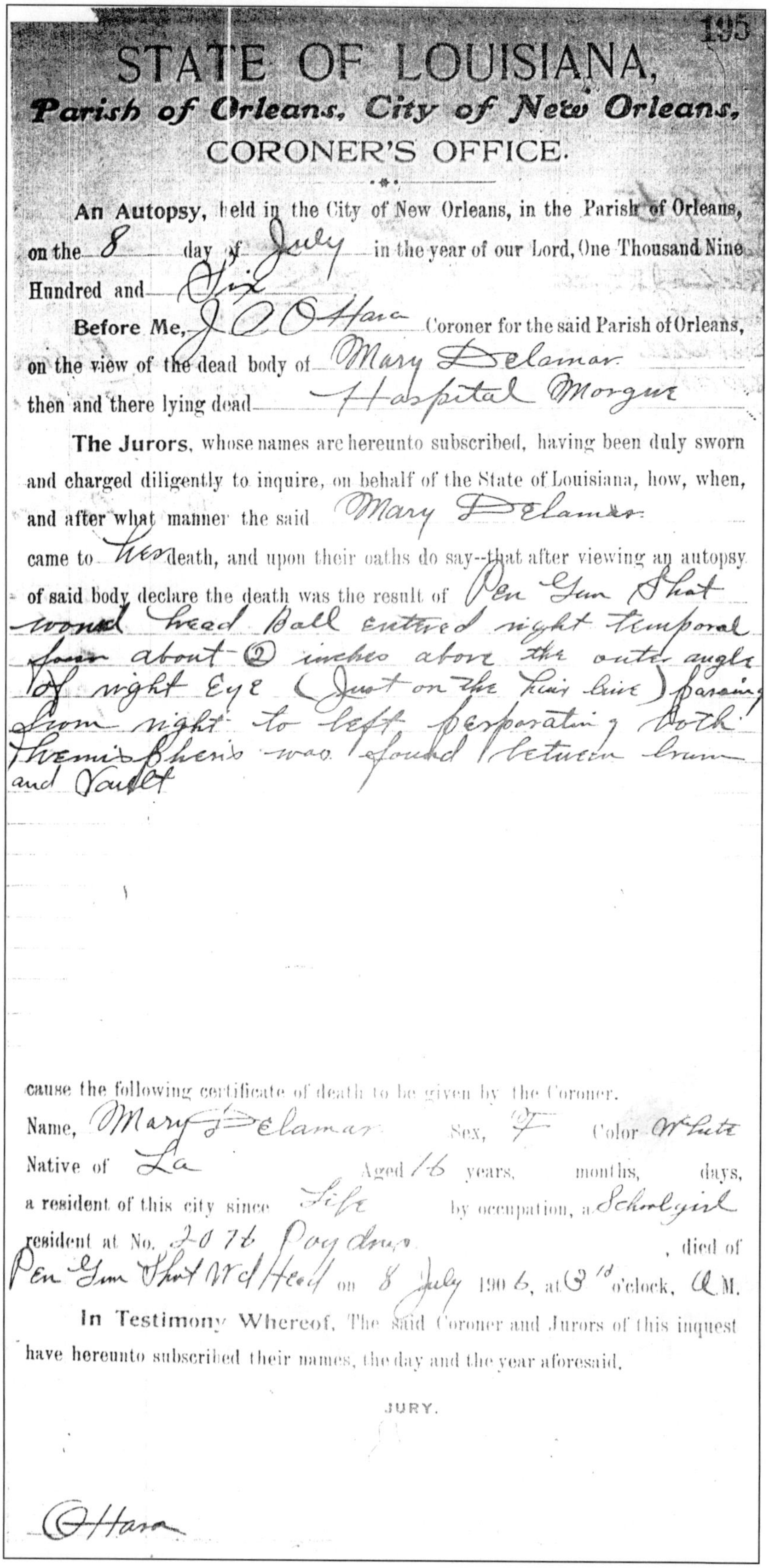
195

STATE OF LOUISIANA,
Parish of Orleans, City of New Orleans,
CORONER'S OFFICE.

An Autopsy, held in the City of New Orleans, in the Parish of Orleans, on the 8 day of July in the year of our Lord, One Thousand Nine Hundred and Six

Before Me, J. O. O'Hara Coroner for the said Parish of Orleans, on the view of the dead body of Mary Delamar then and there lying dead Hospital Morgue

The Jurors, whose names are hereunto subscribed, having been duly sworn and charged diligently to inquire, on behalf of the State of Louisiana, how, when, and after what manner the said Mary Delamar came to her death, and upon their oaths do say--that after viewing an autopsy of said body declare the death was the result of Pen Gun Shot wound head Ball entered right temporal fossa about (2) inches above the outer angle of right Eye (Just on the hair line) passing from right to left perforating both Hemispheres was found between brain and vault

cause the following certificate of death to be given by the Coroner.

Name, Mary Delamar Sex, F Color White

Native of La Aged 16 years, months, days,

a resident of this city since Life by occupation, a Schoolgirl

resident at No. 2076 Poydras , died of

Pen Gun Shot Wd Head on 8 July 1906, at 9 10 o'clock, a.M.

In Testimony Whereof, The said Coroner and Jurors of this inquest have hereunto subscribed their names, the day and the year aforesaid.

JURY.

O'Hara

Figure 1-1 Autopsy of sixteen-year-old Mary Delamar, Autopsy Records, 1904–1913, Orleans Parish, Louisiana. *FHL 906700, item 4.*

---

## FINDING FAMILY BIBLES ON THE WEB

The Bible Archives
www.geocities.com/Heartland/Fields/2403
Free database to assist you in locating family Bibles.

Bible Records Web site
www.biblerecords.com
Tracy St. Claire collects family Bibles from eBay and antique stores, then posts them on her site.

Cyndi's List—Family Bibles
www.cyndislist.com/bibles.htm
Links to more than one hundred sites relating to family Bibles.

eBay
www.ebay.com
Do a search under "family bible" to see if your long-lost family Bible is on the auction block.

Family Bible Records Registry
www.foulke.org
A registry of family Bible owners and transcriptions of Bible pages.

Genealogy: Family Bible Records
www.genealinks.com/bible.htm
Links to family Bible record sites.

---

a hit rate of nearly 25 percent in getting a lost Bible back home. And if you want to make a donation of your family's Bible to be put online, she'll accept photocopies, JPEGs, and text files.

4. **Check eBay and other online auction sites.** Although you might be bidding against St. Claire, you can expect to pay between ten and two hundred dollars for a family Bible. "I often get comments from people stating that it isn't fair for me to bid on eBay," says St. Claire, "and that I might outbid a legitimate descendant. I think it is more important for the Bible to be available to all descendants, and secondarily important for a descendant to own the original. Also, my budget doesn't permit me to pay too much for these Bibles, so I'm easily outbid." Besides, you can still buy it from St. Claire after she transcribes and digitizes the pages.

5. **Check research repositories in the locality where your ancestors lived.** Many public libraries, historical societies, state libraries and archives, and academic libraries have their catalogs online, but they may not include their manuscript holdings online, of which family Bibles would be part. Still, it's worth checking. For links to state archival and manuscript repositories go to < http://lcweb.loc.gov/coll/nucmc/other.html>. The Library of Virginia, which also cov-

ers areas outside of Virginia, has an extensive collection of family Bibles. Images for some of their collection are online as well. You can search their collection at <http://eagle.vsla.edu/bible/>. Some repositories may have a published inventory of their family Bibles, such as the Library of Virginia's *A Guide to Bible Records in the Archives Branch, Virginia State Library*, compiled by Lyndon H. Hart (Richmond: Virginia State Library, 1985).

**Library/Archive Source**

**A useful tool to find Bible records hidden in libraries and archives is the** *National Union Catalog of Manuscript Collections,* **also known as NUCMC.** NUCMC has been published annually since 1959 by the Library of Congress, which requests repositories from all over the country to report their manuscript holdings, such as family Bibles, letters, diaries, and other papers. Cataloged in NUCMC are descriptions of approximately 72,300 manuscript collections from personal, family, and corporate papers, located in more than 1,400 different repositories. You can find volumes for 1959 through 1993 in the reference sections of university and metropolitan libraries. You can search volumes from 1986 forward on the Web at <http://lcweb.loc.gov/coll/nucmc/>. *Index to Personal Names in the National Union Catalog of Manuscript Collections, 1959–1984* is a two-volume printed reference that indexes all the personal and family names appearing in the descriptions of manuscript collections that were cataloged in the annual volumes for those dates—a total of about 200,000 names. This index isn't on the Web, but when you locate a copy in a repository, it is a quick and easy way to check your family surnames.

6. **Check research repositories known for collecting Bible records.** Some research repositories, such as the library of the National Society, Daughters of the American Revolution (DAR) in Washington, DC, and the New England Historic Genealogical Society (NEHGS) in Boston, are known for their collections of Bible records. The DAR library catalog is online at <www.dar.org/library/onlinlib.html>. In a word or phrase search, type in "bible records" and away you'll go. The manuscript department of the NEHGS has been collecting family Bible records for more than 150 years. The department has put part of its records on CD-ROM (more forthcoming), and they are available for purchase at <www.newengland ancestors.org>. Also check for Bible records at the National Archives <www.nara.g ov> and in the Library of Congress catalogs <www.loc.gov>.

7. **Check the Family History Library.** The Family History Library in Salt Lake City, Utah, has many family Bible records on microfilm. Check its catalog online at <www.familysearch.org/Eng/Library/FHLC/frameset_fhlc.asp>. Do a place search, and type in the state in which your ancestors lived. Then look for the subject heading of "bible records." Narrow your search even further by typing in the county where your ancestors lived. If you're working with the Internet or CD-ROM version of the catalog, which you can purchase from the FamilySearch Web site, you can do a keyword search of the catalog for the word "bible" and browse through more than 9,200 entries.

**For More Info**

For more information on using the Family History Library, its centers, or online, consult *Your Guide to the Family History Library* by Paula Stuart Warren and James W. Warren (Cincinnati: Betterway Books, 2001).

8. **Search for military pension files.** Men and women who applied for military pensions from the Revolutionary or Civil wars had to prove births, marriages, and deaths of immediate family members in order to receive their pensions. Many times, they tore out the pertinent pages from the family Bible because

there was no way to make photocopies. If submitted, you'll find these Bible pages among military pension files. For details on obtaining these records, see James C. Neagles's *U.S. Military Records* (Salt Lake City: Ancestry, 1994). You can also obtain forms for ordering military records at the National Archives Web site <www.nara.gov>.

9. **Look in genealogical periodicals.** A good place to look for transcriptions of family Bible entries is state and national genealogical journals. Check for these in the *Periodical Source Index* (PERSI), which you can view on CD-ROM at the Family History Library, at one of its worldwide Family History Centers, or in the genealogical sections of public libraries. The PERSI CD-ROM is also available for purchase at Ancestry.com, or you can use it online at their Web site for the subscriber's fee. If you find Bible entries published in a journal, ask your genealogical librarian if the repository has the publication. If not, you can order the article on interlibrary loan from your public library or from the Allen County Public Library, which creates PERSI. Write to that library's Genealogy Department, P.O. Box 2270, Fort Wayne, IN 46802, for the current photocopying fee and for an order form. Or, download the form online by following the links at <www.acpl.lib.in.us/genealogy/persi.html>.

Of course, also check for family Bibles in antique stores and used bookstores in the locality where your ancestors lived. When and if you find a family Bible, check all of the pages. There may be prayer or funeral cards, letters, postcards, news clippings, or other notations giving you clues to death information. In the Cobb family Bible, Marsha Hoffman Rising found a postcard written to Justus Cobb by his brother, H.E. Cobb, reporting their father's death:

Irwin, Ia Jan 18-96

Dear Brother

Father Died this morning. Could not get you over the Telephone. Will be thare [*sic*] Tomorrow by one o'clock. Make arangements [*sic*] down thare [*sic*].

Your Bro
H.E. Cobb

This is the only source she has ever found documenting the death of Justus Cobb senior.

## BODIES IN TRANSIT

*Mrs. Gibbs died first—long time ago, in fact. She went out to visit her daughter Rebecca, who married an insurance man in Canton, Ohio, and died there—pneumonia—but her body was brought back here.*
—*Thornton Wilder,* Our Town

From about the mid nineteenth century forward, whenever a body was moved from one locality to another, a permit followed it and marked its progress. (See figure 1-3 on page 11.) Once the railroad connected the East and West coasts,

**Figure 1-2** Bible page, T.A. Johnson Papers, University of West Florida, John C. Pace Library. *FHL 1870508, item 1.*

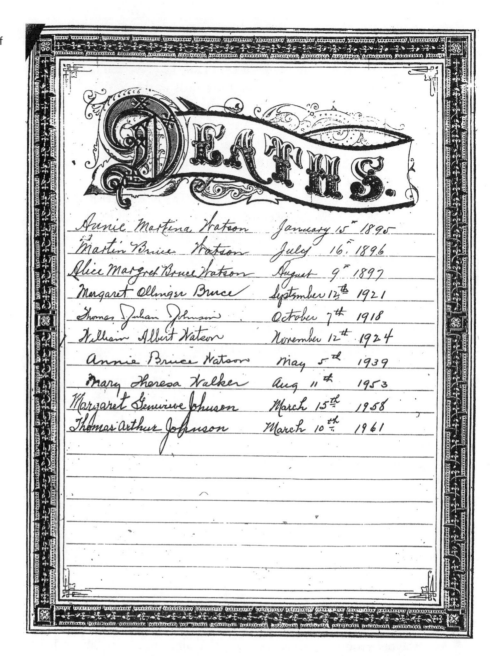

it became easier to transport bodies. So, if Uncle Harry died while he was on vacation or visiting relatives, his body could be shipped back home for burial. Likewise, relatives might have buried Grandma, then the family moved, Grandpa died, and the family wanted to bury the couple together. Grandpa might be shipped to where Grandma was buried, or the family might exhume Grandma's body and bring her to the new locale. (See chapter two, Grave Openings, for more information.) Regardless of the scenario for moving a body, all required a permit. Look for burial removals and permits at the town, city, or county level. You also might find duplicate records in funeral home records.

As a body traveled en route, you might find extant records of its journey at various stopping points. The Department of Health in New York City, for

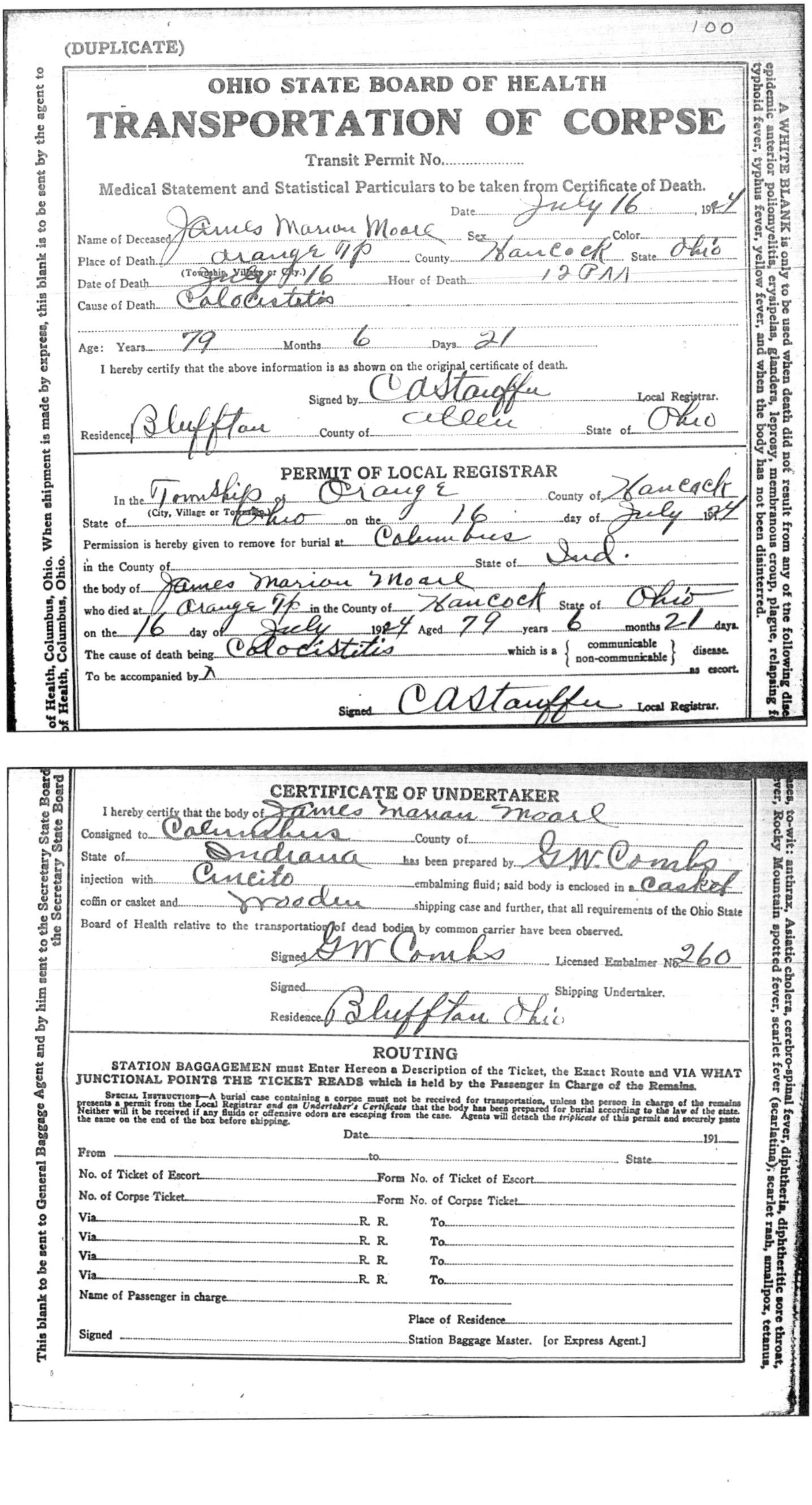
100

(DUPLICATE)

OHIO STATE BOARD OF HEALTH

TRANSPORTATION OF CORPSE

Transit Permit No....................

Medical Statement and Statistical Particulars to be taken from Certificate of Death.

Date July 16 1924

Name of Deceased James Marion Moore Sex Color

Place of Death Orange Tp County Hancock State Ohio

(Township, Village or City.)

Date of Death July 16 Hour of Death 12 PM

Cause of Death Colocistitis

Age: Years 79 Months 6 Days 21

I hereby certify that the above information is as shown on the original certificate of death.

Signed by C A Stauffer Local Registrar.

Residence Bluffton County of Allen State of Ohio

PERMIT OF LOCAL REGISTRAR

In the Township of Orange County of Hancock

(City, Village or Township)

State of Ohio on the 16 day of July 1924

Permission is hereby given to remove for burial at Columbus

in the County of State of Ind.

the body of James Marion Moore

who died at Orange Tp in the County of Hancock State of Ohio

on the 16 day of July 1924 Aged 79 years 6 months 21 days.

The cause of death being Colocistitis which is a { communicable / non-communicable } disease.

To be accompanied by ^ as escort.

Signed C A Stauffer Local Registrar.

A WHITE BLANK is only to be used when death did not result from any of the following diseases, to-wit: anthrax, Asiatic cholera, cerebro-spinal fever, diphtheria, diphtheritic sore throat, epidemic anterior poliomyelitis, erysipelas, glanders, leprosy, membranous croup, plague, relapsing fever, Rocky Mountain spotted fever, scarlet fever (scarlatina), scarlet rash, smallpox, tetanus, typhoid fever, typhus fever, yellow fever, and when the body has not been disinterred.

This blank to be sent to General Baggage Agent and by him sent to the Secretary State Board of Health, Columbus, Ohio. When shipment is made by express, this blank is to be sent by the agent to the Secretary State Board of Health, Columbus, Ohio.

CERTIFICATE OF UNDERTAKER

I hereby certify that the body of James Marian Moore

Consigned to Columbus County of

State of Indiana has been prepared by G.W. Combs

injection with Eucito embalming fluid; said body is enclosed in a Casket

coffin or casket and Wooden shipping case and further, that all requirements of the Ohio State Board of Health relative to the transportation of dead bodies by common carrier have been observed.

Signed G W Combs Licensed Embalmer No. 260

Signed Shipping Undertaker.

Residence Bluffton Ohio

ROUTING

STATION BAGGAGEMEN must Enter Hereon a Description of the Ticket, the Exact Route and VIA WHAT JUNCTIONAL POINTS THE TICKET READS which is held by the Passenger in Charge of the Remains.

SPECIAL INSTRUCTIONS—A burial case containing a corpse must not be received for transportation, unless the person in charge of the remains presents a permit from the Local Registrar and an Undertaker's Certificate that the body has been prepared for burial according to the law of the state. Neither will it be received if any fluids or offensive odors are escaping from the case. Agents will detach the triplicate of this permit and securely paste the same on the end of the box before shipping.

Date 191

From to State

No. of Ticket of Escort Form No. of Ticket of Escort

No. of Corpse Ticket Form No. of Corpse Ticket

Via R. R. To

Via R. R. To

Via R. R. To

Via R. R. To

Name of Passenger in charge

Place of Residence

Signed Station Baggage Master. [or Express Agent.]

**Figure 1-3** Transportation of Corpse, James Marion Moore, Burial removal and burial-transit permits, 1909–1991, for Orange and Union townships, Hancock Co., Ohio. *FHL 1908776, item 9.*

**Figure 1-4** Burial Permit, Christa Main, Burial removal and burial-transit permits, 1909–1991, for Orange and Union townships, Hancock Co., Ohio.
*FHL 1908776, item 9.*

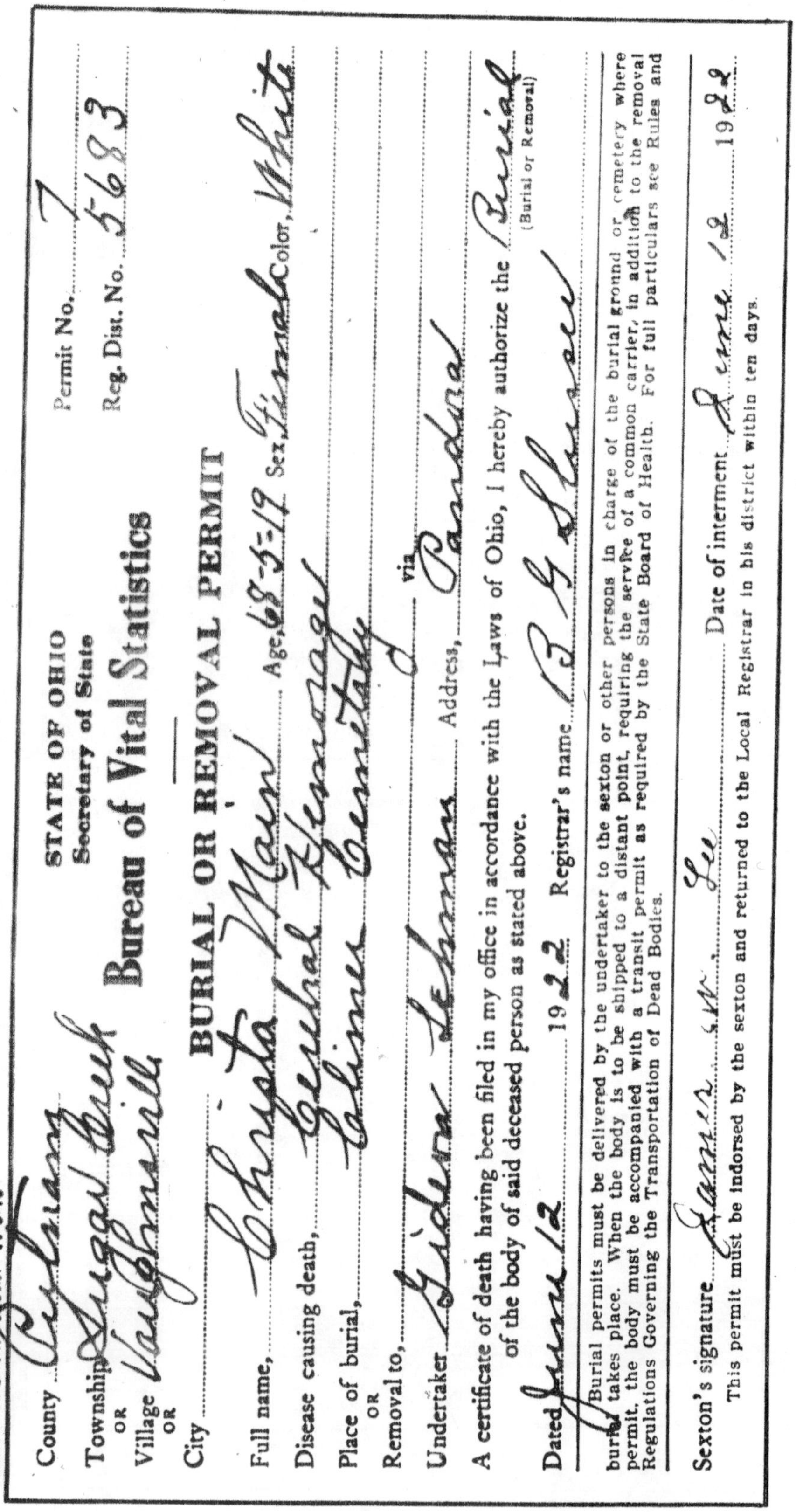

Form V. S. 14. 100M. 11-5-15

STATE OF OHIO
Secretary of State
**Bureau of Vital Statistics**

Permit No. 7
Reg. Dist. No. 5683

County Putnam
Township Sugar Creek
OR
Village Vaughnsville
OR
City

**BURIAL OR REMOVAL PERMIT**

Full name, Christa Main Age, 68-5-19 Sex, Female Color, White
Disease causing death, Cerebral Hemorrhage
Place of burial, Olimes Cemetery
OR
Removal to, via
Undertaker Gideon Lehman Address, Pandora

A certificate of death having been filed in my office in accordance with the Laws of Ohio, I hereby authorize the Burial (Burial or Removal) of the body of said deceased person as stated above.

Dated June 12 1922 Registrar's name B. G. Schwer

Burial permits must be delivered by the undertaker to the sexton or other persons in charge of the burial ground or cemetery where burial takes place. When the body is to be shipped to a distant point, requiring the service of a common carrier, in addition to the removal permit, the body must be accompanied with a transit permit as required by the State Board of Health. For full particulars see Rules and Regulations Governing the Transportation of Dead Bodies.

Sexton's signature James W. Lee Date of interment June 12 1922

This permit must be indorsed by the sexton and returned to the Local Registrar in his district within ten days.

example, kept a register of bodies in transit from 1859 to 1894 (on three rolls of microfilm, FHL 1671686, -87, and -88). No doubt their most famous body to travel through the city was that of Abraham Lincoln. The remains of the assassinated president passed through New York on 24 April 1865, from Washington, DC, to the president's final resting place in Springfield, Illinois. The register gave the following information:

Age: 56 years 2 months
Nativity: Kentucky
Place of Death: Washington, D.C.
Disease: Pistol Shot
Date of Death: April 15/65
Place of Interment: Springfield, Ill.
Name and Residence of Person having charge of the Body: P. Relyea

## BURIAL PERMITS

Just as a permit is needed to relocate or transport a body, it is also required to bury someone. Burial permits, or a certificate of disposition of remains, are required before a body can be buried or cremated. An example appears in figure 1-4 on page 12. You might find burial permits as early as the mid nineteenth century, but typically these are more common in the twentieth century. Look for these records at the town or county level. Also check for microfilmed copies in the holdings of the Family History Library, and among historical societies and local libraries.

## CITY DIRECTORIES

A city directory is an alphabetical list of inhabitants and businesses in a given locality. Some cities published directories as early as the 1700s, while others began publication in the 1800s. Information varies from city to city, but you may find a person's death date listed, or, as in the case of the Columbus, Ohio, city directory of 1889–1890, a list of all deaths in that city from 1 July 1888 to 1 July 1889 (see figure 1-5 on page 14). A clue to watch for is a man being listed, then disappearing the next year with his wife listed as ''widow'' or ''widow of _____.'' **Keep in mind, however, that just because someone disappears from a city directory does not mean that person died.** He or she could have moved or was simply missed for that year, so keep checking for several years after a person's disappearance. Look for city directories in the Family History Library (or through loan at one of its centers), at repositories in the area to which the directory pertains, and at the Library of Congress.

**Reminder**

## CORONERS' RECORDS

If you learn or suspect that an ancestor died from uncertain or unusual circumstances—accidental death (e.g., drowning, burns, exposure, drug overdose,

**Figure 1-5** Deaths in Columbus from July 1, 1888, to July 1, 1889, 1889–1890, Columbus City Directory. *FHL 1000887.*

**D. M. MOORE,** 519 NORTH HIGH
A Perfect Fit and Best Workmanship Guaranteed.

R. L. POLK & CO.'S    [ 51 ]    COLUMBUS DIRECTORY.

## DEATHS IN COLUMBUS,

FROM JULY 1, 1888, TO JULY 1, 1889.

| Name and Age. | Date of Death. |
| --- | --- |
| Adams Edw J, 26 | Aug 21, 1888 |
| Adamson Susanna, 29 | March 9, 1889 |
| Agler Lottie, 93 | May 9, 1889 |
| Akin Anna W, 36 | Oct 11, 1888 |
| Akin Harriett E, 88 | Sept 20, 1888 |
| Allen Mrs A J | Jan 18, 1889 |
| Alvord George, 66 | May 8, 1889 |
| Ambrose Sr Marg, 27 | Aug 23, 1888 |
| Anderson Olive, 54 | Oct 12, 1888 |
| Anthony Louis, 33 | Aug 4, 1888 |
| Aoi Emil, 36 | Feb 16, 1889 |
| Armen Ella, 26 | June 13, 1889 |
| Armstrong Mary E, 52 | July 10, 1888 |
| Armstrong Mary E, 52 | March 10, 1889 |
| Assmann Louisa, 24 | Feb 2, 1889 |
| Austin Mary, 35 | May 1, 1889 |
| Ayers Catherine, 29 | Aug 26, 1888 |
| Badger Alma, 36 | July 17, 1888 |
| Baker Ada, 52 | March 8, 1889 |
| Baldwin Barbara A, 28 | Dec 15, 1888 |
| Bals Christina, 39 | July 10, 1888 |
| Ball George, 71 | Feb 27, 1889 |
| Ball John J, 69 | June 6, 1889 |
| Barber Amy B, 53 | Feb 10, 1889 |
| Barber Elizabeth, 68 | April 21, 1889 |
| Barrett Alice, 23 | Oct 3, 1888 |
| Bassett Margaret, 26 | Aug 23, 1888 |
| Bauer Jacob, 61 | May 5, 1889 |
| Bauer Leonhard, 58 | May 8, 1889 |
| Bauer Valentine, 51 | Feb 24, 1889 |
| Bauman Mary S, 72 | Jan 10, 1889 |
| Bay Charles, 21 | Sept 27, 1888 |
| Beach William H, 40 | Aug 2, 1888 |
| Becker Rebecca, 79 | March 5, 1889 |
| Beeson Margareth, 68 | July 21, 1888 |
| Belknap David G, 40 | April 22, 1889 |
| Bennett Frank, 23 | Aug 3, 1888 |
| Bergman Francis, 32 | July 3, 1888 |
| Bevelhymer James N, 36 | Dec 20, 1888 |
| Bidlingmaier Mrs Fred, 38 | Apr 27, 1889 |
| Binkham Lucinda, 69 | Feb 17, 1889 |
| Blair Rose, 19 | July 29, 1888 |
| Bohlander Jacob, 33 | Dec 6, 1888 |
| Bopp Annie M, 27 | Dec 29, 1888 |
| Botts Annie, 32 | Feb 12, 1889 |
| Bowers Elizabeth, 68 | Jan 14, 1889 |
| Bowers Susan E, 37 | Aug 29, 1888 |
| Bowers Riley, 19 | May 31, 1889 |
| Boyd Margaret, 86 | July 27, 1888 |

| Name and Age. | Date of Death. |
| --- | --- |
| Bracken John, 42 | Dec 1, 1888 |
| Bragg J H, 37 | Oct 16, 1888 |
| Brame Taylor, 21 | Feb 13 1889 |
| Bramenberger Mary, 24 | Mar 10, 1889 |
| Brandenburg Willis, 23 | Sept 20, 1888 |
| Bray William, 63 | Nov 2, 1888 |
| Bright John W, 23 | Nov 12, 1888 |
| Brinkman Theodore, 58 | Oct 25, 1888 |
| Britton Clara, 27 | Oct 16, 1888 |
| Brockhoven Anna M, 79 | Jan 19, 1889 |
| Brokaw Catherine A, 30 | Mar 28, 1889 |
| Brooks Emma L, 49 | Feb 17, 1889 |
| Brown Anson, 68 | Feb 25, 1889 |
| Brown William, 40 | Aug 28, 1889 |
| Browne Julia, 23 | Oct 28, 1888 |
| Brun Louis, 27 | Nov 13, 1888 |
| Bryant John O, 45 | June 26, 1889 |
| Buckrels John, 67 | Aug 22, 1888 |
| Buehler Adie, 23 | Sept 2, 1888 |
| Buerstleise George, 55 | April 2, 1889 |
| Bunn Eliza S, 60 | May 1, 1889 |
| Burckhardt Jacob, 19 | Oct 7, 1888 |
| Burger Ira, 55 | Mar 7, 1889 |
| Burk Joseph S, 52 | July 10, 1888 |
| Burns John C, 24 | May 22, 1889 |
| Bush Mary, 59 | Dec 11, 1888 |
| Butler Edward, 50 | March 10, 1889 |
| Butler John, 80 | July 2, 1889 |
| Butler Josephine K, 41 | Nov 29, 1889 |
| Butler Margaret, 77 | Jan 4, 1889 |
| Butler Mary J, 68 | March 19, 1889 |
| Byron John W, 30 | Sept 10, 1888 |
| Byrne Arthur, 88 | Jan 1, 1889 |
| Callaghan Thomas, 83 | April 16, 1889 |
| Cameron Anna B, 20 | Nov 7, 1888 |
| Cananay John, 70 | Dec 15, 1888 |
| Caren Emma J, 22 | March 26, 1889 |
| Carlisle Charlotte, 58 | Oct 3, 1888 |
| Carter Eliza J, 51 | Sept 24, 1888 |
| Casey Cornelius, 24 | June 27, 1889 |
| Cassell William W, 21 | Jan 29, 1889 |
| Catrell William R, 65 | April 20, 1889 |
| Chapman Harriet, 83 | July 31, 1888 |
| Chittenden Helen K, 33 | March 12, 1889 |
| Chorlton Samuel C, 54 | May 1, 1889 |
| Clark Gus, 49 | March 17, 1889 |
| Clark Mary A, 44 | April 5, 1889 |
| Clark Patrick J, 50 | July 5, 1888 |
| Close John, 28 | Feb 28, 1889 |

*J. S. Ricketts & Son,* Real Estate Bought, Sold and Exchanged In Any Part of the County. 142 W. 2d Av

J. B. ROMANS, FLORIST, 31 North High Street.

mine explosion), alcoholism, suicide, murder, or criminal negligence—then look for a coroner's record. Records for Alexander Agnew, a worker in a sawmill, appear in figures 1-6 and 1-7 on pages 16 and 17. Illness was a leading cause of death for children in previous centuries, but children also were prone to accidental deaths, such as drowning and burns. **If you have a child in your family history who died young, but you don't know the cause of death, check for a coroner's report.** These records often predate vital registration and might be the only record you'll find on a particular child or person. Following is an example showing a child who died from suffocation. Included in the coroner's report was an undated and unnamed news clipping about the death.

> Scott County, Iowa, Coroner's Records, 1850-1960, FHL 1819309
> Name: Francis Lucile Engel
> Address: 1442½ W 3rd St.
> Age: 1 mo. Occupation: infant
> Date of Death: Feb. 29, [19]20
> Hour of Death 5 a.m.
> Cause of Death: Suffication [*sic*] sleeping with mother.
> Date of injury: no     Date of Inquest: no
> Hour of Inquest: no     Autopsy by: no
> Undertaker: Runge

> **Babe Suffocates Beside Parents**
> Mr. and Mrs. Ed Engel, 1442½ West Third street, Davenport, woke up Sunday morning to find their infant daughter, who was lying in bed with them, suffocated. The parents thought the child ill at first but when medical aid was summoned, it was found that she was dead.
>
> The coroner was called but decided that no inquest was necessary. Surviving are the parents and two grandparents, Nicholans Engel and Mrs. Sarah J. Patterson of Davenport. The body was taken this morning to Alexis, Ill., for interment.

Both medical examiners and coroners investigate suspicious deaths. The position of coroner, however, predates that of the medical examiner. The coroner, an elected position, was responsible for examining all dead bodies and for looking for signs of foul play. No special education was required, nor was it necessary to be a doctor. By the late nineteenth century, however, many urban areas and states began replacing the coroner with the medical examiner, who was a physician. Some states still use the elected coroner system or a combination of both.

If the coroner determined the death was from criminal negligence or murder, then he held an inquest, and in the records of the inquest you will find some meaty information. Jurors were appointed, and witnesses were called to testify. Some of these witnesses may be relatives, and typically not only their names and relationship to the deceased were recorded, but also their residences. If you're intrigued by medical facts, you'll find the postmortem findings (autopsies) especially fascinating. Also in coroners' records, you may find an inventory of the deceased's personal effects that were found on the body (see figure 1-7).

Coroners' records can provide you with some unexpected details about immigrant ancestors. From Kenneth Scott's *Coroners' Reports, New York City,*

homicide, *n.* The slaying of one human being by another. There are four kinds of homicide: felonious, excusable, justifiable, and praiseworthy, but it makes no great difference to the person slain whether he fell by one kind or another—the classification is for the advantage of lawyers.

——Ambrose Bierce
*The Devil's Dictionary*

**Figure 1-6** Inquest on Alexander Agnew, Coroners' Inquest Records, 1867–1950, Lake County, California. *FHL 1754048.*

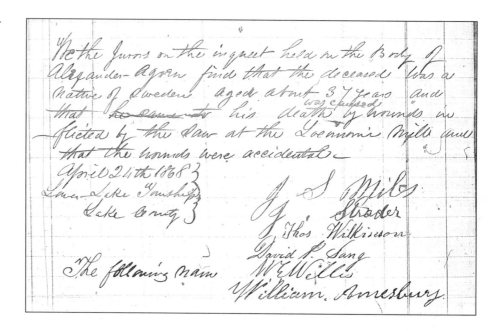

*1843–1849*, thirty-year-old Mary Hogan, who was born in Ireland, died in New York City from apoplexy in 1847. Catharine Hogan, her sister, told the coroner that they had arrived in the United States about six weeks earlier on the ship *Alexander Stewart*.

You might find coroners' records abstracted and published. For New York City, for example, Kenneth Scott abstracted the coroners' reports for 1823–1842 and 1843–1849, and these were published in two volumes by the New York Genealogical and Biographical Society in 1989 and 1991, respectively (*Coroners' Reports, New York City, 1823–1842* and *Coroners' Reports, New York City, 1843–1849*). More were abstracted in the society's journal, *New York Genealogical and Biographical Record* (see the bibliography for complete information). The original records are on microfilm at New York City's Municipal Archives, 31 Chambers Street, Manhattan, or through the Family History Library. To illustrate what types of causes of death could warrant calling in the coroner, here are a few examples from the 1843–1849 volumes. Notice that even "old age" might require a coroner's investigation if the cause of death was initially uncertain or a person died alone.

> Hyde, Dryer. Old age, b. Westchester Co., age 72 yrs. and 15 days. Edward Hyde is a son of dec'd. (25 May 1849)
>
> Husted, Thomas. Disease of heart, b. Conn., age 60, husband of Prudence Husted. (13 Dec. 1848)
>
> Mills, Francis Drake. Accidentally fell from 2nd story window, b. Mass., age between 2 and 3 yrs., son of Drake Mills. (7 June 1843)
>
> Vanderbilt, Elizabeth. Suicide by cutting throat with razor, b. Rockland Co., N.Y., age 34, wife of Cornelius Vanderbilt. Dec'd has lost a child about 9 months ago. Dr. Richard J. Dusenbury has attended the family for a full 3 years past. (14 Apr. 1845)

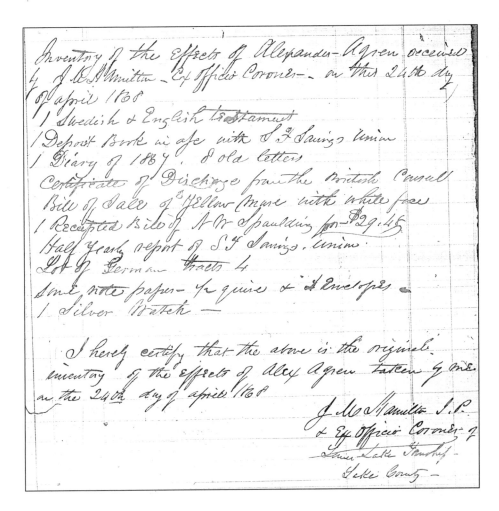

**Figure 1-7** Inventory of the Effects of Alexander Agnew, Coroner's Inquest Records, 1867–1950, Lake County, California. *FHL 1754048.*

Cavalier, Isaac (colored). Disease of liver and lungs, accelerated by inhuman treatment by his landlord, b. Philadelphia, age 39. His widow is Ann Cavalier. (27 Nov. 1842)

Gedney, Rachael. Old age, b. Mamaroneck, Westchester Co., age 107. Mary Powell is a granddaughter of dec'd. A daughter of dec'd and mother of Mary Powell is still alive, age 77. The mother of the dec'd died at 105. She had lived for a while at New Haven. (27 Nov. 1848)

Coyle, Cornelius. Criminal neglect by intoxicated parents, John and Julia Coyle, b. NYC, age between 3 and 4 mos. (18 Feb. 1843)

Coroner and medical examiner files are usually open to the public, and, if not, family history research is generally a legitimate reason to gain access to them. Some coroners' reports prior to the twentieth century have been microfilmed and are available through the Family History Library or through one of its worldwide branch centers; in fact, when you enter "coroner's records" as a keyword search in the CD-ROM version of the catalog, there are more than 230 entries.

You might also find information on obtaining coroner or medical examiner records on the Internet, although it's doubtful you'll find the actual records

## CORONER/MEDICAL EXAMINER JURISDICTIONS

### States Using State Chief Medical Examiners

| | |
|---|---|
| Connecticut | New Mexico |
| Delaware | North Carolina |
| District of Columbia | Oklahoma |
| Iowa | Oregon |
| Maine | Rhode Island |
| Maryland | Tennessee |
| Massachusetts | Utah |
| Mississippi | Vermont |
| New Hampshire | Virginia |
| New Jersey | West Virginia |

### States Using District/County Medical Examiners

Arizona
Florida
Michigan

### States Using Coroner Systems

| | |
|---|---|
| Colorado | North Dakota |
| Idaho | Ohio |
| Kansas | Pennsylvania |
| Louisiana | South Dakota |
| Nebraska | Wyoming |
| Nevada | |

### States Using Medical Examiner and Coroner Systems

| | |
|---|---|
| Alabama | Minnesota |
| Alaska | Missouri |
| Arkansas | Montana |
| California | New York |
| Georgia | South Carolina |
| Hawaii | Texas |
| Illinois | Washington |
| Indiana | Wisconsin |
| Kentucky | |

*Source: Death Investigation in the United States and Canada* (Atlanta, Ga.: U.S. Department of Health and Human Services, 1992), page 9, as adapted in Kenneth V. Iserson, *Death to Dust: What Happens to Dead Bodies*, page 139.

online. In your search engine, type the word "coroner" followed by the locality of interest. Also look under "medical examiner." The State of Connecticut Office of the Chief Medical Examiner <www.state.ct.us/ocme> claims that its database has more than 150,000 records. In the future the office hopes to have the capabilities to electronically request and transmit records, transfer fees, and even file death certificates.

First check to see if the records you need have been microfilmed by the Family History Library. If not, you will need to write for the records, visit the coroner's office yourself, or hire someone to check the records for you. You can find coroners' or medical examiners' records at one of three governmental jurisdictions: city, county, or state. (See page 18 for the jurisdictions.) Historical documents may have been transferred to a historical society or archive, which is the case with New York City coroners' records, mentioned previously.

**Follow up your research into coroners' records with newspaper research.** There might be an obituary, and if the death was unusual, such as in a case where a coroner was required, it may also appear as a feature story. If the death was from criminal negligence or murder, then not only will there be subsequent articles, but you might also find court records when the case went to trial. Be sure to check the newspaper again during the trial to see if there were additional articles.

**Research Tip**

## DEATH CERTIFICATES

Death certificates are the official documents that record people's deaths. Like most records, they weren't created and kept for genealogists who would one day want to learn about their family histories; they were created for statistical purposes and to determine the frequency and distribution of fatal diseases. Statewide death registration is fairly recent. Many states did not have mandatory reporting of deaths until the early twentieth century. Thomas J. Kemp's *International Vital Records Handbook,* current edition, tells when death and other vital registration began in each state, and it also provides forms, lists fees for obtaining records, and lists Web sites for each state's vital records office. Or, see *Where to Write for Vital Records* from the National Center for Health Statistics, available online at <www.cdc.gov/nchs/howto/w2w/w2welcom .htm>. Many states now post on the Internet ordering procedures and fees to obtain vital records; some also include indexes. Keep in mind that some states have restrictions on obtaining vital records, or you must prove that you are a descendant.

Modern death certificates are completed by several people. If a person dies in a hospital, nursing home, or other institution, then the nurse or staff member fills in the time and date of death. The doctor fills in the cause, then the funeral director or someone on the staff obtains the rest of the information from an "informant" (see page 24). The information may then be retyped onto a new, blank form, which the funeral director takes to the doctor for his or her signature. After the doctor signs the form, the funeral director takes it to the registrar to get a burial permit. A copy of the death certificate might go to the funeral home. If you are having problems obtaining a death certificate from a state vital statistics office, you might be able to get a copy from the funeral home. (See Funeral Home Records on page 27.) Another place to look for a death

## YEAR STATES BEGAN DEATH REGISTRATION

| | | | |
|---|---|---|---|
| Alabama | 1908 | Montana | 1907 |
| Alaska | 1913 | Nebraska | 1905 |
| Arizona | 1909 | Nevada | 1911 |
| Arkansas | 1914 | New Hampshire | 1905 |
| California | 1905 | New Jersey | 1848 |
| Colorado | 1907 | New Mexico | 1919 |
| Connecticut | 1897 | New York | 1880 |
| Delaware | 1881 | North Carolina | 1913 |
| District of Columbia | 1855 | North Dakota | 1908 |
| Florida | 1899 | Ohio | 1909 |
| Georgia | 1919 | Oklahoma | 1908 |
| Hawaii | 1896 | Oregon | 1903 |
| Idaho | 1911 | Pennsylvania | 1906 |
| Illinois | 1916 | Rhode Island | 1852 |
| Indiana | 1900 | South Carolina | 1915 |
| Iowa | 1880 | South Dakota | 1905 |
| Kansas | 1911 | Tennessee | 1914 |
| Kentucky | 1911 | Texas | 1903 |
| Louisiana | 1914 | Utah | 1905 |
| Maine | 1892 | Vermont | 1857 |
| Maryland | 1898 | Virginia | 1912 |
| Massachusetts | 1841 | Washington | 1907 |
| Michigan | 1867 | West Virginia | 1917 |
| Minnesota | 1900 | Wisconsin | 1907 |
| Mississippi | 1912 | Wyoming | 1909 |
| Missouri | 1910 | | |

certificate is in the deceased's estate file (see Wills, Administrations, and Probate on page 42).

The more recent the death certificate, the more information it is likely to contain, although keep in mind that errors in information do occur. Typically, modern death certificates give the following details: place of death; conditions contributing to the death; name of the deceased; personal and statistical particulars (sex; race; marital status; name of spouse; date of birth, place of birth; age in years, months, and days; occupation; parents' names and birthplaces); medical aspects of death (date of death, how long the physician attended the deceased, time of death, cause of death, duration of illness or disease, contributing factors, whether or not an autopsy was performed, signature of attending physician); name and address of the informant and sometimes the relationship to the deceased; place of burial, cremation, or removal; date of burial; name and address of undertaker or funeral home. Death certificates might also contain a Social Security number, how long the deceased resided in the United States and in that particular community, and whether the deceased was a war veteran or in the military.

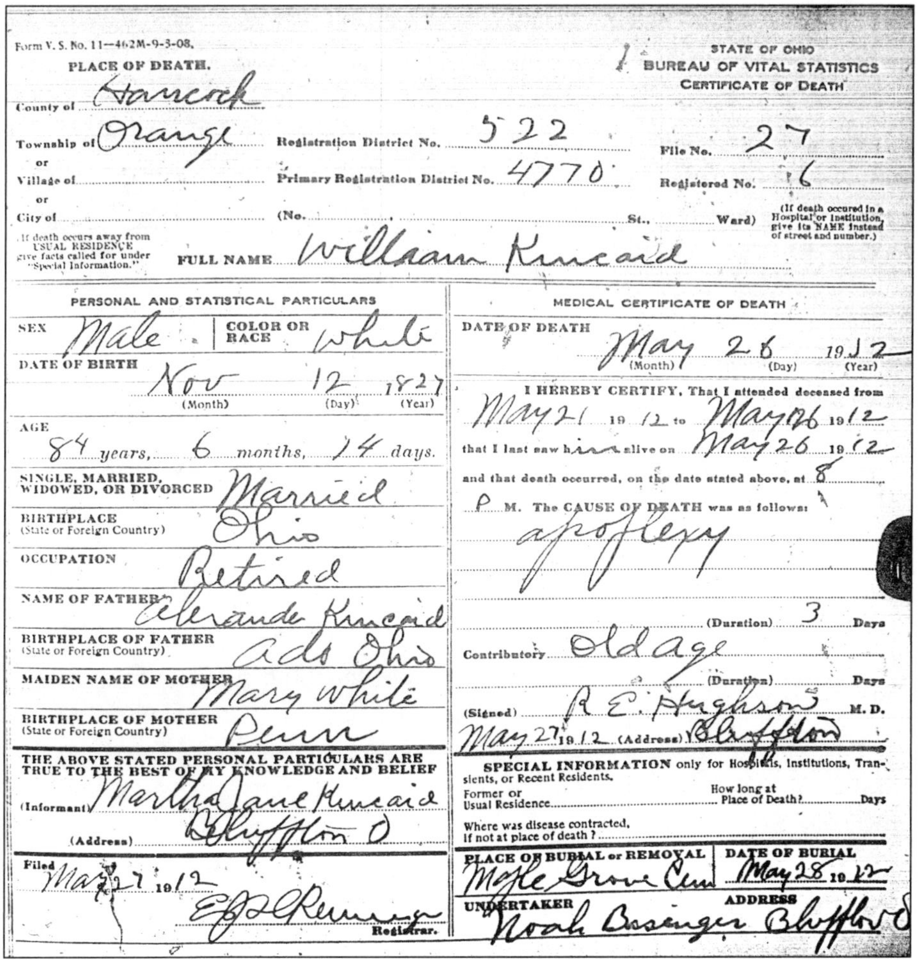

Form V. S. No. 11—462M-9-3-08.
STATE OF OHIO
BUREAU OF VITAL STATISTICS
CERTIFICATE OF DEATH
PLACE OF DEATH.
County of Hancock
Township of Orange Registration District No. 522 File No. 27
or
Village of Primary Registration District No. 4770 Registered No. 6
or
City of (No. St., Ward) (If death occured in a Hospital or Institution, give its NAME instead of street and number.)
(If death occurs away from USUAL RESIDENCE give facts called for under "Special Information.")
FULL NAME William Kincaid

PERSONAL AND STATISTICAL PARTICULARS
SEX Male COLOR OR RACE White
DATE OF BIRTH Nov 12 1827 (Month) (Day) (Year)
AGE 84 years, 6 months, 14 days.
SINGLE, MARRIED, WIDOWED, OR DIVORCED Married
BIRTHPLACE (State or Foreign Country) Ohio
OCCUPATION Retired
NAME OF FATHER Alexander Kincaid
BIRTHPLACE OF FATHER (State or Foreign Country) Ads Ohio
MAIDEN NAME OF MOTHER Mary White
BIRTHPLACE OF MOTHER (State or Foreign Country) Penn
THE ABOVE STATED PERSONAL PARTICULARS ARE TRUE TO THE BEST OF MY KNOWLEDGE AND BELIEF
(Informant) Martha Jane Kincaid
(Address) Bluffton O
Filed May 27 1912
E. F. Renninger Registrar.

MEDICAL CERTIFICATE OF DEATH
DATE OF DEATH May 26 1912 (Month) (Day) (Year)
I HEREBY CERTIFY, That I attended deceased from May 21 1912 to May 26 1912
that I last saw him alive on May 26 1912
and that death occurred, on the date stated above, at 8 P. M. The CAUSE OF DEATH was as follows:
apoplexy
(Duration) 3 Days
Contributory Old age
(Duration) Days
(Signed) R. E. Hughson M. D.
May 27 1912 (Address) Bluffton
SPECIAL INFORMATION only for Hospitals, Institutions, Transients, or Recent Residents.
Former or Usual Residence How long at Place of Death? Days
Where was disease contracted, if not at place of death?
PLACE OF BURIAL or REMOVAL Maple Grove Cem DATE OF BURIAL May 28 1912
UNDERTAKER Noah Basinger ADDRESS Bluffton O

**Figure 1-8** Death certificate of William Kincaid, Ohio Death Certificates, 1908–1912. *FHL 1908776, item 2.*

## DEATH CERTIFICATES TODAY

Unexpectedly, I have learned some lessons about the reliability of death certificates and other records by being present for six family deaths in the last ten or twelve years. When we first met, my husband, Rick, had three dear grandparents in their nineties, living in nursing homes. They died over a period of several years in the early 1990s. My parents, in their eighties, both died in hospice in 1999. Rick's mother, Carol, died at 76 in 2001, in a hospital, shortly after heart surgery. In addition to many life lessons, here is what I learned about how death certificates were compiled in these institutions.

In the grandparents' cases, it was their well-informed, grown children who supplied the genealogical information, sometimes confirmed by Rick, the family historian. In the cases of both my parents and my mother-in-law, I gave the information. I was the best equipped to do so for my parents, and very well-equipped, also emotionally, for my in-laws. Indeed, when I gave Carol's information, I was on a hospital telephone making arrangements with a crematorium representative with my father-in-law, Rick, and his sister nearby. So I could confirm each piece of information with the group. Thus I have in my mind a good model for how families may report this kind of information.

I learned less satisfying examples of how institutions and medical professionals report information. The last three deaths are the ones where I was directly involved in completing the death certificates. In all three cases, cremation was preferred. Normal practice was that the crematory representative would compile and actually prepare the death certificate, which I could then retrieve from the county health department. They correctly listed themselves as the "funeral director or person acting as such." Through conversation with family, genealogical information was correct. Through institutional records, exact times and dates of death were correct in every case. Some information could be misleading to later researchers, however. For example, my home address became my parents' residence on the certificates, even though it never was except for official purposes. A thoughtful analyst would also see, however, that the place of death was hospice.

The disturbing discoveries, for me, had to do with medical practices. On every certificate there is a place "to be completed only by certifying physician" or "physician in attendance." In all six cases, Dr. Somebody signed. In the last three cases, I know how that signature was obtained. The doctor's name would come from the hospital or hospice because the family was unsure which of the string of recent doctors was the doctor of record. Sometimes the one chosen as such, after the fact, surprised the family. Then the crematory representative literally tracked down Dr. Somebody by telephone and car, rushing in or camping out to get his signature. In all six cases, the loved one died with nurses and family, but no doctor, present at the time of death. In the five cases that were nursing home or hospice patients, the Dr. Somebody who signed had not been to see that patient in at least weeks if not months!

This, then, calls into question causes of death as well. I have learned that medical personnel really do not know, perhaps cannot know, the cause of death in an elderly person who has had many health problems. So someone lists causes or picks one. In the cases of Rick's grandparents, I could see that the same handwriting filled out the death certificate, causes of death and all, but it was not the same hand as the doctor's signature. It appeared to be the funeral director's hand. Presumably, causes of death thus copied come from medical records where doctors have written diagnoses. The causes included terms that mean starvation, while in the nursing home. Rick and I later realized this meant intravenous feeding was withheld in a manner that the family had not intended.

On one of the later death certificates, where I was more involved, I noted one cause of death only, and a span of years identified as "interval between onset and death." The cause and interval match the illegible signature of the doctor, who had not seen the patient in months. True, the one cause listed was surely one of the causes of death in a long-term sense, but there were several others, and the interval was wrong.

My advice is to question every piece of information on death certificates. I would not assume, as some genealogists do, that old, second-hand information from family is less reliable than contemporary information from modern institutions. I also face each death certificate, obituary, or other remnant of someone's passing with a new respect and sensitivity, knowing what the processes are like in our supposedly modern, advanced society.

—Katherine Scott Sturdevant

## Analyzing Information on Death Certificates

While death certificates are what genealogists call a primary source—that is, a record created at the time of the event—the information on the certificate contains both firsthand and secondhand knowledge. The firsthand knowledge is the information the physician or an attendant provided on the cause of death, date of death, and contributing factors. Understand, however, that even this information can be in error. According to Kenneth V. Iserson, M.D., in *Death to Dust: What Happens to Dead Bodies?* (page 21), the cause of death and the deceased's age have a 29 percent error rate, with death certificates of minorities having the most mistakes. He also says that about the same percent incorrectly report whether or not an autopsy was performed. Likewise, the cause of death can be obscured or covered up on a death certificate to protect a person's reputation and privacy; for example, instead of "suicide" you might find the cause of death as "accidental," or instead of "abortion" you might find "uterine bleeding" or "hemorrhaging."

**For More Info**

For more information on nineteenth-century causes of death, see William B. Saxbe Jr.'s "Nineteenth-Century Death Records: How Dependable Are They?" and Dr. Saxbe's lectures, "Read Between the Lines: Interpreting Modern Death Records" (NGS 00-W-41) and "What Killed Aunt Rhody? Interpreting Old Death Records" (NGS 00-W-30), available for purchase at <www.audiotapes.com>.

**Given nineteenth-century medical knowledge, the cause of death could be totally erroneous based on what we know today about diseases.** Diagnoses were not supported by any kinds of tests, such as X rays, blood tests, or microscopic examinations of tissues. They were based on signs and symptoms only, and many diseases have similar symptoms. It's difficult, if not impossible, to determine a modern equivalent to a nineteenth-century cause of death. While Appendix C gives definitions of common causes of death, keep in mind that the diagnosis on a death certificate, or any source that records the cause of death for that matter, might not be correct. On the 1870 mortality schedule (see page 34 for mortality schedules) of Boscawen, Merrimack County, New Hampshire, for example, fifty-two-year-old Geroge W. Blood's cause of death was "masturbation." Now as everyone knows, you can go blind from that, but you can't die from it.

Even today, unless an autopsy is performed, the cause of death is usually based on the patient's medical history, clinical signs, and tests done before the patient died. Because we have sophisticated medical testing prior to death, such as CAT scans and MRIs, physicians are usually confident in their diagnoses.

The informant on the death certificate is the person who provided second-hand information about the deceased, such as date and place of birth, and parents' names and birthplaces. Your research will reveal the relationship of the informant to the deceased, if the death certificate does not give that information. The informant related details about the deceased from what other family members or the deceased told him or her, so you cannot be certain of its accuracy without confirming the information in other records. Also keep in mind that the informant may not be thinking clearly due to grief; informants have been known to accidentally give their own mother's maiden names, for example, instead of the deceased's. On the other hand, if the informant happened to be the family genealogist, this information could be more reliable than anything else on the record.

## DEATH REGISTERS

**Important**

**Some towns, cities, and counties kept death registers, which might predate statewide registration or were the basis for reporting to the state.** Prior to statewide registration, reporting a death might not have been mandatory, so you could find some of your ancestors recorded and not others. Some of these registers may be quite detailed, giving the name of the deceased, date of death, cause of death, marital status, age, occupation, parents' names, and birthplace; others may simply give the name of the deceased and the date of death. Others might also be accompanied by a permit for burial or removal.

Virginia, for example, began statewide vital registration of deaths in 1912, but you can find county death registers from as early as 1853, some of which also include slave deaths. The state commissioner of revenue registered deaths for each county, and then turned over the books to the clerk of each county court. The clerk then made copies for his office and for the state auditor. The information between the state and county books varies, and the county copy

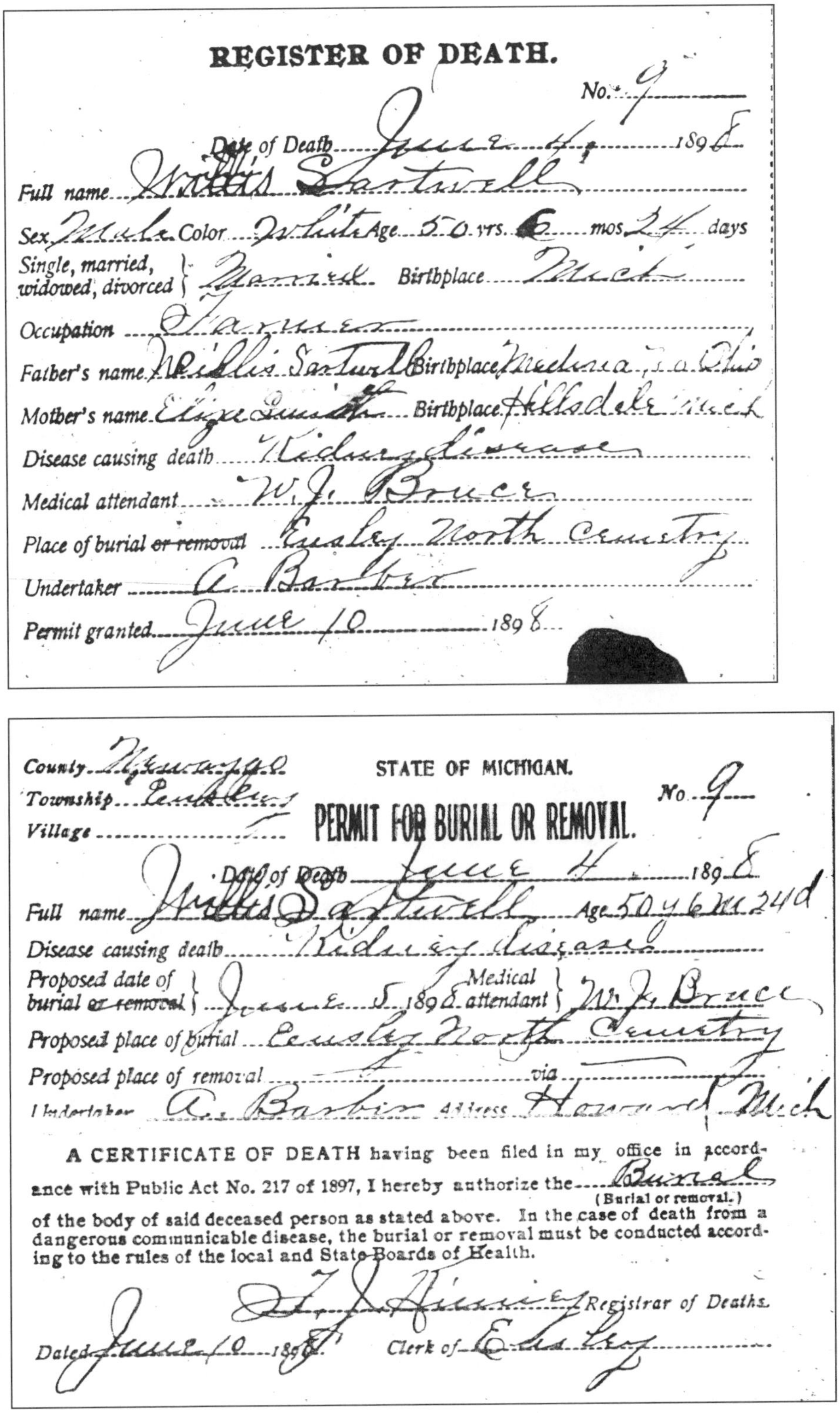

REGISTER OF DEATH.

No. 9

Date of Death June 4 1898

Full name Willis Sartwell

Sex Male Color White Age 50 yrs. 6 mos. 24 days

Single, married, widowed, divorced Married Birthplace Mich

Occupation Farmer

Father's name Willis Sartwell Birthplace Medina Co Ohio

Mother's name Eliza Smith Birthplace Hillsdale Mich

Disease causing death Kidney disease

Medical attendant W. J. Bruce

Place of burial ~~or removal~~ Ensley North Cemetery

Undertaker A. Barber

Permit granted June 10 1898

County Newaygo

STATE OF MICHIGAN.

Township Ensley

Village —

No. 9

PERMIT FOR BURIAL OR REMOVAL.

Date of Death June 4 1898

Full name Willis Sartwell Age 50 y 6 m 24 d

Disease causing death Kidney disease

Proposed date of burial ~~or removal~~ June 5 1898 Medical attendant W. J. Bruce

Proposed place of burial Ensley North Cemetery

Proposed place of removal — via —

Undertaker A. Barber Address Howard City Mich

A CERTIFICATE OF DEATH having been filed in my office in accordance with Public Act No. 217 of 1897, I hereby authorize the Burial (Burial or removal.) of the body of said deceased person as stated above. In the case of death from a dangerous communicable disease, the burial or removal must be conducted according to the rules of the local and State Boards of Health.

F. J. Hinnie Registrar of Deaths.

Dated June 10 1898 Clerk of Ensley

**Figure 1-9** Register of Death and Permit for Burial or Removal for Willis Sartwell, Ensley Township, Newaygo County, Michigan, 1897–1949. *FHL 1321916, item 2.*

may contain transcription errors. The Virginia registers—depending on which copy you are looking at—give the name of the deceased, race, name of owner of slave, sex, place of death, parents' or spouse's names, birthplace, occupation,

\di'fin\ *vb*

**Definitions**

Watch for the terms "entombed" and "interred" in records. Entombment means burial in an above-ground vault, while interment is typically burial underground.

last place of residence, cause of death, and the attending physician, if any; however, sometimes the information is incomplete, and not all deaths were reported. Those that were might have been reported several months after the death, and there is no way to identify the informant. Both the state and county copies are on microfilm at the Family History Library or through its branches.

## DEATHS AT SEA

Deaths, along with births and marriages, occurring during a voyage should be recorded on the passenger list, sometimes on the last page of the entire list for that passage. Only cryptic notations might appear next to the original entry of the passenger, so be sure to always check the last page. (For information on how to find and use passenger arrival lists, see *A Genealogist's Guide to Discovering Your Immigrant and Ethnic Ancestors*, [Cincinnati: Betterway Books, 2001] chapter six.) On the ship *Utopia*, for example, which left Naples and arrived at New York City on 23 April 1883 (National Archives microfilm M237, roll 464), Sav. Rubetro appeared as a forty-eight-year-old laborer. A notation on the same page for Rubetro's entry recorded his death aboard the *Utopia* on 21 April 1883 of pneumonia. (For burials at sea, see page 159.) The death might then be recorded either at the port of arrival or at the family members' final destination, so check both places.

## FUNERAL, MEMORIAL, AND PRAYER CARDS

Memorial and funeral cards became popular in the 1880s. Like today, the cards were printed with the vital statistics of the deceased and a verse; sometimes a photograph of the deceased was included. They were mass produced, however, until the 1920s. (See figure 1-10 on page 27). According to Jay Ruby in *Secure the Shadow: Death and Photography in America* (page 131), the companies that manufactured and printed these cards all had the same procedure. H.F. Wendell and Company, for instance,

> would pay a penny an obituary to women from all over the United States who would collect the notices from the local newspapers and mail them to him. The women were recruited with small ads in dozens of small-town newspapers. Based on the information obtained from the obituary, a card would be printed on speculation and sent with a catalog and other promotional material.

If a photograph of the deceased accompanied the obituary, the photo would be included; if not, people might modify the cards themselves to add a photograph.

Funeral cards have evolved over time and are now typically issued by the funeral home or church. **Look for these little cards tucked inside Bibles or among family papers.** On one side of the card, there might be an illustration of a saint or other religious emblem. On the other side, you'll find a prayer or Bible verse, along with the name of the deceased and vital statistics, usually birth and death

**Hidden Treasures**

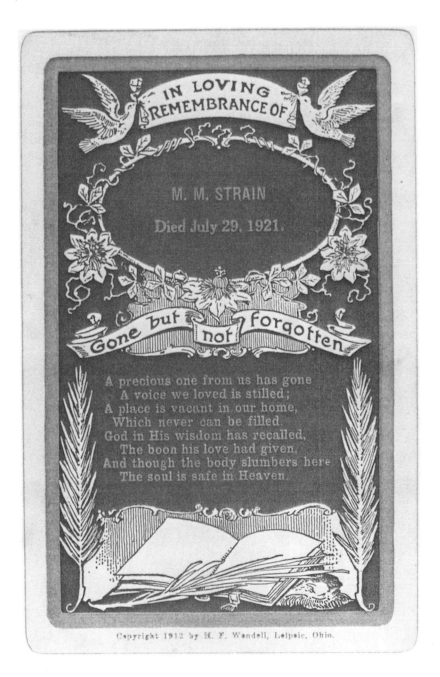

information. Some cards are "memorial obituaries," where the obituary is clipped from the newspaper and encased in plastic.

## FUNERAL HOME RECORDS

While most funeral homes have no problem accommodating genealogists in their requests for ancestors' records, keep in mind that funeral home records are private records, and the funeral home is within its rights to restrict or deny access. Because funeral home records are private, the content varies from one funeral home to another and from one time period to another. (See figures 1-11

**Figure 1-11** Record of Funeral for Sarah Ann Daniels, Flamm Funeral Home, Rexburg, Madison Co., Idaho.
*FHL 1531432, item 2.*

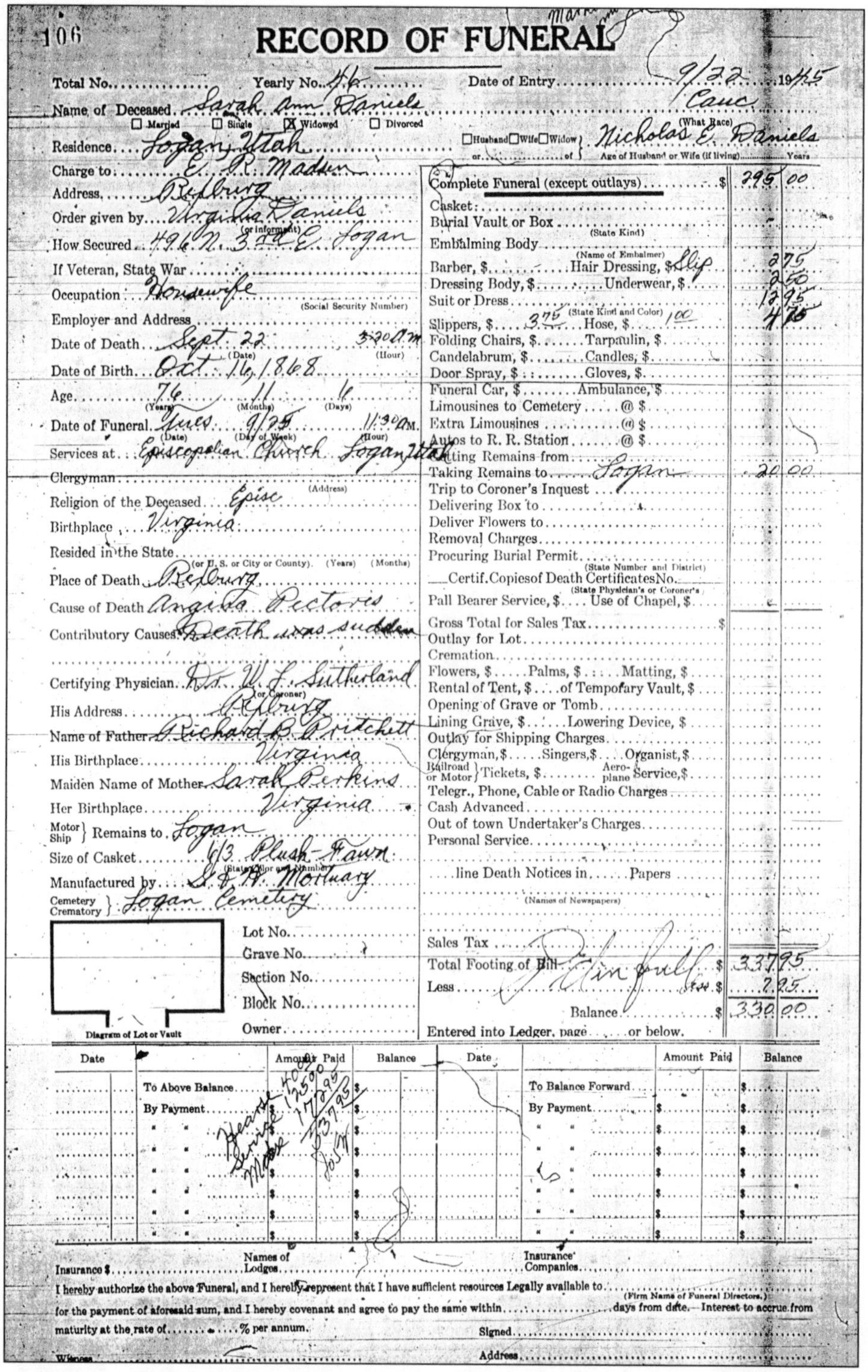
106 RECORD OF FUNERAL

Total No.............. Yearly No. 46 .......... Date of Entry 9/22 1945

Name of Deceased Sarah Ann Daniels (What Race) Cauc

☐ Married ☐ Single ☒ Widowed ☐ Divorced

Residence Logan, Utah ☐Husband☐Wife☐Widow of Nicholas E. Daniels (Age of Husband or Wife (if living)) Years

Charge to E. R. Madsen

Address Rexburg

Order given by Virginia Daniels (or informant)

How Secured 496 N. 3rd E. Logan

If Veteran, State War

Occupation Housewife

Employer and Address (Social Security Number)

Date of Death Sept 22 (Date) 3:20 A.M. (Hour)

Date of Birth Oct. 16, 1868

Age 76 (Years) 11 (Months) 6 (Days)

Date of Funeral Tues 9/25 (Date) (Day of Week) 11:30 A.M. (Hour)

Services at Episcopalian Church Logan Utah

Clergyman (Address)

Religion of the Deceased Episc

Birthplace Virginia

Resided in the State (or U.S. or City or County) (Years) (Months)

Place of Death Rexburg

Cause of Death Angina Pectoris

Contributory Causes Death was sudden

Certifying Physician Dr. W. L. Sutherland (or Coroner)

His Address Rexburg

Name of Father Richard B. Pritchett

His Birthplace Virginia

Maiden Name of Mother Sarah Perkins

Her Birthplace Virginia

Motor/Ship Remains to Logan

Size of Casket 6/3 Plush-Fawn (State Color and Number)

Manufactured by S & H Mortuary

Cemetery/Crematory Logan Cemetery

Lot No. / Grave No. / Section No. / Block No. / Owner

Diagram of Lot or Vault

Complete Funeral (except outlays) $ 295 00

Casket

Burial Vault or Box (State Kind)

Embalming Body (Name of Embalmer)

Barber, $ Hair Dressing, $ Slip 2 75

Dressing Body, $ Underwear, $ 2 50

Suit or Dress (State Kind and Color) 12 95

Slippers, $ 3.75 Hose, $ 1.00 4 75

Folding Chairs, $ Tarpaulin, $

Candelabrum, $ Candles, $

Door Spray, $ Gloves, $

Funeral Car, $ Ambulance, $

Limousines to Cemetery @ $

Extra Limousines @ $

Autos to R. R. Station @ $

Getting Remains from

Taking Remains to Logan 20 00

Trip to Coroner's Inquest

Delivering Box to

Deliver Flowers to

Removal Charges

Procuring Burial Permit (State Number and District)

Certif. Copies of Death Certificates No. (State Physician's or Coroner's)

Pall Bearer Service, $ Use of Chapel, $

Gross Total for Sales Tax $

Outlay for Lot

Cremation

Flowers, $ Palms, $ Matting, $

Rental of Tent, $ of Temporary Vault, $

Opening of Grave or Tomb

Lining Grave, $ Lowering Device, $

Outlay for Shipping Charges

Clergyman, $ Singers, $ Organist, $

Railroad or Motor Tickets, $ Aero-plane Service, $

Telegr., Phone, Cable or Radio Charges

Cash Advanced

Out of town Undertaker's Charges

Personal Service

line Death Notices in Papers (Names of Newspapers)

Sales Tax

Total Footing of Bill $ 337 95

Less $ 7 95

Balance $ 330 00

Entered into Ledger, page or below.

| Date | | Amount Paid | Balance | Date | | Amount Paid | Balance |
|---|---|---|---|---|---|---|---|
| | To Above Balance | | $ | | To Balance Forward | | $ |
| | By Payment | | | | By Payment | $ | $ |

Insurance $ Names of Lodges Insurance Companies

I hereby authorize the above Funeral, and I hereby represent that I have sufficient resources Legally available to (Firm Name of Funeral Directors) for the payment of aforesaid sum, and I hereby covenant and agree to pay the same within days from date. Interest to accrue from maturity at the rate of % per annum.

Signed

Witness Address

and 1-12 on pages 28 and 29.) Some records are greatly detailed, giving not only similar information to what you'll find on a death certificate, but also names of all immediate family members, and the costs of the funeral, right down to the slippers the deceased wore when buried.

According to the National Funeral Directors Association, there are more than 22,100 funeral homes in America today, and 85 percent are family owned.

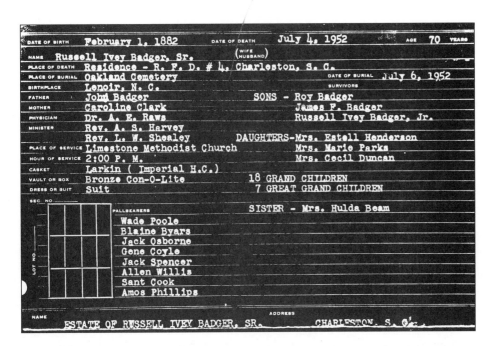

**Figure 1-12** Funeral Record for Russell Ivey Badger Sr., Shuford Hatcher Funeral Home, Gaffney, Cherokee Co., South Carolina.
*FHL Microfiche 6019354, #2.*

**Sources**

**Three guides will help you locate funeral homes:** *American Blue Book of Funeral Directors* (published every even-numbered year), *The National Yellow Book of Funeral Directors* (published annually), and *The Red Book* (National Directory of Morticians, published annually). One of these directories should be available in your public library's reference section; if not, your local funeral home should have a directory. Or, go online to <www.funeralnet.com> and type in the locality where your ancestors died to find a funeral home in the area. This database is compiled from *The National Yellow Book of Funeral Directors*. (For other online funeral home records, see chapter two, Virtual Cemeteries, Obituaries, and Funeral Homes, on page 75.)

If the records you seek are for a funeral home that no longer exists, check for the records at active funeral homes, the local or state historical society, the local public library, or on microfilm or abstracted at the Family History Library.

If your ancestor or relative was an undertaker, look for his advertisements in city directories and newspapers. Before 1882, there was no national organization for funeral directors, and only a few state organizations had been founded, such as the Michigan Funeral Directors Association in 1880 and the Pennsylvania Funeral Directors Association and Wisconsin Funeral Directors Association, both in 1881. (For links and addresses of state funeral directors associations, go online to <http://nfda.org/membership/assoc.html>.) After 1882, there are a few national organizations you can try for information:

National Funeral Directors Association, founded in 1882
13625 Bishop's Dr., Brookfield, WI 53005
Toll-free: (800) 228-6332, Phone: (262) 789-1880, Fax: (262) 789-6977
E-mail: nfda@nfda.org, Web site: www.nfda.org
Cremation Association of North America, founded in 1913
401 N. Michigan Ave., Chicago, IL 60611
Phone: (312) 644-6610, Fax: (312) 321-4098

E-mail: CANA@sba.com, Web site: www.cremationassociation.org
Jewish Funeral Directors of America, organized in 1932
   Seaport Landing, 150 Lynnway, Suite 506, Lynn, MA 01902
   Phone: (781) 477-9300, Fax: (781) 477-9393
   E-mail: info@jfda.org, Web site: www.jfda.org

Another source to check for undertakers is the surviving manufacturing or industry schedules of the 1810, 1820, 1850, 1860, 1870, and 1880 censuses. As you'll learn in chapter six, most early-day undertakers were cabinetmakers or were involved in other skilled trades besides undertaking. They made coffins themselves until caskets began to be mass-produced in factories. Charles Williams of Fredericksburg, Spotsylvania County, Virginia, was recorded on the 1860 manufacturing schedule (transcribed at <http://departments.mwc.edu/hipr/www/fbg60man.htm>). His occupation was cabinetmaker and undertaker, with $4,000 of capital invested. He worked mostly with white pine, but also used yellow pine and eight to nine other different types of woods. He made cabinets and coffins by hand.

Some of these schedules are available through the Family History Library, but most are held at the National Archives or its branches. For more information on accessing manufacturing and industry schedules, see Kathleen W. Hinckley's *Your Guide to the Federal Census* (Cincinnati: Betterway Books, 2002).

## INSTITUTIONAL RECORDS
### Hospitals, Asylums, Sanatoriums, Almshouses, Prisons

If your ancestor died as an inmate of a hospital, asylum, sanatorium (such as a tuberculin sanatorium), almshouse (poorhouse), or prison, then the death would have been recorded in that institution's registers. (See figure 1-13 on page 31.) These registers, which may predate statewide vital registration, might be in a separate book of deaths, or the deaths could be mixed in with the main register book. Likewise, the information will vary from institution to institution and from one time period to the next. Early registers might only give you a name and the date of death. Later registers likely will contain more details. The records of Charity Hospital in New Orleans, Louisiana, for example, give the name of the deceased, date of admission, nativity, occupation, last residence, age, race, marital status, date of death, malady, and by whom buried (medical college, friends, spouse, etc.). This information was given as early as 1850.

It can be tricky to find these registers. The Family History Library has a good collection of institutional records. Check the catalog for both the state, county, and city where the institution was located. Or, try a keyword search by typing in "hospital" or "hospital death," "prison" or "prison death," and so forth, then browse what's available. Also look for published record abstracts. If you have ancestors in Georgia, for example, check out *The Georgia Black Book: Morbid, Macabre, and Sometimes Disgusting Records of Genealogical Value*, and volume two: *The Georgia Black Book: More Morbid, Macabre, and Sometimes Disgusting Records of Genealogical Value, Just When You Thought It*

**DEATH**

Name: *Snyder, Joseph*

Address:

Male ✓    Age *66*    Married ✓

Female    Race *W*    Single

Natural

Suicide ✓ *By drowning in a bucket of water*

Execution

Not Known ✓

Time and date of death: *September 8-1869*

Where death took place: *Cell 78 South Corridor*

Date Admitted: *Sept 4 1869*    Committed By:

Charge: *Murder*    Disposition:

Sentence:

Cause of death: *Suicide – By drowning in a bucket of water*

Doctor:

Turned over to Coroner:

Turned over to Anatomical Board:

If known where buried:

Buried by: *Family*

Remarks:

*MRe*
Guard

RS-22  5 6-42  500

**Figure 1-13** Death record for Joseph Snyder, Philadelphia Jail and Penitentiary Death Register, 1819–1914. *FHL 975749.*

*Was Safe to Get Back Into Genealogy*), by Robert Scott Davis Jr., Louise Moxley, and Colleen Elliott (Easley, S.C.: Southern Historical Press, 1982, 1987). Here, you'll find references to murders, murder victims, murderers, insane asylum inmates, thieves, and other misfits of society.

To learn if an institution and its records still exist—perhaps under a different name—write to the town, city, county, or state historical society. Ask if a particular institution is still in operation, what the current name and location are, and where the records might be housed for the time period you're interested in.

**Remember, access to the more recent records may be restricted because of privacy laws.** Medical records of any kind are almost always impossible to get unless they are yours or you can prove you are the next of kin to the deceased person whose records you are seeking.

**Reminder**

## MONUMENT MAKERS' RECORDS

People have long marked the final resting places of loved ones with some kind of marker, even if only a stack of stones. Horizontal flat tombstones and vertical

**Quotes**

When I first came to Spoon River
I did not know whether what they told me
Was true or false.
They would bring me the epitaph
And stand around the shop while I worked
And say "He was so kind," "He was wonderful,"
"She was the sweetest woman," "He was a consistent Christian."
And I chiseled for them whatever they wished,
All in ignorance of its truth.
But later, as I lived among the people here,
I knew how near to the life
Were the epitaphs that were ordered for them as they died.
But still I chiseled whatever they paid me to chisel
And made myself party to the false chronicles
Of the stones,
Even as the historian does who writes
Without knowing the truth,
Or because he is influenced to hide it.

—Richard Bone in Edgar Lee Masters' *Spoon River Anthology*

**Notes**

The excerpt from John Custis's will was quoted in "The Funerary Monuments and Burial Patterns of Colonial Tidewater Virginia, 1607–1776," by Elizabeth A. Crowell and Norman Vardney Mackie III, *Markers* 7 (1990): 103–138, at 112–113.

headstones abound in cemeteries, some elaborately carved, others simply with the name of the deceased. There were probably few full-time stone carvers in early America. Most people who made gravestones did so as a sideline to their main trade, such as masonry, woodcarving, cabinetry, and so on. In colonial New England, there were plenty of stone quarries, so headstones did not have to be imported. Local carvers kept few headstones in stock, however; most were carved on an as-needed basis. In colonial Tidewater Virginia, where there were no stone quarries, headstones were imported from England. Several months to a few years could pass from the time between death and the placement of a marker, regardless of whether it was carved locally or imported. In fact, a marker may not even be purchased until many months or years after the death when the family could afford it.

Finding evidence of ordering and carving headstones may be difficult for the colonial period, but you may find notations in wills, inventories, and settlements of the deceased's estate. John Custis of Virginia stipulated in his 1749 will that his executor should

lay out and expend as soon as possible after my decease out of my estate the sum of one hundred pounds sterling, money of Great Britain to buy a handsome tombstone of the most durable stone that can be purchased for pillars very decent and handsome to lay over my dead body . . . and if by any accident the tombstone and appurtenances should be lost broke or any waies miscarry in coming in from England or any other ways whatsoever in that case my positive will is and I earnestly require it that my heir or executors immediately send to England for such another stone exactly with the same appurtenances of the same price until one shall come safe to hand according to my will. . . .

Stone carvers sometimes identified their work by carving their initials or name into the base of the stone, usually on the back. Frequently you will find that the stone has sunk so you can no longer read it. If the stone is sturdily in the ground, you can safely dig the dirt away for a few inches to see if there are carver's initials or a name. But please firmly replace the dirt. (It's best to check with the cemetery sexton before you start digging, of course. You wouldn't want to be falsely arrested for grave robbing and have a felony on your record.)

If you have an ancestor who was a New England stone carver, or you want to learn more about the carver who chiseled your ancestor's headstone, see Theodore Chase and Laurel K. Gabel's *Gravestone Chronicles I* and *II,* and Harriette Merrifield Forbes's *Gravestones of Early New England and the Men Who Made Them, 1653–1800,* as well as back issues of *Markers,* the journal of the Association for Gravestone Studies. Also check the industry and manufacturing schedules for stone carvers (see page 30), as well as city directories and newspapers for advertisements.

Rural folk who did not have access to a stone carver might make homemade markers or purchase them from mail-order catalogs, such as Sears, Roebuck. According to the 1902 edition of the *Sears, Roebuck Catalogue,* for $5.10 to $7.65, consumers could purchase a marker and base made from Vermont marble. "For sunk name and date letters, 6 cents each; for sunk verse letters 2½ cents each." Even the freight charges were reasonable by today's standards: twenty-five to fifty cents per one hundred pounds for delivery east of the Mississippi River; fifty cents to one dollar per one hundred pounds for delivery south of the Ohio River; and one dollar to a dollar and a half for delivery west of the Mississippi River and east of the Rocky Mountains. If you lived farther west, the amount increased proportionally. Headstones ranged in weight from 125 to 206 pounds for a standard marker and base.

For headstones and monuments since the mid nineteenth century, you might find the name of the monument maker in funeral home or cemetery records, or you might find the name of the carver listed among those paid out of the deceased's estate (see Wills, Administrations, and Probate on page 42). Once you have the monument maker's name, check city and telephone directories to see if the business is still in operation. Many of these businesses are family run, and the person operating it today may be the descendant of several generations of stone carvers.

As with other private business records, the content and existence of monument makers' records will vary greatly. At best, you'll find the name of the person who purchased the marker, the inscription that was to go on it, the composition of the marker (marble, granite, etc.), the measurements of the marker, the cost, and the dates it was ordered and erected.

Be on the lookout for new stones replacing older ones. Methods for determining this are discussed in chapter two.

---

**THE END OF AN ARTISAN**

My great-grandfather Alexander Stuart was born in 1847 in Arbroath, Scotland, and later lived in Wisconsin, Illinois, Minnesota, and Kansas. His occupation was tombstone carver as were so many of his fellow Scotsmen. Alexander and his brother Robert stayed busy in this industry for many years. The work they did was exquisite. One cemetery in Salina, Kansas, holds many of their creations as do others in Wisconsin and Illinois.

Alexander was buried near St. Paul, Minnesota, in a large cemetery. As a fledgling genealogist, I visited the cemetery to see the magnificent stone that marked his grave. My father or grandfather had never taken me to the cemetery even though we didn't live far from it. I went to the cemetery office to check the location of the graves of Alexander and his wife, Emma (Slaker), and jotted down the information. I did ask if it might be a family plot, but these were the only two burials that were family. As I walked out the door, the employee cheerfully said, "By the way, there is no marker at that site." My reaction was that this person was confused. I found the burial site, and sure enough, Alexander and Emma lie in unmarked graves. That sent a weird feeling throughout my body.

So why doesn't this master carver have a beautiful marker? Research shows he died poor and almost totally blind from glaucoma, no longer able to work. A good extended family project might be to have a marker placed for Alexander and Emma. Maybe in 2002 to mark the 150th anniversary of his arrival in the United States.

—Paula Stuart Warren

## MORTALITY SCHEDULES

Mortality schedules will give you the name of the deceased, sex, age, "color," whether free or slave, marital status, place of birth (state, territory, or country), month the death occurred, occupation, disease or cause of death, and the number of days ill.

These supplemental schedules to the federal census were taken for the census years 1850, 1860, 1870, and 1880 (see figure 1-14). They list the people who died during the twelve-month period prior to the official federal census date. More precisely, they cover the time span of 1 June through 31 May of 1849–1850, 1859–1860, 1869–1870, 1879–1880. A mortality schedule was also taken in conjunction with the 1900 census for those states that did not yet have statewide death registration, but after the information had been statistically compiled, the originals were supposed to be destroyed. Only one state's mortality schedules for 1900 are known to have survived—Minnesota—and are published. See James W. Warren's *Minnesota 1900 Census Mortality Schedule* (St. Paul, Minn.: Warren Research and Marketing, 1992).

Some federal mortality schedules have been indexed by the Accelerated In-

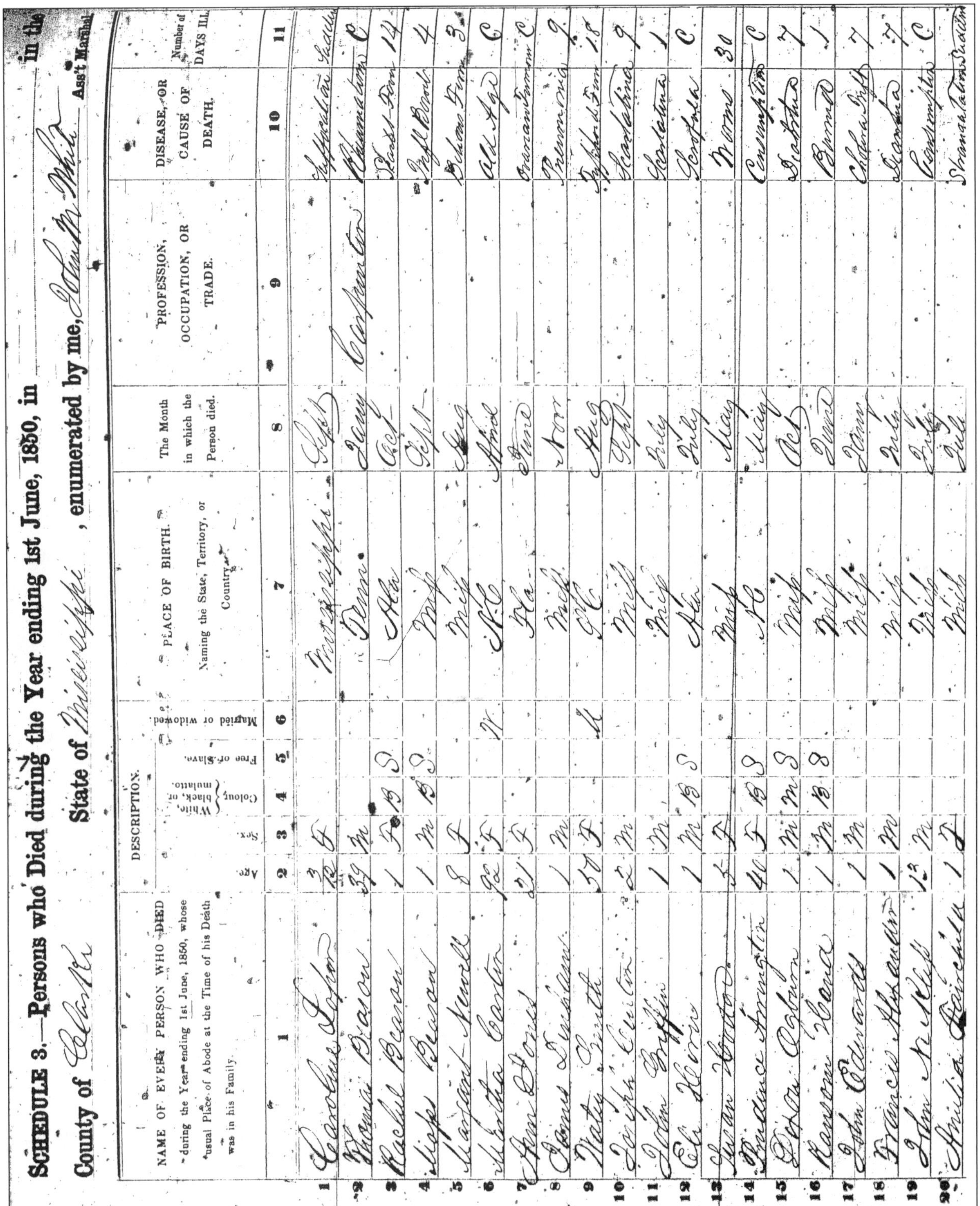

SCHEDULE 3.—Persons who Died during the Year ending 1st June, 1850, in County of _Clark_ State of _Mississippi_, enumerated by me, _John M. White_, Ass't Marshal.

| NAME OF EVERY PERSON WHO DIED during the Year ending 1st June, 1850, whose usual Place of Abode at the Time of his Death was in his Family. | DESCRIPTION. | | | | | PLACE OF BIRTH. Naming the State, Territory, or Country. | The Month in which the Person died. | PROFESSION, OCCUPATION, OR TRADE. | DISEASE, OR CAUSE OF DEATH. | Number of DAYS Ill. |
|---|---|---|---|---|---|---|---|---|---|---|
| | Age | Sex | White, {Colour} black, or mulatto. | Free or Slave. | Married or widowed. | | | | | |
| 1 | 2 | 3 | 4 | 5 | 6 | 7 | 8 | 9 | 10 | 11 |

Figure 1-14  1850 Mortality Schedule, Mississippi, Clark County.
*FHL 1550803.*

dexing Systems on microfiche (available through the Family History Library), and some are being indexed on CD-ROM. If your ancestor was considerate enough to die during one of these twelve-month periods for these census years, make sure you check the mortality schedules, even though omissions occurred. (For more information on mortality schedules, see Kathleen W. Hinckley's *Your Guide to the Federal Census*.)

Mortality schedules were sometimes taken as part of state censuses, as well. These censuses were usually taken during the five-year period in between federal censuses, although the information can vary from what the federal mortality schedules reported. For example, the 1855 state census for New York included deaths in the previous year but not names of the decedents, while some of the other state mortality schedules used the same column headings as the federal ones. See Ann S. Lainhart's *State Census Records* (Baltimore: Genealogical Publishing Co., 2000) for information on finding state mortality schedules.

## NECROLOGIES AND OTHER SOURCES

**Sources**

If your ancestor belonged to an organization, society, church, union, or other association, check the group's publications for necrologies. **This listing of the recently deceased may be published annually in newsletters, journals, or yearbooks.** You might find full obituaries in these publications as well. Realize that there might be misinformation or typographical errors in just about any source, so always verify with other records.

### American Medical Association's Deceased Physician File

If you have an ancestor who was a medical doctor, you may find an obituary and other information, such as medical schools attended and biographical data, in the files of the American Medical Association's (AMA) Deceased American Physicians, 1864–1970. This file is available on 237 reels of microfilm at the Family History Library or through one of its centers. The names are arranged in alphabetical order, so it is easy to search. Some Canadian physicians also are included. The National Genealogical Society (4527 Seventeenth Street North, Arlington, VA 22207-2399) also has the AMA files and will search each name you submit for fifteen dollars; **however, if you have several names to check, it is more economical to rent the microfilm from a Family History Center.**

**Money Saver**

## OBITUARIES AND DEATH NOTICES

*According to obituary notices, a mean and useless citizen never dies.*
—*Anonymous*

For the locality where your ancestor lived and died (which may be two different places), check newspapers for an obituary or death notice. Death notices are fairly straightforward, giving the name of the deceased, usually the date of death, where the service will be held, and possibly the place of burial.

Here is a typical notice from *The Sunday Republican*, St. Louis, Missouri, 15 April 1855:

> DIED
>
> Yesterday afternoon, MARY JANE ERMESH, aged 19 years, after a lingering illness. Her funeral will take place this afternoon, at 4 o'clock, from the residence of her brother-in-law, James Carlisle, No. 13 Fourth street, opposite the Court House. Friends and acquaintances of the family are invited to attend without further notice.
>
> —Philadelphia, Cincinnati and Zanesville (Ohio) papers please copy.

Note the last line about Philadelphia, Cincinnati, and Zanesville newspapers copying the death notice. **This is an important clue that tells you other family and friends of the deceased must be in these cities.** If you were not certain where your ancestor originated or where other relatives might reside, this is your lead. Not all death notices carry this tag line, however.

**Important**

Obituaries give more detail than death notices and are a news item sometimes written by the newspaper staff from information provided by the funeral home. When I worked at the *Ranchland News* in Simla, Colorado, the funeral home would fax us a form that had been completed by the undertaker after interviewing a family member. We then took the bare-bones information to write the obituary. I noticed the obituaries I wrote used more of the genealogical details than those written by my fellow reporters. If only all obituaries could be written by genealogists.

Some nineteenth-century obituaries recorded mostly aspects of a person's character and were considered a eulogy to the deceased, such as the following obituary from an uncited clipping:

> Mary Stuart Fitzhugh, died on August 31, 1881, at the residence of her son-in-law, Mr. T.A. Marshall, the widow of James Madison Fitzhugh, and daughter of David Stuart of King George County, Va., age seventy-one years.
>
> She had been a member of the Episcopal Church since 1831 and having served her Lord for half a century, death possessed no terrors for her, but was looked upon and awaited calmly and patiently as a translation to a better and brighter world, as a means of being reunited to her husband and children who had preceded her. . . .
>
> So when the summons came it found her calm, peaceful, self-possessed, and hopeful, relying upon the Savior in whom she had trusted, and though at intervals suffering the most agonizing pain, her constant prayer was "Lord, take thy servant to thyself." No murmur, no petition for relief from pain, no request for recovery to health, simply, "Lord, take me home."
>
> In so brief a notice we cannot dwell upon the virtues of the deceased lady. In all the relations of life, as a wife, mother, friend and neighbor she endeavored to fulfill her duty, and her sweet patience and resignation under trials, the most severe loss of husband and children, reverses of fortune, and years of physical suffering endeared her to all who knew her. Her consider-

ation for others was such that even on her death bed she expressed herself as being glad that her children were not there to witness her suffering.

Thanking those around her for their unwearied attention, she said, "My time has come to die; this is my last day upon earth; but I do not fear death. I am ready and willing to go." Then she tried to sing a hymn which her husband had sung when dying, "There is room in Paradise for me," and beckoned to some celestial visitant invisible to our mortal sight, but hovering probably above her ready to waft her spirit across the dark river to realms of perpetual bliss. . . .

Other obituaries were more like minibiographies, like the following obituary for Joseph Burden (contributed by Marsha Hoffman Rising, CG), as published in the *Tri-Weekly Patriot* (Springfield, Missouri), 5 February 1867. Notice the leads to follow for land and courthouse records and genealogical records. Unfortunately, the place of Burden's burial is not included. In these early obituaries, it's usually hit or miss whether the name of the cemetery will be included.

Joseph Burden, long a prominent citizen of Greene county, was born on the Cumberland River in Tennessee in 1796; married a lady from Georgia and moved into this county in the fall of 1833. He settled on a farm which John Fulbright had opened up, the current location of the Berry Hospital. In 1841, he built the house on Boonville street just north of the square, where Gen. N.R. Smith's widow resides, and there for about twelve years kept a boarding house. He then built the hotel now kept by Henry Matlock in the extreme north of town.

In 1856, he bought what was known as the "Campbell Reserve"—the lot reserved by John P. Campbell for himself, in the original fifty acres granted to the county for the town site, upon which the first house in Springfield was originally built by Campbell in 1830. It was situated next west of Major McElhany's residence. It was a double log house with a hall between the two wings and by 1867 it had been weather-boarded, for the purpose of modernizing and enlarging it.

In this house Joseph Burden died in January last. His widow and five children survive him. He held various local offices for his long life, and was regarded with much respect by his fellow citizens of all classes.

**Reminder**

**Recent immigrants might place obituaries in foreign-language newspapers instead of American, English-language newspapers.** The drawback is that most foreign-language papers aren't indexed, even for vital information, so you will need to narrow the date of death to within a short time frame for easier searching. The Immigration History Research Center, University of Minnesota, 826 Berry Street, St. Paul, MN 55114, <www1.umn.edu/ihrc>, has the best collection of foreign and ethnic newspapers. (See Suzanna Moody and Joel Wurl's, *The Immigration History Research Center: A Guide to Collections* [New York: Greenwood Press, 1991] for more information.) You may obtain many of the newspapers on microfilm at this facility through interlibrary loan.

The cause of death might or might not appear in the obituary, but for the latter part of the twentieth century and for today's obituaries, you may get a clue to the cause of death by looking at where the family requested donations be sent. Watch for the words "died suddenly," which might indicate an accidental death, suicide, or murder—or it could simply mean a heart attack or a stroke. The words "lingering" or "long illness" could suggest heart disease, tuberculosis, or cancer.

Those who might not ordinarily be featured on the front page of the newspaper could end up there because they died in an unusual way. **If you have a family story of someone dying in an accident or unusual death, also look for an article.** John Norris, for example, didn't do anything particularly newsworthy in life, but in death he made the front page, much to the chagrin of his relatives (see below). There was never an obituary for Mary Clark, but a news article appeared two weeks before her death when she unsuccessfully (at the time) attempted to take her life in 1908.

Look at all the record leads offered by this one article: death certificate, coroner's record, military records, funeral records, church records, cemetery records, possibly hospital records.

**Research Tip**

**J.G. Norris, 56, Dies of Exposure in One-Room Home**
(*Greenwich Time*, 7 Jan. 1948, p. 1, col. 4, and p. 2)
John G. Norris, 56, was found dead of exposure in his one-room shack on Almira Dr. at 2:20 p.m. yesterday [6 January 1948]. He was found by his nephew, Arthur Doran, of Almira Dr., who had been sent by his mother to bring his uncle to the Doran home for dinner.

Found locked in the unheated shack with Mr. Norris were two nine-week-old puppies. Scratch marks were found on Mr. Norris' face, indicating the dogs had attempted to awaken their master.

Mr. Norris was lying on the bed in the 8-by-10-foot shack when Doran broke into the room. He was fully clothed, but had taken his shoes off. Blankets were piled over him. On his head was his cap.

In the shack was a coal stove and a supply of fuel. The stove was cold, police reported, and had apparently been unlit for some time. There were no windows in the shack, but investigating authorities reported the temperature inside was as cold as it was outside the frame building.

Mr. Norris, who had been ill for the past several years, was last seen walking on Pemberwick Rd. at 2 p.m. Medical Examiner Ralph W. Crane fixed the time of death as sometime during the night of Jan. 5. Death was caused by exposure, he said. . . .

Mr. Norris was known for his affection for dogs. Outside the shack in which he lived, were several pets who played with policemen when they arrived at the scene yesterday afternoon.

Under a doctor's care for the past year, Mr. Norris had undergone several operations in Greenwich Hospital in the past decade.

He was born in Greenwich, the son of the late David and Delia Gordon Norris. He is survived by four sisters, Mrs. William Doran and Mrs. Charles

Guiffra of Greenwich and Mrs. John McCue and Mrs. P.M. Fitzhugh of Harrison, N.Y.

Mr. Norris was a veteran of World War I, having served with the 71st Regiment.

Funeral Services will be held from the Frank M. Reilly Funeral Residence Saturday at 8:30 a.m. Requiem Mass will be celebrated at St. Roch's Church at 9 a.m. Burial will be at St. Mary's Cemetery. Friends may call after 2 p.m. Thursday.

Estate settlements and sales appear in newspapers, helping narrow down the time an ancestor died. Also check for personal and local news items at least a week to a month before and a week after the death for relatives coming to the person's deathbed or for the funeral. By collecting obituaries and news items on all siblings of your ancestor, you might be able to piece together three or four generations of a family. (See the case study in Appendix D.)

You might also come across colorful stories about ancestors who didn't die, such as this one from the *San Francisco Chronicle* 31 August 1914, p. 14, col. 5:

**Youth Disappointed in Love Wants to Die**
Special Dispatch to The Chronicle.
STOCKTON, August 30.—Believing that Miss Mamie Freitas, with whom he was madly infatuated, had wearied of his attentions, Joseph de Bartalo, aged 22, fired a bullet into his abdomen yesterday and is lying at the Emergency Hospital in a dying condition.

De Bartalo told the physicians, just before being placed on the operating table, that he had been keeping company with Miss Freitas for five months and that when she refused to speak to him yesterday he feared their romance was about to end and decided to kill himself. Hastening to his home, following the episode, De Bartalo shut himself in his room and fired the bullet. Relatives heard the report and rushed to his assistance.

Miss Freitas called at the hospital to see her lover. She admitted having refused to speak to him, but declared that the quarrel was of a minor nature.

## Finding Obituaries, Newspapers, and Indexes

*Obituaries: A Guide to Sources*, 2nd ed., by Betty M. Jarboe, is a bibliography of books and articles that index or abstract obituaries and death notices from newspapers and periodicals. It also includes references to annuals and yearbooks that contain necrologies, as well as transcripts of published cemetery records and tombstones. This guide is arranged geographically, but as the compiler points out in the introduction, this work does not contain everything published, and it was published in 1989, so sources after that date would not be included. Nonetheless, it is a good starting point.

To find newspapers, go to the *Gale Directory of Publications and Broadcast Media*, which you can find in the reference sections of most libraries. The directory is arranged by state, then city. It will tell when the newspaper was established and give the address where you can write. If the newspaper is out of print, try Clarence Brigham's *A History and Bibliography of American Newspapers, 1690–1820* and Winifred Gregory's *American Newspapers, 1821–1936*. Also look for the Library of Congress publication *Newspapers in Microform.*

Another resource is the United States Newspaper Program <www.neh.gov/projects/usnp.html>, a national effort to locate, catalog, and preserve on microfilm newspapers published in the United States from the eighteenth century to the present. On the Newspaper Program's Web site, you'll find a state-by-state listing of projects, how many newspapers have been cataloged, and links to state repositories housing microfilm collections.

**Many newspapers have been microfilmed, and the films are usually kept at local libraries and historical societies.** Volunteers at these facilities sometimes index vital events, such as births, marriages, and deaths, onto index cards. Sometimes the library or historical society will interlibrary loan the microfilmed copies of the newspapers. If not, write to the repository and ask if its newspaper has been indexed and request a search.

Some metropolitan newspapers have published indexes, such as *The New York Times*. While you might not think your ancestor living in Kansas would do anything worthwhile enough to justify a death notice or obituary in *The New York Times*, you never know. Furthermore, many people can claim a distant relative who was newsworthy. Most people have never heard of Edward Ward Carmack, an early twentieth-century senator from Tennessee. Carmack certainly didn't do anything meritorious to give him a spot in the history books. Those researching him were fortunate that he was assassinated in 1908 so that his death made *The New York Times*.

There are three types of indexes for *The New York Times*.

1. *The New York Times Index* is published annually and is widely available in large public and academic libraries. This index begins in 1851 and covers articles by subject; for example, you would look under "deaths" to see if an obituary appeared for your ancestor or a relative. You can also identify the dates of national events, then search other, unindexed papers. For example, you can look in the *Index* to find out when Civil War casualty lists were published.

2. *The New York Times Obituary Index* covers 1858 through 1968, with a supplement covering 1969 through 1978. This is an index to obituaries only, not death notices. The *Obituary Index* was compiled from the *Index* and covers those names/obituaries that appeared under the heading of "Deaths" in the *Index*. It lists mostly prominent people, but there are more than 390,000 entries. For death notices since 1997, check *The New York Times* online at <www.nytimes.com>.

3. The *Personal Name Index to The New York Times Index* covers 1851 through 1974, with supplements covering 1975 through 1996. This index only covers names from the *Index* and references the pages in the *Index*. Keep in mind that not every name in the *Times* was indexed—only names within headlines, not those within articles.

Microfilm Source

Let's go back to Edward Ward Carmack and see in which of the three indexes he appeared. Since the item about his assassination was not an obituary, his name is not in the *Obituary Index*. The *Index* listed his name, but it was cross-referenced to the subject heading of "murders." The *Personal Name Index* listed him by name. In short, check all three indexes, and look under names and subjects.

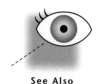

**See Also**

For online obituaries, see chapter two, Virtual Cemeteries, Obituaries, and Funeral Homes, on page 75.

## SOCIAL SECURITY DEATH INDEX

The Social Security Death Index contains entries on more than 66 million deceased people who had Social Security numbers and whose deaths were reported to the Social Security Administration. (Many deaths are and were not reported to the Social Security Administration, especially if the deceased was not receiving any benefits.) The index covers reported deaths from 1962 (when the Social Security Administration began computerizing its records) to the present, although there may be some records from as early as 1937. The information contained in the Social Security Death Index varies slightly, but typically you'll find the person's name, date of birth, date of death (or date it was reported), the state of residence when the person applied for a Social Security number, and the place where the final payment was sent.

Some genealogical software programs, such as Family Tree Maker, come with the Death Index on CD-ROM, but you can access the index at no cost at the Family History Library, at one of its centers, or online at one of these sites:

- www.familysearch.org/Eng/Search/frameset_search.asp?PAGE=ssdi/search_ssdi.asp
- www.ancestry.com/search/rectype/vital/ssdi/main.htm
- http://ssdi.genealogy.rootsweb.com/cgi-bin/ssdi.cgi

You do not need to know a person's Social Security number to gain access to the index; simply type in the person's name. However, you will need to know some identifying information—such as a birth year—in case there are several people by the same name. No middle names or initials are used in the database. Using the information obtained from the Death Index, you may then send for the original form SS-5, "Application for a Social Security Number," by writing to the Freedom of Information Officer, 4-H-8 Annex Bldg., 6401 Security Boulevard, Baltimore, MD 21235. There is a twenty-seven dollar fee for this service. Form SS-5 won't give you any further information on the person's death, but it will give you the applicant's birth date and place, parents' names (including mother's maiden name), employer's name, and where the person resided at the time of death. If you use the Social Security Death Index on Ancestry.com, it will generate a form letter for you. Once you have confirmed you have the right person, send for his or her death certificate, which will give you more clues and information for further research.

## WILLS, ADMINISTRATIONS, AND PROBATE

*Let's choose executors and talk of wills: And yet not so, for what can we bequeath Save our deposèd bodies to the ground?*
—*William Shakespeare*, Richard II, *Act 3, Scene 2, lines 148–150*

Probate is a process by which property and items of the deceased are transferred to heirs. Wills or administrations are the documents that specify these transfers. When a person dies leaving a valid will, that person is said to have died "testate." When a person dies leaving no valid will, then that person is said to have died "intestate." Not everyone leaves a will, and not all wills get recorded. Those that are recorded are generally indexed. Wills are usually probated in the court that has jurisdiction where the person resided at the time of death.

**Though a will does not give you the person's date of death, you can narrow down the date to between the date when the person made the will and the date it was entered into probate and recorded.** For example, Townshend Dade made his will on 9 April 1761, and it was entered into the Stafford County, Virginia, probate court on 9 June 1761 (Deed and Will Book 1748–1763, page 391). So we can say that Townshend Dade died between 9 April and 9 June 1761. Once in a while, you will find recorded the date the person died when the will was admitted into probate. In New York, for example, a petition that gives the date of death has been required since 1830.

**Research Tip**

Usually wills have a statement in the opening paragraph that reads something like, "I will that all my just debts and funeral expenses be paid." On occasion, however, you will find the testator specifying a cemetery in which to be buried, the kind of tombstone, and even the foliage and upkeep of the grave. Here are a few examples:

From the will of Rachel Wilson, dated 18 August 1886, recorded 5 June 1888, Polk Co., Missouri, Wills B:13–14, FHL 944903:

> . . . and my grave furnished with tombstones of the same quality of the
> stones furnished for Jesse Neils grave. . . .

From the will of Frederich Schroder, dated 21 February 1874, recorded 9 March 1874, Hamilton Co., Ohio, Wills 31:35–37, FHL 355112:

> . . . 2nd. That on my burial place shall be erected a monument of Italian
> Marble at a cost of not more than Four hundred ($400) Dollars, with my
> name together with the name of my deceased wife, be cut in suitable form.
> 3rd. I bequeath to the German Protestant Churchyard on Walnut Hills
> as an endowment fund of Two hundred dollars ($200) and wish that it
> be made the duty of the Trustees, to look after the interest of the above
> named Two hundred Dollars, to be applied for the beautifying of my
> grave. . . .

Perhaps one of the most detailed instructions for burial comes from the will of William D. Gallager, dated 27 March 1869, recorded 9 February 1871, Hamilton Co., Ohio, Wills 19:154–159, FHL 0355106:

> . . . 1st My son in law William H. Sayre and myself having purchased a Lot
> in Spring Grove Cemetery Lot No. 9 Sec. 99, each being the owner of one
> half and as I have removed the Remains of my late wife Rachel B. Gallager
> there it is my desire when I die that my remains shall be buried in said lot
> besides my late wife Rachel B. Gallager and that my Executors shall have a

tomb made similar to the one over the remains of my late wife and have it placed over my remains and purchase among other ornaments to improve the lot as they may think Best to do. . . . 5th I also bequeath and desire my Executors shall invest . . . Three hundred dollars $300 in the hands of the Trustees of the Spring Grove Cemetery to be applied yearly to keep the lot owned by W.H. Sayre and myself in complete repair and Particular the Graves of myself and wife and my daughter Emma and Husband and children graves not only in repair but to plant a reasonable amount of Flowers on or around our Graves. . . . I am particular about this matter from the fact that I find when the old folks die . . . [that] their . . . Graves are very often neglected. 6th I also bequeath $100 One Hundred Dollars and desire my Executors shall place it in the hands if safe of the Trustees of a Church in New Castle Delaware where my Mother is buried as a Permanent investment the interest of which to be applied yearly in Keeping her grave in order and planting flowers around her grave in season if the Church is not safe then invest it in some other safe place. When in Philadelphia I tried but in vain to find the remains of my father to have it removed with my mother in New Castle Del. But the heathens had sold his house to build a big church this they call Christianity <u>heathens would not do so.</u> 7th Out of the high regard I entertained for the Parents of my late wife and the memory of the undying love she entertained for her mother when living I Bequeath one hundred dollars $100 and desire my Executors will place it or invest it in the hands of the Trustees if they are safe as a Permanent investment of the Baptist Church I believe is called the Hope Church standing on Budd or New Market St. between Poplar and Lanail [?] St. in . . . Philadelphia where the remains of Mrs. Boon is interred the interest of which to be expended yearly in Keeping their grave in order and planting flowers around it for ever. . . .

Ironically, and despite all of his painstaking efforts, no stone remains in Spring Grove Cemetery to mark William Gallager's grave.

One type of will that may be more valuable in determining a time of death is a "nuncupative will," one that is dictated orally by someone on his or her deathbed. This type of will must be written within a short time period for it to be valid. Realize, however, that someone can be on his or her deathbed for months, so the date a will was dictated may not be close to the death date at all.

**Notes**

**Administrations are filed when there was no will, and these files have all the same value as would a will file,** except you won't have the date of a will to help narrow the date of death, nor will you have the deceased's specific instructions about where to be buried. Papers in an administration file, however, may give the exact date of death, and the account may show the amount paid for the coffin, the grave marker, and the undertaker.

In addition to the will or administration, look for the inventory of the deceased's estate and the list of debts. These are usually recorded in separate books, or they are among loose papers in the probate packet. Within these documents you might find how much was paid out of the estate, when the coffin was ordered, and other details pertaining to the burial. One of the best ways to estimate the date of death is by finding in the probate the date the physician billed for his last visit and the date the coffin was made and the burial clothes were purchased. In the estate file of William Able, Polk County, Missouri, Probate Box 4, Marsha Hoffman Rising found that Dr. Jewett made his last visit on 19 August 1842. John Toler built a black walnut coffin for six dollars on 22 August 1842. So we can narrow William Able's death down to between the nineteenth and the twenty-second of August in that year.

## Finding Wills and Administrations

Probate packets, wills, and administrations recorded in clerk's books are held at the county courthouse, and in some New England states, in the town or a probate district, unless the records have been transferred to a county or state archive. Not all states call their probate courts the same thing. The jurisdiction where your ancestor's will or administration is recorded might be called the superior court, a circuit court, a district court, a chancery court, a register of wills, or a surrogate's court. Check the current edition of *The Handy Book for Genealogists* (Logan, Utah: Everton Publishers, 1991) or *Ancestry's Red Book* (Salt Lake City, Utah: Ancestry, 1989) for county courthouse addresses and the name of the appropriate jurisdiction.

When you find a will in a clerk's will book, you are looking at the recorded will, not the original. **Ask if the "probate packet" still exists, as this should contain all the surviving documents generated during the probate process, including the original will.** Contested wills and records are kept in the court of the original probate, usually within this packet. If the original will still exists, you will want to check it because errors could have been made when the clerk hand-copied it into the will book. Sometimes the recorded will is all that has survived.

Tip

Here are tips for finding your ancestors' wills or administrations:

1. Working from the date your ancestor died, check microfilmed indexes of wills and administrations through the Family History Library. Look under the county and state your ancestor last resided or died in, then under "probate records." This will give you a list of what is available on microfilm. Sometimes the library has the index to probate records, but the actual records have not been filmed. Even so, being able to search the index yourself is always better than relying on a clerk who may not check for other relatives or under variant spellings. Remember, the indexes and the records will not be online; you'll need to order the microfilm through one of the 3,400 worldwide Family History Centers.

2. Once you have the volume and page number from the index, if the library has the records on film, then order the relevant film(s). If not, use the address given in the *Handy Book* or *Red Book* to write to the courthouse for the records.

3. If the library does not have the index on microfilm for the time period in which your ancestor died, write directly to the probate clerk and ask if your ancestor left a will. Give your ancestor's full name, date of death, and any other identifying information. Don't forget to include a self-addressed, stamped envelope so the clerk can tell you if the repository has the record and what the

fee will be to obtain a copy. Remember, too, to ask if the entire probate packet still exists and how much it would be to copy it.

## WHAT'S NEXT?

One of these records has hopefully pointed you in the right direction toward finding your ancestor's final resting place. However, if you're still unsure about where the grave is or in which cemetery, there are more resources in the next chapter for you to check.

# TWO

# Locating Graves, Cemeteries, and Their Records

MORTIMER BREWSTER: *"You mean you're going to bury Mr. Hotchkiss in the cellar?"*

MARTHA BREWSTER: *"Oh, yes, dear—that's what we did with the others."*

—*Joseph Kesselring's* Arsenic and Old Lace

F inding an ancestor's grave can be easy, or it can be one of the most difficult tasks at hand. While I can guarantee that practically all of your ancestors were indeed buried somewhere, unfortunately, not all of them have grave markers. As you'll read in chapter three, some headstones were nothing more than rough-cut boulders. Others weren't made from durable materials. Some graves may have never had a marker, and if your ancestors were buried in someone's cellar, you probably haven't a prayer of finding them.

If your ancestor died since the late nineteenth century, you may easily learn where that person was buried through home sources (funeral cards and oral history). Death certificates and obituaries usually carry this information, too, or they may include the name of the funeral home, which might still have a record of where the body was buried (see chapter one).

For ancestors who died before the late nineteenth century, discovering where they were buried may require more creativity. You need to know the locality where the ancestor died, since this was likely where the person also was buried. Shipping bodies to distant locations didn't become feasible until the Civil War, simply because there was no good method of preserving a body for transit.

Keep in mind, too, that grave markers sometimes have a way of disappearing entirely or ending up in places you would never suspect. I've heard of old headstones being used for stone walkways; as building materials, like bricks; and as cornerstones for fireplaces. New owners who inherit an old, rundown cemetery on their property with just a few fallen over headstones may move

## SOMETIMES DEAD RELATIVES FIND YOU

It all began with a routine trip to the local genealogical society. The new quarterlies were on display. It won't take long, I thought. I will just quickly glance at the queries to see if any of them apply to my pioneer families. One jumped off the page! "Help! Seeking descendants of Robert Sharp buried in Sunset Hill Cemetery, Warrensburg, Missouri. Decisions required about mausoleum."

It was my husband's second great-grandfather! A telephone call that evening revealed that the roof of the mausoleum had collapsed, damaging the coffins and exposing the crypt. The five bodies had been removed to the local mortuary, but the kindly funeral director did not know how much longer he would be able to keep them. The cemetery association was a private one and had funds only for maintenance, not repairs. The only descendants that had been located were not interested in the problem.

My husband, Dean, traveled to the ancestral home. The cemetery committee recommended the mausoleum be razed and the bodies buried. Law required that vaults be provided for the evicted residents. This could all be provided at the bargain basement price of $6,000 to $8,000! Concern, respect, and regard for our ancestors is one thing. But this was another. We could think of a few other things to do with that amount of money!

We contacted two other descendants. Neither were interested in providing the funds. We contemplated how long it could take to find descendants who would contribute enough money to put these unfortunate folks in the ground—where they never wanted to be in the first place. Perhaps a compromise was possible. How about cremating the bodies, replacing the remains where they were, and fixing the mausoleum so that it would not constitute a hazard? The funeral director was willing, but he would need death certificates in order to cremate them. Only one of the deceased persons had lived into the death certificate era. Fortunately, my husband is a physician.

An image immediately developed in my mind—my husband, with stethoscope appropriately placed, bending over a pile of bones and pronouncing them "really most sincerely dead" (as the coroner said in the movie *The Wizard of Oz*). Dean had a better idea. He called the Bureau of Vital Statistics. It wasn't easy to find a way around the rules, but we finally located a reasonable bureaucrat. We would need notarized statements that Dean was indeed a bona fide descendant and that he took responsibility for the disposal of their remains. We provided all the family statistics for the funeral director, produced the notarized statement, and for $600 he agreed to handle the matter.

But, before the remains became ashes, Dean wanted to be absolutely sure that the people who were supposed to be there were indeed the ones who were. He made another trip to the ancestral home, camera in hand. Now we know how well preserved someone remains after 120 years in a mausoleum!

—Marsha Hoffman Rising

these to another locality, donate them to a museum, or store them in their garage. Sad, I know, but true.

Following are ideas and resources to help you locate your ancestors' graves and the cemeteries where they were buried.

## CEMETERY LOCATORS AND SURVEYS

Several guides will help you locate cemeteries and obtain records. *Cemeteries of the U.S.: A Guide to Contact Information for U.S. Cemeteries and Their Records*, edited by Deborah M. Burek, lists more than 22,000 cemeteries in all fifty states and major military cemeteries in U.S. territories and foreign countries. Arranged by state, then county, an entry from Lancaster County, Pennsylvania, for example, shows the type of information you can find in this source:

Greenwood Cemetery

719 Highland Ave., Lancaster, PA 17603

Phone: (717) 392-1224

Terry Shamberger, President

Years of Operation: 1889-Present. Affiliations: non-sectarian. Facilities: chapel, mausoleum, and crematorium. Services: cemetery is open 24 hours for visitation; office hours are 8:30 A.M.-5 P.M. Monday-Friday and 9 A.M.-1 P.M. on Saturday. Cemetery Records: housed on-site; available for searches; no appointment necessary; searches by office personnel only.

A few statewide guides exist that inventory all of the cemeteries, including private family burial grounds and isolated graves, and give directions and information. In the *Colorado Cemetery Directory*, edited by Kay R. Merrill (Denver: Colorado Council of Genealogical Societies, 1985), for example, the directory gives the following information for each cemetery listed: location, type of cemetery (public, private, etc.), year of first burial, status (still in use, abandoned, etc.), record custodian, if inscriptions have been transcribed and published, and where that publication is available. Here are a few examples:

Brett Cemetery; c[irca] 1 mile west of Edwards, Eagle Co., on U.S. 6, on knoll back of ranch buildings at the mouth of East Lake Creek (probably Sec. 6, T5S, R82W, 6th P.M.); Private, family; 1st known burial 1884, last 1931; maintained by owners; James Brett Owner; inscriptions [published]; at Denver Public Library.

Unknown Child, Grave of; c. 2½ miles south of Elbert, Elbert Co. (Sec. 15, T10S, R64W, 6th P.M.); single grave; killed by Indians; abandoned; no records available.

Sakala Cemetery; 8 miles southeast of Fondis, Elbert Co., on County Road 86 (Sec. 20, T10S, R61W, 6th P.M.); community now private; 1st marked burial 1906, last 1950; Russian Orthodox Cross used on most tombstones; occasional use; published inscriptions in *The Colorado Genealogist* 41:135.

**Research Tip**

## IN SEARCH OF A CEMETERY

Unlike libraries or other repositories, some of the cemeteries that are the final resting places of our ancestors are not easy to locate on maps. In fact, many of these cemeteries do not show up on any of the maps that we have at our disposal today. Modern technology offers an answer to the question of where the cemetery is.

Few people realize that the United States Geographic Survey Web site <http:// mapping.usgs.gov/> will give you information on more than just towns through its Geographic Names Information System Query Form <http://geonames.usgs. gov/pls/gnis/web_query.gnis_web_query_form.> In fact, you can type in the name of the cemetery and then be given the county, state, type of feature, latitude, longitude, and USGS map for each entry in the GNIS database that meets your search criteria.

When looking for the location of a cemetery, the latitude and longitude will help you not only to pin down the exact location of the cemetery, but also get driving directions to that cemetery. You can't find this information on the GNIS site, but you can use the latitude and longitude information in conjunction with another Web site to create a map and accompanying driving directions for printing.

Armed with the latitude and longitude, visit the MapBlast Web site <www.mapbl ast.com.> This is the only one I have found that includes searching via latitude and longitude in the Advanced Search section of the Directions tab. But you need to make a small change to the information taken from the GNIS database. For instance, the Greenlawn Cemetery, located in Franklin County, Ohio, has a latitude of 395625N and a longitude of 0830157W. You would need to alter these numbers slightly for MapBlast to recognize them. The latitude must be entered as 39.5625 (leave the N off) and the longitude needs to be entered as -83.0157 (leave the W off). You may need to experiment with these based on the numbers you get from the GNIS database.

After typing in the place from which you drive, you can then get directions from the hotel or your home to the cemetery in question. These directions can include turn-by-turn images to make it even easier to locate the cemetery or other landmark in question.

—Rhonda McClure

Here are some of the other statewide directories:

*Association of Municipal Historians of New York State Cemeteries Name/ Location Inventory, 1995–1997.* Bowie, Md.: Heritage Books, 1999.

*Burial Grounds of Vermont.* Bradford, Vt.: The Vermont Old Cemetery Association, 1991.

*California Cemetery Inscription Sources: Print and Microform,* by Elizabeth

Gorrell Kot and Shirley Pugh Thomson. Vallejo, Calif.: Indices Publishing, 1994.

*Cemetery Locations in Wisconsin.* Janesville, Wisc.: Origins, 1998.

*A Directory of Cemeteries and Funeral Homes in Washington State.* Orting, Wash.: Heritage Quest, 1990.

*Massachusetts Cemeteries*, by David Lambert. Boston: New England Historic Genealogical Society, 2002.

*Missouri Cemetery Inscription Sources: Print and Microform*, by Elizabeth Gorrell Kot and Shirley Pugh Thomson. Vallejo, Calif.: Indices Publishing, 1995.

*Ohio Cemeteries.* Mansfield, Ohio: Ohio Genealogical Society, 1978.

*Ohio Cemeteries Addendum.* Baltimore, Md.: Gateway Press, 1990.

Another method of locating cemeteries is the U.S. Geological Survey's Geographic Name Information System <http://mapping.usgs.gov/www/gnis/gnisform.html>. Type in the locality and the keyword "cemetery" in the "Feature Type" to pull up a list of cemeteries in that area.

**Idea Generator**

**If you know the area where your ancestor was buried, but you haven't figured out where the cemetery is, ask the local town folk or the historian.** Small, rural, and defunct cemeteries may be impossible to find otherwise. When I was looking for remote rural cemeteries to include in my eastern Colorado transcribing project, all I had to do was mention the word cemetery to some of the old-timers, and they would tell me about the graves on so-and-so's property. Also check with the funeral directors in surrounding towns. For example, in the eastern Colorado rural community where I live, the closest funeral home is twenty-four miles away. The nearest monument maker is sixty miles away, but both companies would know the locations of the cemeteries they service. Other people to ask are county maintenance crews, county surveyors, sheriffs, and public utility crews. A rather laborious, last-resort process would be to read the deeds for the county—assuming you're dealing with a small one—which mention areas reserved for burial grounds.

You might also try contacting the International Cemetery and Funeral Association, which has more than six thousand members:

International Cemetery and Funeral Association, founded in 1887 as the American Cemetery Association

1895 Preston White Dr., Suite 220, Reston, VA 20191

Toll-free: (800) 645-7700, Phone: (703) 391-8400, Fax: (703) 391-8416

E-mail: gen4@icfa.org    Web site: www.icfa.org

## City Directories

As mentioned in chapter one, a city directory is an alphabetical list of inhabitants and businesses in a given locality. **Through this source you can find names of cemeteries, funeral homes, and monument makers that your ancestors might have patronized.** Many city directories have classified business sections with ads. Look under these keywords:

**Notes**

- cemeteries

- monument makers
- tombstones
- funeral directors
- undertakers
- embalmers

Figure 2-1 on page 53 shows undertakers' ads from a Cincinnati city directory. Some major city directories are available on microfilm at the Family History Library and may be borrowed through any Family History Center. The Library of Congress in Washington, DC, has the largest collection of city directories, many of which are on microfilm and microfiche, but the Library of Congress is not a lending library. You would have to go there to use the directories, or hire someone to search them. Typically, you can find city directories at the public or state libraries to which the directory pertains. Primary Source Media at <www.citydirectories.psmedia.com> has more than two hundred city directories for nearly one hundred cities online. Some of these directories date from 1859, with major cities having better coverage. Some directories may be accessed for free, but you will need to pay a subscriber's fee for full use.

## County, Local, and Family Histories

Other sources to try for locating where your ancestors were buried are published family histories and local and county histories. Descendants and residents submitted information on their families for publication in county histories, usually paying a fee for the entry to be published; therefore, information content and accuracy varies. **Although local and county histories are known for their inaccurate information about ancestors, you might still find the clue you need to locate a grave or cemetery.** For example, on page 480 of *El Paso County [Colorado] Heritage*, by Juanita L. and John P. Breckenridge (Colorado Springs, Colo.: Curits Media Corp., 1985), Mariman Johnson "died 17 June 1929 and [was] buried [in] Ramah, Colo." This sketch doesn't name the cemetery, but at least it tells in what town Mariman was buried. (Ramah, by the way, has only one cemetery.) In this same history on page 604, Harriet Polders "passed away and was laid to rest [next to] her husband George in the Evergreen Cemetery in Colorado Springs, Colorado." You might also find causes of death, especially if the death was unusual. Again, from the El Paso County history, on page 606, Henry Pring Jr. "was killed when he was forty-seven, being thrown from a buggy by a runaway horse," and Aubrey Jasper "was killed by lightning at the age of sixteen."

Local and county histories might also provide you with the history and location of the cemeteries in the area. In the history *Clay City and Harrison Township, Clay County, Indiana* (Clay City, Ind.: Clay City Centennial Committee, 1973), page 328, Duncan Cemetery is described:

> Sometime prior to his death in 1860, George W. Duncan set aside the southeast corner of land he owned and occupied as a cemetery. This plot is the

**Warning**

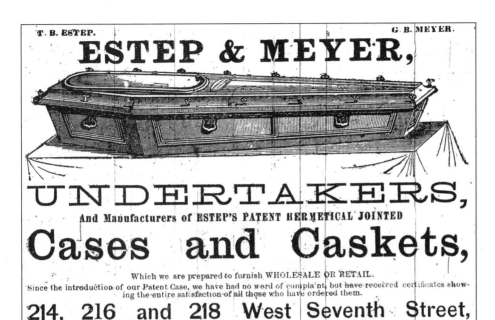

**Figure 2-1** City directory ads for undertakers. Estep & Meyer undertakers, and John P. Epply, undertaker. *1869 Williams' Cincinnati City Directory.*

southeast corner of the west half of the northeast quarter of Section 21, Township 10 North, Range 6 West. It is still in use (1972).

If your ancestor was discussed in a published family history, an earlier genealogist may have located the grave and recorded its whereabouts. Here are some places to check for published family histories:

1. **The Family History Library.** The Family History Library has more than seventy thousand biography and family history volumes. The entire library holdings are searchable online (see page 8) by several different categories; one category is surname. The results will be a list of books that focus specifically on your family of interest as well as books that might contain your surname as an "allied" branch.

2. **Public libraries with genealogy and local history departments.** Many public libraries with genealogy and local history collections now make their catalogs available online. For the locality where your ancestors lived, look for an online library catalog, then check if the repository has any published genealogies on your family. A major genealogy department with more than 38,000 published family histories is Ft. Wayne, Indiana's Allen County Public Library. Its catalog is online at <www.acpl.lib.in.us/genealogy/whoweare.html>.

3. **Genealogical Library Master Catalog.** This is a three-CD-ROM set available for purchase. It lists more than 300,000 family histories, local histories, and genealogical sources in libraries across the United States. You can learn more about this set at OneLibrary.com.

4. **Commercial online sites.** You can also check for published family histories on Internet sites such as GenealogyLibrary.com, which has collected nearly 3,000 family history books. These concentrate mostly on works published between 1880 and 1920 that are now in the public domain. The site adds three new family histories each day. For a monthly subscriber fee, you can access the collection. Another site that is beginning to publish family histories is Virtually Remembered.com. The histories on this site have not been previously published, but are ones that people are contributing now.

5. **Family Web pages.** Also online you might find electronically published family histories. Some researchers find it more cost-effective to publish their genealogies electronically on their own home pages.

If you find a published genealogy at the Family History Library that has been microfilmed, you may order a copy of the film through your local Family History Center. If it has not been microfilmed, then you need to visit the library or have someone check the book for you. If, however, the only existing copy is in a library that won't loan it through interlibrary loan, try locating a copy through an online used bookstore. If that doesn't work, you'll have to add making a trip to that repository to your to-do list.

## Diaries and Letters

**If you are lucky enough to have diaries and letters among your family history papers, make sure you read these for possible clues to death and place of burial.** When Mary-

**For More Info**

For more resources to help you find published family histories, see Sharon DeBartolo Carmack's "An Open Book," *Family Tree Magazine* (June 2000): 24–29.

**Hidden Treasures**

ellen Harshbarger McVicker was working on her doctoral dissertation about cemeteries in the Boonslick region of Missouri, she used the Mitchell family graveyard in Cooper County, Missouri, as a case study. Thomas Mitchell had kept a diary, and on 29 May 1888, he recorded information about the family plots after he and Jimmy, his African-American farmhand, and two other hands had gone to the burial ground for its annual repair and cleanup. Following are the opening paragraphs of a detailed account of who's buried there.

> Jimmy, myself, and two other hands went to Mr. Viertel's my early home, and refenced with mulberry posts, one plank and three wires, the graves of my People. We trimmed up the trees and improved the general appearance of things very much. The ground fenced is twelve steps east and west by twenty four north and south. My grandmother Mitchell rests here since Oct. 27, 1820. Her grave is near the centre of the lot and was perhaps the first one buried here. It is covered with a large limestone slab—and my grandfather Mitchell who died Aug. 13, 1839 in the 73rd year of his age rests by her side on the south. My great grandparents on my mother's side, John and Mary Miller, he at age 88 and she at 86 years, rest here also at the end of their pilgrimage. They were Presbyterians of the straightest sect. . . .

Of course, existing diaries and letters, if not already in your possession, can be difficult to find, so **here are some tips and sources for trying to track them down.**

1. Ask relatives if they possess any ancestors' diaries or letters.
2. Put queries in genealogical magazines and on the Web, seeking diaries or letters that may be in the possession of distant "genealogy" cousins.
3. Check the Internet. Several Web sites are digitizing old diaries and posting them. Type the keywords "diary" and "diaries" into a search engine.
4. Write to historical societies, archives, and libraries in your ancestor's locality to see if a diary or any letters were deposited there.
5. Check reference guides to help locate diaries and letters in repositories, such as the *National Union Catalog of Manuscript Collections*, discussed in chapter one under Bible Records. Other sources are

*American Diaries: An Annotated Bibliography of Published American Diaries and Journals*, by Laura Arksey, Nancy Pries, and Marcia Reed. Detroit, Mich.: Gale Research Co., 1983, 1987.

*New England Diaries, 1602–1800. A Descriptive Catalogue of Diaries, Orderly Books and Sea Journals*, compiled by Harriette Merrifield Forbes. New York: Russell and Russell, 1976; originally published privately 1923.

*The Published Diaries and Letters of American Women: An Annotated Bibliography*, compiled by Joyce D. Goodfriend. Boston: G.K. Hall and Co., 1987.

*American Diaries: An Annotated Bibliography of American Diaries Written Prior to the Year 1861*, compiled by William Matthews. Berkeley: University of California Press, 1945.

*American Diaries in Manuscript, 1580–1954: A Descriptive Bibliography,*

**Notes**

This excerpt is quoted in Maryellen's excellent case study, "The Mitchell Family Burial Ground: A Case Study in a Boonslick Family Burial Ground," must reading for anyone restoring a family graveyard <http://mo-river.net/history/boonslick/chapter 3.htm.> Her full dissertation, "Reflections of Change: Death and Cemeteries in the Boonslick Region of Missouri," is at <http://mo-river.net/history/boonslick/index.htm.>

**Tip**

**Figure 2-2** Deed between Enon Babtist [*sic*] Church and Charles B. Dyer for burial lot, Hamilton Co., Ohio, Cemetery Deeds 1:8. *FHL 344600.*

compiled by William Matthews. Athens: The University of Georgia Press, 1974.

Don't forget also to look for published diaries, including published diary anthologies, and diaries and letters of your ancestor's friends, relatives, and neighbors, which may contain notations about your ancestor's death and burial.

## CEMETERY DEEDS

Just as you would receive a deed showing your ownership to a piece of land, you get an original deed when you buy a cemetery plot. A copy is typically recorded in one of two places: with the town or county—either in traditional deed books or in one designated for the cemetery—or with the cemetery sexton. In these records, you'll find the names of the buyer and seller (grantor and grantee), as well as the amount paid for the plot, the lot number, and where it is located in the cemetery. (See figure 2-2 on page 56.)

Within regular land deeds you can sometimes find where family plots were located. For example, in Greene County, Missouri, Deed Book E:192, on 17 January 1850, Arthur N. and Mary Davis sold to Tapley Daniel, for $700, the NE ¼ of section 24 township 30 range 22, except for the fifty-foot square at the graveyard. Obviously, the Davises did not want to sell the family burial plot when they vacated the land.

## CEMETERY PLAT MAPS

While you may not find plat maps for defunct or family cemeteries, those cemeteries still open for interments should have some sort of map or register so that grave diggers don't accidentally dig a fresh grave over one in use. Check for cemetery plat maps at the cemetery office or with town or county offices. Cemetery maps will give the name of the person or persons occupying graves. (See figure 2-3 on page 58.) Some maps may give more detailed information, such as the date of burial. In some cases, the maps might have been created in modern times if other cemetery records have been lost and burials are still taking place; therefore, you won't find everyone who's buried in the cemetery on the map. If the grave is unmarked or the marker is missing, then that person's grave won't be on the map.

## CEMETERY TRANSCRIPTIONS

If you haven't already noticed, genealogists love cemeteries. It's their favorite place to hang out, and frankly, if it weren't for the need to see an ancestor's tombstone, some genealogists might never venture outdoors and leave their computers or the library. Thoughtful and kindhearted genealogists get bees in their bonnets while they're in the fresh air and decide to copy down all of the tombstone inscriptions. Then they publish the inscriptions in a book or on the Internet so others will have access to them. Genealogical societies, cemetery

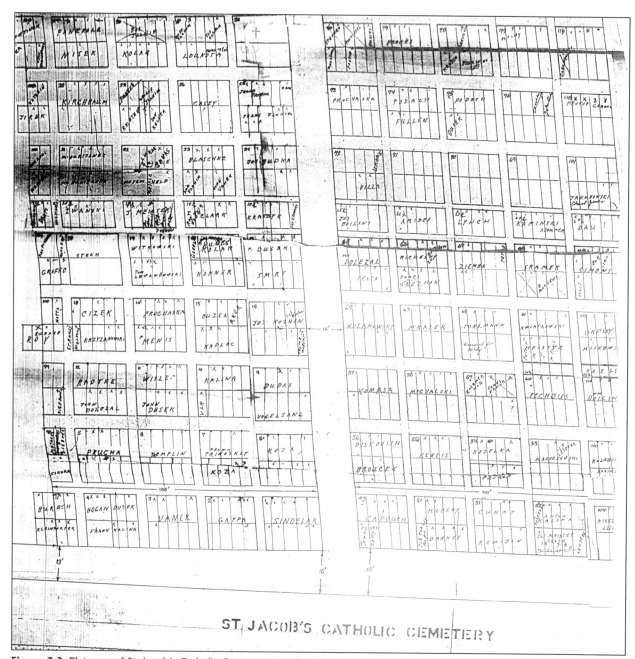

**Figure 2-3** Plat map of St. Jacob's Catholic Cemetery, North Judson, Indiana.
*FHL 1638079, item 16.*

associations, and other organizations, such as the National Society, Daughters of the American Revolution (DAR), often take on cemetery transcribing projects. You can check the DAR library catalog online at <www.dar.org/library/onlinlib.html>. Some cemetery transcripts may be published; others may be available only in manuscript form or on index cards. The New England Historic Genealogical Society in Boston, Massachusetts, for example, has a large collection of cemetery transcriptions in manuscript form. Check to see if the area you're interested in has a state, county, or town cemetery association, historical society, or genealogical society that may have a card file or manuscript collection of transcribed inscriptions.

Between 1935 and 1943, the Works Progress Administration (WPA) Historical Records Survey undertook a cemetery survey project. It was done on a county by county basis—although not every county took part—so the end results varied. Some have typed manuscripts; others have card files. Some contain just the tombstone inscriptions; others have maps of the county showing cemetery locations. Some augmented the project with newspaper obituaries and death notices. Some only recorded the war dead or veterans. Unfortunately, these WPA cemetery transcripts are not centrally housed, and you will need to check county repositories and state libraries and archives for them. The Saving Graves Web site is compiling a master index to the WPA cemetery project that will be available online with links to the transcriptions or where the records are housed <www.savinggraves.com/wpa/index.htm>. If you are aware of any of these projects in your locality, please e-mail your name and contact information to wpaproject@savinggraves.com. Also check the online library catalog of the DAR mentioned previously, since they have a large collection of WPA Historical Records Survey projects.

To find published cemetery transcriptions, check the catalog of the Family History Library. Once there, enter the locality where you believe your ancestor was buried. Then look for the subject heading "cemetery." This library has, perhaps, the largest collection of published cemetery transcriptions. *Obituaries: A Guide to Sources*, 2d ed., by Betty M. Jarboe, mentioned in chapter one, also lists published cemetery transcriptions. Many transcriptions are now being published online. See the listings on page 75 under Virtual Cemeteries, Obituaries, and Funeral Homes.

## Analyzing Published Cemetery Transcriptions

The only problem with published cemetery transcriptions, both paper-and-ink and online versions, is there is no set standard when it comes to formatting the information for publication. I randomly surveyed about thirty published

### CEMETERY SERENDIPITY

My husband, Steve, and I were in Dade County, Missouri, visiting relatives, both alive and dead. I knew one of his ancestors was buried in a particular cemetery since I had found the inscription in a book of cemetery transcriptions a few months earlier at the Family History Library in Salt Lake City. The transcription was published a few years earlier, so the stone still had to be legible. We walked row after row after row and couldn't find the headstone I was seeking. It was a hot July day, so we took a break under one of the only shade trees in the cemetery, Steve choosing to sit on a tombstone. Exasperated that I couldn't find the woman I was looking for and ready to start my row-by-row hunt again, I happened to look down and saw that Steve was sitting on the tombstone I had been looking for!

cemetery transcriptions from a variety of localities while I was at the Family History Library. They are as individual as snowflakes, and good and not-so-good ones exist.

- Some included plat maps of the cemetery.
- Some looked like computer database printouts.
- Some arranged the inscriptions in alphabetical order. (Horrors! **This destroys possible family connections and the original layout of the graves.**)
- Some were augmented with genealogical information, but among these were some that didn't tell where that information came from nor was the information distinguishable from what was on the headstone.
- Some gave only the life span of the deceased in years and didn't include any other information. Some probably presented "died in her 47th year" as "aged 47 years," and some probably did the math to determine a birth year, which is only approximate, at best.
- Most gave directions to the cemetery.
- Some gave the history of the cemetery.
- Some gave all the information on the stone, but neglected to tell you the starting point of the transcriptions, so there's no way to tell where in the cemetery the graves are located.
- None included what gravestone art was on the marker, which can be an important clue in your research (see chapter five).
- The overwhelming majority never noted the composition of the stone to indicate the age of the grave.
- For some, it was impossible to tell if the information came from the compiler walking the cemetery and transcribing the stones, or if the compiler was publishing information from the cemetery records, or both.

As you can see, cemetery transcripts are not all created equally. **Yes, they are wonderful research tools and finding aids, but like any other secondary source of information, it pays to go to the original.** There could also be typographical errors in the compilation, and you won't know for sure if it was the transcriber's mistake or a stonecutter's error until you see the stone for yourself (or a picture of it, if you need to have someone view the stone for you).

For example, in O.E. Pilson's compilation *Tombstone Inscriptions of the Cemeteries of Patrick County, Virginia* (Baltimore: Gateway Press, 1984), page 49, Jacob Shough's date of death from his headstone is given as 11 February 1892. The problem is Jacob's will was proved 7 February 1892 (Patrick Co., Va., Wills 8:113–114), three days before he supposedly died. Since a person typically has to die before that person's will can be entered into probate, either Pilson's date is a typo or the marker carries the error. In this case, you don't even have to see the gravestone to know there's a mistake somewhere, but it would still be a good idea to know where the error lies.

## CHURCH GRAVEYARDS

If you discover through other sources that your ancestor belonged to a church, check to see whether the church has burial registers, and if your ancestor was

**NOT ALL TRANSCRIPTIONS ARE CREATED EQUAL**

Several years ago, my husband and I were researching his family in Dallas County, Alabama. At the library in Selma, we came across a book of local cemetery records and found the cemetery in which many of his ancestors and connections were buried. The book listed the names and dates of birth and death on the tombstones. A short time later, we came across another cemetery book with the same cemetery included. This book had full transcriptions of everything on the tombstone. The other book had left out so much information. This book also had directions to the cemetery and the exact row and placement of each grave.

—Regina Hines Ellison

buried in the church graveyard. If the church no longer exists, then the extant records may be with another church of the same denomination in the area, deposited with a local historical or church archive, or microfilmed and available through the Family History Library.

## FAMILY BURIAL GROUNDS

Family cemeteries on private property are often the most difficult to find. If you're unable to travel to the area to ask locals where a family plot might be, here are a couple of avenues to try:

- Write to the local postmaster or mistress (if it's a small community). That person may be able to put you in touch with someone, such as a town historian, who knows where the cemetery is.
- Write to the county surveyor's office, and ask if they know about family burial plots in the area.
- Put an ad in the local newspaper or write a letter to the editor, asking if anyone knows the whereabouts of the family cemetery.
- Post queries on genealogical and cemetery Web sites (see Virtual Cemeteries, Obituaries, and Funeral Homes on page 75).

Other places to contact are the local or county genealogical or historical societies or cemetery associations. These groups often have done an inventory or made transcriptions of all the cemeteries in the area.

## GRAVES ALONG THE OREGON-CALIFORNIA TRAILS

Thousands of pioneers died on their journey west along the Oregon and California trails and were buried along the trails where they died. According to John D. Unruh Jr. in *The Plains Across: The Overland Emigrants and the Trans-*

---

### BURIED IN ALPHABETICAL ORDER?

We stopped just as soon as we pulled into the cemetery, looking for Grandma and Grandpa Stone's graves. It had been a long trip with our young daughter, Ginger, and we piled out eagerly.

"Here's Junior Bowlan," said Marleen. His mother, father, and some uncles had graves there, too, so we studied them for a moment.

"And there's Bobby Brown," I added as I looked to the next row. "I wonder where Grandma Stone is buried."

Ginger pointed far out over the cemetery. "She's buried over there," she declared.

I looked out to where she was pointing and wondered if she had a premonition. "What makes you think she isn't right here close?" I asked.

She pointed at the Bowlan and Brown headstones near us. "Daddy," she said indignantly. "This is the 'B' section."

—Lin Stone

---

*Mississippi West, 1840–60* (Urbana: University of Illinois Press, 1979), pages 408–409,

> Disease was far and away the number one killer, accounting for nearly nine out of every ten deaths. Although the emigrant was never completely safe from the scourge of epidemic disease, the initial portion of the trail to Fort Laramie, otherwise the easiest segment of the journey, occasioned the most disease-induced deaths. . . . Slightly over half of the burials had occurred east of Fort Laramie, nearly three-fourths prior to Fort Hall, and the last 21 percent beyond Fort Boise. . . . Diarrhea, tuberculosis, smallpox, mumps, and a host of other illnesses downed travelers, but the chief afflictions were cholera, mountain fever, and scurvy.

Unruh's research showed that in 1850 and 1852, most emigrants who died before reaching Fort Laramie died from cholera. If they managed to get beyond that point, "they encountered what was commonly termed 'mountain fever.' Either Rocky Mountain spotted fever or Colorado tick fever, the disease was less virulent than cholera but deadly enough." If emigrants survived past that point, "the last portion of the journey found them most susceptible to scurvy as months without sufficient fruits and vegetables began to take their toll." Accidents such as drowning and careless handling of firearms were the next common causes of deaths along the trails.

Historians disagree on the total number of deaths along the Overland Trail. Some estimate as many as thirty thousand, but Marsha Hoffman Rising, CG, FASG, believes the number is considerably less, perhaps around five thousand.

This is based on her attempts to actually document the identities of those who died on the Overland Trail. After four years of study, she has been able to identify only 1,700. "Many of the published sources appear to be duplicating deaths," said Rising. "For example, Robert Burchard was mentioned in a diary as having died on 17 June 1850, and in the newspaper, he was reported as dying on June 19. Both reported he originated from Osage, Missouri, but one source says he died along the Platte River, the other says he died 170 miles west of Fort Kearney but was buried along the Platte River. This is obviously the same man, but if a researcher were just counting numbers of deaths from sources, Burchard probably would have been counted twice."

Many graves were not marked to protect the body from human predators, but a few hundred marked graves are still visible. The Graves and Sites Committee of the Oregon-California Trails Association, P.O. Box 1019, Independence, MO 64051-0519, <http://octa-trails.org>, works to identify graves, mark unidentified ones, and preserve those that remain. They have published *Graves and Sites on the Oregon and California Trails* by Randy Brown and Reg Duffin. This book tells where each identified grave is located, who owns the property, how to gain access to the site, and what biographical information about the pioneer is known.

## GRAVE OPENINGS AND TRANSFERS

After I gave a lecture on cemetery research to one genealogical society, a lady raised her hand with a question. She wanted to know how she could tell if her ancestor was really buried where his grave was marked. If you, too, have had this burning question and want to have a grave opened—just to make sure your ancestor is really there—you can do this in one of two ways. You can open the grave yourself, but you'd be charged with a felony; or you can have it done legally by petitioning the court (see figure 2-5 on page 67). Both methods create quite a bit of paperwork, but the latter doesn't involve any jail time. Either way will cost you a pretty penny. Typically, you can't just walk into the cemetery office and ask for a grave to be opened without good cause. Good cause would be transferring the body to a new resting place (and not to your backyard) or for a postmortem exhumation (and not one done by you). Records of grave openings and transfers will be on file with the cemetery office, and when the body was transferred, the funeral home that handled the body will have a record as well (see chapter one, Bodies in Transit, on page 9).

## RELOCATED AND DEFUNCT CEMETERIES

Cemeteries get relocated all the time because of changes in the use of the land. There generally is a record of this when it happens. A model reinterment project will include painstaking efforts to record everyone who was buried in the original cemetery and where remains are moved to in the new cemetery. Even unmarked graves get attention, with researchers attempting to identify the remains from other sources.

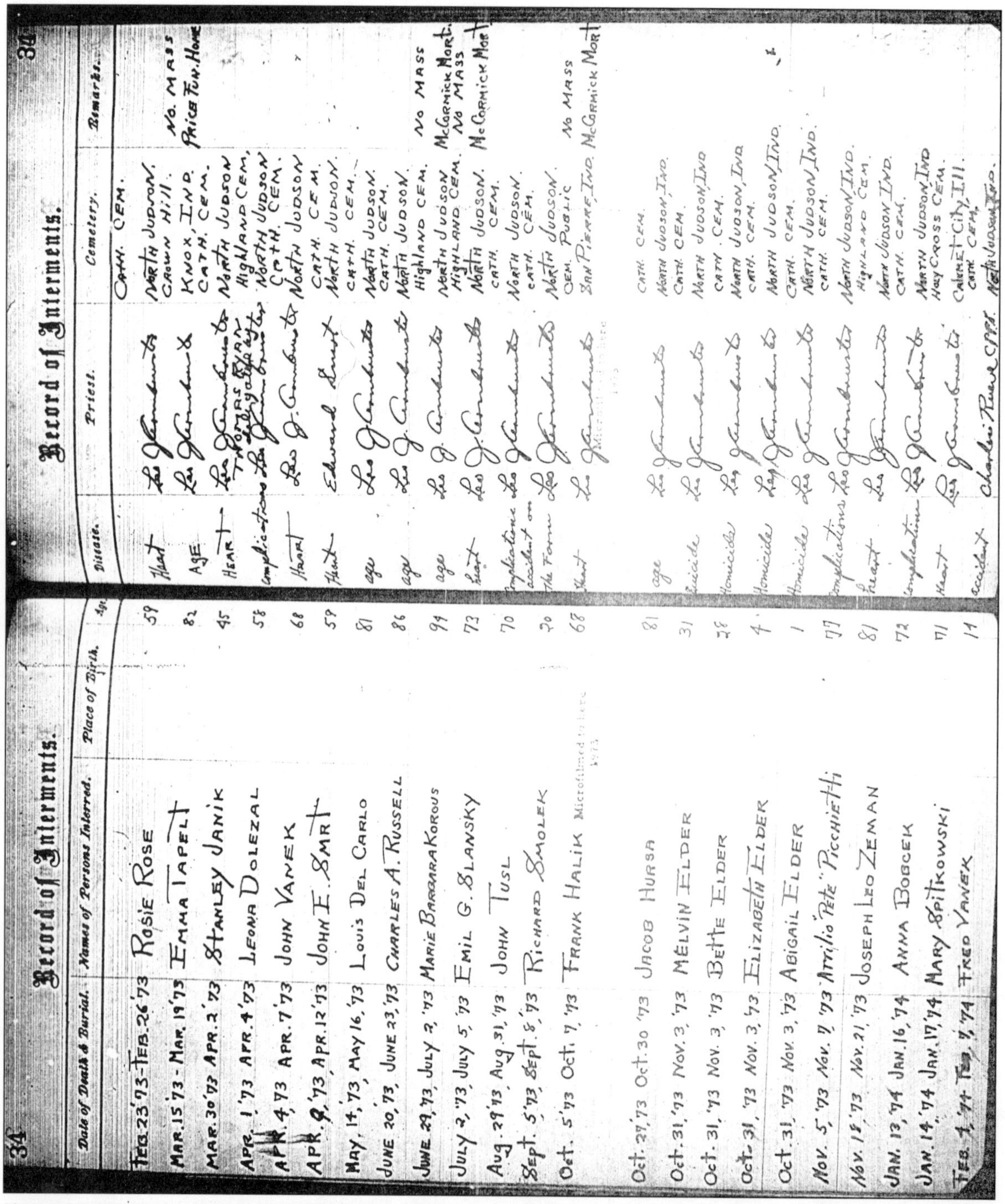

**Figure 2-4** St. Jacob's Interments, 1894–1989, Parish of Cyril and Methodius, North Judson, Starke Co., Indiana. Note the Elder family's causes of death. *FHL 1638079, item 18.*

According to *Relocated Cemeteries in Oklahoma and Parts of Arkansas-Kansas-Texas* by Madeline S. Mills and Helen R. Mullenax (Tulsa, Okla.: the authors, 1974), "throughout the State of Oklahoma, and parts of Arkansas, Kansas, and Texas, there were numerous cemeteries which had to be relocated due to the construction of the Arkansas River navigational system, various flood control projects, and the expansion of the Fort Sill Army Installation in

## NEW CONSTRUCTION FINDS OLD CEMETERY

"A sliver of human bone found at a city-owned parking lot in Staten Island offers new evidence of a 19th Century cemetery for quarantined immigrants—and may jeopardize construction of a $40-million court complex on the site."

So opened the article "A Clue to Immigrants' Sad Past: Cemetery find could jeopardize court construction" in *Newsday* on 2 February 2001, page A12. Testing confirmed that the bone fragment, likely from a female shinbone, was more than one hundred years old, and it was found on the northernmost corner of a 578-space parking lot, near Hyatt Street.

As it turned out, the land was the site of a quarantine hospital that opened in 1799 after "an outbreak of communicable diseases, including typhoid, cholera, tuberculosis, smallpox and yellow fever." The diseases "were traced to immigrants arriving in New York." The hospital, known as Marine Hospital, operated until 1858. Those who died in the hospital were buried in an adjoining cemetery until 1849. After that, the hospital bought property to use as its cemetery in a neighboring town.

Unfortunately, no one knows how many bodies were buried on the hospital's site, but Staten Island officials think "anywhere from 700 to several thousand immigrants are interred there."

Because sick immigrants were known to bribe their way out of the hospital or escape, spreading infectious disease across New York City, a group of angry citizens set the hospital ablaze in 1858 after carrying the sick and dying patients into the street. And, naturally, all the records went up in smoke.

Oklahoma. This book shows the locations of the original cemeteries, the people buried in them . . . and the relocation cemeteries."

Another major cemetery relocation project was through the Tennessee Valley Authority. The Master File Relocation Card Index for Grave and Cemetery Removal and Relocation, 1934–1954, is on microfilm at the Family History Library. The index lists the cemetery name, name of the deceased, date of birth, date of death, age, type and condition of marker and inscription, nearest living relative or source of information, source's address, and relationship to the deceased. States involved were Tennessee, Alabama, Mississippi, North Carolina, Georgia, Kentucky, and Virginia. Indexes for all of these states are available at the Family History Library.

San Francisco, California, is an interesting case of cemetery relocation. Because of space, concerns over public health, and crime, burials within the city of San Francisco became illegal in 1902. The city and county board of supervisors mandated that interments in Laurel Hill and Calvary cemeteries be removed. Ongoing disputes arose, of course, which weren't resolved until the 1940s. In an attempt to solve the problem of what to do with the exhumed bodies, Roman Catholic Archbishop Patrick Riordan blessed a potato field five miles south of the city. This site became the incorporated city of Colma, California, where "the dead outnumber the living." For a time line of San Francisco cemeteries, see City of the Silent Web site at <www.notfrisco.com/colmatales/timeline.htm l>. For a chart detailing "Where the Dead Went," covering dates when San Francisco cemeteries were in operation and their fates, see <www.notfrisco .com/colmatales/sfgen.html>. Today, only two cemeteries remain in the city of San Francisco—the San Francisco National Cemetery at the Presidio and the Mission Dolores Cemetery—but both no longer allow burials.

Sometimes acts of nature, flooding in particular, moved cemeteries. When the Missouri River flooded on 12 July 1993, it severely damaged the cemetery in Hardin, Ray County, Missouri. According to the *News-Leader* of 11 July 1998, page 3A, out of 1,576 burials, 793 remains were lost. Of those, 645 bodies were recovered, but only 120 could be identified. The remaining 525 were reinterred in the north side of the cemetery in a section known as the "Unknown Section." These graves are marked with small stones, and a marker at the cemetery entrance explains the unfortunate circumstances.

**Sources**

**If you suspect that a cemetery has been moved, ask the town hall, county courthouse, local library, or historical society.** Someone there should know where the records would be. Once you narrow down a date when the cemetery would have been relocated, check the local newspapers. There will be articles about the relocation and the seeking of relatives of those being reinterred.

If a cemetery is no longer in use, there probably is no longer a cemetery office or a sexton, and the records may no longer exist. But still check places like the town hall, the county courthouse, and the local historical society to see if any records do exist. Your best bet, however, may be a published book of cemetery inscriptions.

Also keep in mind that sometimes the name of the cemetery will change. In 1934, a WPA transcribing team copied down all the tombstones in New Catholic Cemetery in Greenwich, Connecticut. Today that same cemetery is known as St. Mary's Cemetery. Mount Washington Cemetery in Colorado Springs, Colorado, was founded in 1871, but the name was changed in 1877 to Evergreen Cemetery. Sometimes cemeteries can be known by more than one name and not actually have an official name. These names may be applied informally after the name of the community, the road on which it's located, a farm it's located near, or the name of someone or a family buried there. If you find the name of a cemetery on a record, but you're having trouble locating it, check with the local funeral home or an old-timer of the town. They will likely know the informal name and whether that cemetery is operating under a different name.

## SEXTON'S RECORDS

The person in charge of a cemetery and its records was known as the sexton; today the person is known as the cemetery superintendent. This person might

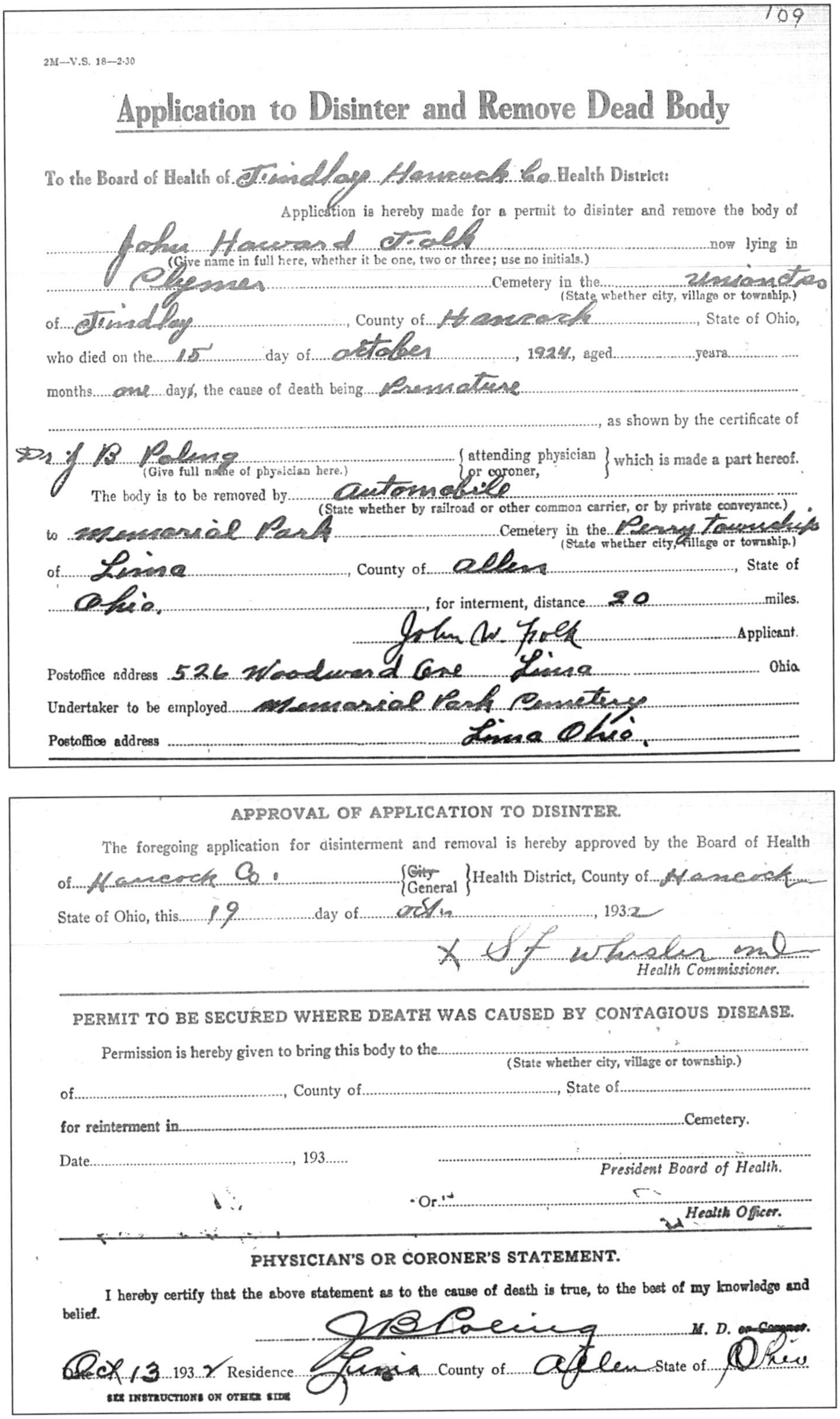

109

2M—V.S. 18—2-30

**Application to Disinter and Remove Dead Body**

To the Board of Health of Findlay Hancock Co Health District:

Application is hereby made for a permit to disinter and remove the body of John Howard Folk now lying in (Give name in full here, whether it be one, two or three; use no initials.) Clymer Cemetery in the Union twp (State whether city, village or township.) of Findlay, County of Hancock, State of Ohio, who died on the 15 day of October, 1924, aged ........ years ........ months one day, the cause of death being Premature ........, as shown by the certificate of Dr J B Poling (Give full name of physician here.) {attending physician / or coroner,} which is made a part hereof.

The body is to be removed by automobile (State whether by railroad or other common carrier, or by private conveyance.) to Memorial Park Cemetery in the Perry Township (State whether city, village or township.) of Lima, County of Allen, State of Ohio, for interment, distance 20 miles.

John W. Folk Applicant.

Postoffice address 526 Woodward Ave Lima Ohio.

Undertaker to be employed Memorial Park Cemetery

Postoffice address Lima Ohio.

**APPROVAL OF APPLICATION TO DISINTER.**

The foregoing application for disinterment and removal is hereby approved by the Board of Health of Hancock Co. {~~City~~ / General} Health District, County of Hancock, State of Ohio, this 19 day of Oct, 1932

S F Whisler MD
Health Commissioner.

**PERMIT TO BE SECURED WHERE DEATH WAS CAUSED BY CONTAGIOUS DISEASE.**

Permission is hereby given to bring this body to the ........ (State whether city, village or township.) of ........, County of ........, State of ........ for reinterment in ........ Cemetery.

Date ........, 193.... ........ President Board of Health.

Or ........ Health Officer.

**PHYSICIAN'S OR CORONER'S STATEMENT.**

I hereby certify that the above statement as to the cause of death is true, to the best of my knowledge and belief.

J B Poling M. D. ~~or Coroner.~~

~~Date~~ Oct 13 1932 Residence Lima County of Allen State of Ohio

SEE INSTRUCTIONS ON OTHER SIDE

**Figure 2-5** Application to Disinter and Remove Dead Body for John Howard Folk, Burial Permits and Removals, 1909–1991, Hancock Co., Ohio. *FHL 1908776, item 9.*

be responsible for a nonsecular or church cemetery, and in early America, he might also handle bell-ringing to toll a person's death and either dig the grave himself or hire someone.

Sexton's records typically give the name of the deceased, the date of burial, and sometimes the age of the deceased and the relationship to a survivor. You might also find the exact location of the grave in the cemetery. Others may include the fee charged for digging the grave, ringing the bell, and erecting the tombstone. Following are examples from the account book of Aaron Van Nostrand, sexton at Grace Episcopal Church of Jamaica, Long Island, New York, 1773–1820, as copied by Josephine C. Frost in 1913 (FHL 17713, item 12):

> 1780 Oct. 24 Gen. Delancy; for Major Weller; digging grave 10/; fun. bell 5/; pall 4/; inviting and attending 16/.
> 1806 John Skimore; sodding and putting up wife's tombstone.
> 1817 Jan. 3 Tunis Van Brunt; grave for Mr. Van deBelt; for his remains broght [*sic*] from Yards, Far Rockaway to Jamaica Church 16/.

You can find a variety of information in visiting the cemetery office or locating the records in a town or city hall: who was buried in a plot, who purchased the plot, who is responsible for the grave's upkeep, such as a relative living in the area. Sometimes the records will tell when the marker was placed and who the stonecutter was. Sometimes you may find an obituary or death certificate among the records. **You may also find named in the records other relatives buried in the plot that are not named on the grave marker.** If you run across a locked tomb or mausoleum that contains the inscriptions inside, you'll need the records to determine who's buried there. If you're trying to locate living relatives, ask if you can attach a card with your name and number to the burial record, so if some long lost cousin happens to be searching for the same ancestors, he or she can find you.

**Notes**

## VETERANS CEMETERIES

Soldiers who died prior to the Civil War were buried either in cemetery plots on posts and forts or right where the death occurred. Even after the Civil War, soldiers of the Regular Army, Union Army, and some Confederate Army and their family members were buried on military installations. Many of the remains were removed, however, to a national cemetery. Check the National Archives microfilm publication M2014, *Burial Records for Military Posts, Camps, and Stations, 1768–1921*. This two-volume register, part of the Records of the Office of the Quartermaster General, Record Group 92, was based on each post's burial records or grave markers. Although there are some entries for eighteenth-century graves, most of the burials occurred between 1860 and 1890. Arranged by military post and rough chronological order of burials, you'll find name, rank, company, regiment, date of death, location of grave (section and number), and remarks, which may include the cause of death or a civilian's relationship to the soldier.

On 17 July 1862, Congress enacted legislation authorizing the purchase of land to be used as national cemeteries "for soldiers who shall have died in the service of the country." In that year, fourteen national cemeteries were established:

| Cemetery | Location |
|---|---|
| Alexandria | Alexandria, Virginia |
| Annapolis | Annapolis, Maryland |
| Antietam | Sharpsburg, Maryland |
| Camp Butler | Springfield, Illinois |
| Cypress Hills | Brooklyn, New York |
| Danville | Danville, Kentucky |
| Fort Leavenworth | Fort Leavenworth, Kansas |
| Fort Scott | Fort Scott, Kansas |
| Keokuk | Keokuk, Iowa |
| Loudon Park | Baltimore, Maryland |
| Mill Springs | Nancy, Kentucky |
| New Albany | New Albany, Indiana |
| Philadelphia | Philadelphia, Pennsylvania |
| Soldiers Home | Washington, DC |

After the Civil War, army crews sought out the remains of Union soldiers who died in battle in order to reinter them in national cemeteries. By 1870, the remains of nearly 300,000 Union soldiers had been buried in national cemeteries. Unfortunately, nearly half of the Union soldiers buried there are unknown. Confederate soldiers buried in federal cemeteries were primarily those who died in Union prison camps.

In 1873, all honorably discharged veterans became eligible for burial in national cemeteries. Jurisdiction of the cemeteries fell under the Department of the Army initially, then the Veterans Administration (now the U.S. Department of Veterans Affairs). The Veterans Administration's National Cemetery System is now known as the National Cemetery Administration.

There are presently 119 national cemeteries in thirty-nine states (and Puerto Rico), with more than two million Americans from every war—the Revolutionary War to the Gulf War—buried there. **For a list of these cemeteries go to the National Cemetery Administration Web site at <www.cem.va.gov/listcem.htm>.** Additionally, the Veterans Millennium Health Care and Benefits Act of 1999 requires the Veterans Administration to establish six more national cemeteries in these cities and states: Atlanta, Georgia; Detroit, Michigan; Miami, Florida; Sacramento, California; Pittsburgh, Pennsylvania; and Oklahoma City, Oklahoma.

## Obtaining Burial Information

The National Cemetery Administration will search its records of the 119 national cemeteries at no cost, and you can request up to a maximum of ten specific names. The only information the administration will provide, however, is whether the individual was buried in a national cemetery and where. You

**See Also**

For information on veterans' markers, see chapter three.

**Internet Source**

## CONFISCATION OF LEE'S PROPERTY

According to the Arlington National Cemetery Web site, Robert E. Lee's property was confiscated by the federal government "when property taxes levied against Arlington estate were not paid in person by Mrs. Lee." The property was offered for public sale in 1864 and purchased by a tax commissioner, then it was appropriated as a national cemetery. After Lee's death in 1870, his grandson, George Washington Custis Lee, brought an action for ejectment in the circuit court in Alexandria (now Arlington) County, Virginia. He "claimed the land had been illegally confiscated, and that, according to his grandfather's will, he was the legal owner. In December 1882, the U.S. Supreme Court, in a 5-4 decision, returned the property to Custis Lee, stating that it had been confiscated without due process." Three months later, the government purchased the property from Lee for $150,000. For more on the history of Arlington Cemetery and Arlington House, go to <www.arlingtoncemetery.org/historical_information/arlington_house.html.>

need no special form, but you need to provide the following information:

- full name, including alternate spellings
- date and place of birth
- date and place of death
- state from which the individual entered active duty
- military service branch

Most requests take about three weeks. Send your request to the U.S. Department of Veterans Affairs, National Cemetery Administration (402B), Burial Location Request, 810 Vermont Ave. NW, Washington, DC 20420.

## Arlington National Cemetery

Located on 200 acres in Virginia, Arlington National Cemetery is the only national cemetery still under the administration of the Department of the Army. More than 260,000 people have been buried at Arlington National Cemetery, which was established in 1864 from the illegally confiscated lands of Confederate General Robert E. Lee. Veterans from all wars from the American Revolution to the Gulf War are buried there, with pre–Civil War dead reinterred after 1900.

Section 27 of the cemetery is the burial site for more than 3,800 former slaves, called "contrabands" during the Civil War. Their headstones are designated with the word "civilian" or "citizen."

To locate an ancestor's grave site, telephone or visit the customer service desk in the Visitors Center. The telephone number is (703) 607-8052. The Visitors Center is open every day of the year except for Christmas Day.

## State Veterans Cemeteries

In addition to national veterans cemeteries, many states have their own state veterans cemeteries. States solely run these grounds even though they may have received some federal funding. Contact the specific cemetery for information on locating an ancestor's grave. **You can find a list of all state veterans cemeteries and contact information at <www.cem.va.gov/lsvc.htm>.**

**Internet Source**

## American Revolution and Civil War Sources

You can check two sources to help locate Revolutionary War veterans' graves. Patricia Law Hatcher's *Abstracts of Graves of Revolutionary Patriots,* four volumes, and the CD-ROM, *The SAR Revolutionary War Graves Register* (Buffalo, N.Y.: Progeny, 2000), are both available at the Family History Library. The *Graves Register* is also available for purchase through the publisher at (800) 565-0018.

Three main works will help you find your Civil War Union soldier's final resting place in a national cemetery:

- *Roll of Honor: Names of Soldiers Who Died in Defense of the American Union, Interred in the National Cemeteries.* Washington, D.C.: Government Printing Office, 1866–1868; reprinted by Genealogical Publishing Co., Baltimore, 1994, 10 vols.
- *The Unpublished Roll of Honor,* by Mark Hughes. Baltimore: Genealogical Publishing Co., 1996.
- *Index to the Roll of Honor,* compiled by Martha and William Reamy. Baltimore: Genealogical Publishing Co., 1995.

If you have a Union veteran in your family history who was buried in a family plot or private cemetery instead of in a national cemetery, all is not lost. There is a card file of Union soldiers' burial places on twenty-two rolls of

### CIVIL WAR BATTLEFIELD DEATH

Vicksburg, May 29th: to Samuel Stephenson, Esq. With feelings of deepest sorrow I seat myself on the battlefield to make a sad record—the death of your most worthy son, John B. Stephenson who was killed yesterday at 2:30 p.m. by a rifle ball passing through his head. He died instantly. The Doctor was the only regimental physician present with our sharpshooters near the fort. [Details of how he was killed and of his character.] We had a coffin made and I procured a bushel of salt to preserve the body so that I think he will be easily removed. We buried him on the field a short distance below where he fell and close along the side of two others of lamented comrades. The board that marks the grave is the lid of a cartridge box and marked "Dr. John B. Stephenson, Co. F 17th Ill. Vol. Inf. May 28th 1863." After the fall of Vicksburg, I think there will be no trouble in moving the body, should you wish it; but at present it would be very difficult to do anything. Signed, J. Moore.

*—Monmouth* [Illinois] *Atlas,* 12 June 1863.
Contributed by Marsha Hoffman Rising, CG, FASG

National Archives microfilm publication M1845, *Card Records of Headstones Provided for Deceased Civil War Veterans, ca. 1879–ca. 1903*. This card file records Union soldiers who died between about 1861 and about 1903, but there are a few War of 1812 and Revolutionary War veterans listed among the cards. The cards are arranged alphabetically by surname, then first name. While not all of the information was completely filled out, the cards were supposed to provide the name of the soldier, rank, company, regiment, place of burial (cemetery's name), location of the cemetery, grave number, date of death, name of the headstone supplier, and date of the contract with the headstone provider. The microfilm is available at the National Archives in Washington, DC, at its thirteen regional records facilities, or at the Family History Library and on loan through its Family History Centers.

For ancestors who served in the Confederacy, check state sources. Individuals and chapters of the United Daughters of the Confederacy have published some rosters of Confederate graves. Also check *Register of Confederate Soldiers, Sailors and Citizens Who Died in Federal Prisons and Military Hospitals in the North, 1861–1865*, on National Archives film M0918, which is also available at the Family History Library on film #1024456.

## WPA Veterans' Graves Registration Project

Beginning in the 1930s, the Works Progress Administration (WPA) undertook a project to register all veterans' graves in each state; however, not all counties in each state participated, so the registers are often incomplete. A few of these projects are available at the Family History Library. Look for others at state historical societies and libraries, as well as at county-level repositories. The Minnesota Historical Society is working to computerize its index of more than 72,000 graves registration reports and to eventually post the reports on its Internet site at <http://mnhs.org>. It is not clear whether this graves registration, begun in 1927, was part of the WPA project (see also Cemetery Transcriptions on page 57.)

## Soldiers Buried Overseas

According to Michael G. Knapp and Constance Potter in their article "Here Rests in Honored Glory: World War I Graves Registration," soldiers who died overseas during World War I "were often buried several times—a quick burial a day, week, or even longer after death; a more formal burial in a local cemetery; and finally burial in an American military cemetery in Europe or a cemetery back in the United States." The Graves Registration Service (GRS) is responsible for keeping records of these burials.

After the war, the GRS sent a questionnaire to each deceased soldier's next of kin, asking whether the person wanted to bring the soldier's remains back to the United States for interment. While the majority of remains were returned home for reburial in either a nonmilitary or national cemetery, many families opted to leave their loved ones in Europe. More than thirty thousand now rest in one of the eight overseas American military cemeteries: six in France, one in Belgium, and one in Great Britain. Additionally, some of the bodies were rein-

# AMERICAN MILITARY BURIED OVERSEAS

## American Military Cemeteries Overseas for World War I Deceased

France          Aisne-Marne American Cemetery and Memorial, 6½ miles north-
                west of Chateau-Thierry, just southwest of Belleau, Aisne

                Meuse-Argonne American Cemetery and Memorial, just east of
                Romagne-Gesnes, Meuse

                Oise-Aisne American Cemetery and Memorial, 1½ miles east of
                Fere-en-Tardenois

                Somme American Cemetery and Memorial, ½ mile southwest of
                Bony, Aisne

                St. Mihiel American Cemetery and Memorial, Thiaucourt,
                Meurthe-et-Moselle

                Suresnes American Cemetery and Memoiral (both WWI and
                WWII), 4 miles west of the center of Paris in the city of Suresnes

Belgium         Flanders Field American Cemetery and Memorial, Waregem

Great Britain   Brookwood American Cemetery and Memorial, southwest of
                Brookwood, Surrey

## American Military Cemeteries Overseas for World War II Deceased

Belgium         Ardennes American Cemetery and Memorial, Neupre

                Henri-Chapelle American Cemetery and Memorial, 2 miles north-
                west of Henri-Chapelle

France          Brittany American Cemetery and Memorial, 1 mile southeast of
                St. James, Manche

                Epinal American Cemetery and Memorial, 4 miles south of Epinal,
                Vosges

                Lorraine American Cemetery and Memorial, ¾ mile north of St.
                Avoid, Moselle

                Normandy American Cemetery and Memorial, on a cliff overlook-
                ing Omaha Beach and the English Channel, east of St-Laurent-
                sur-Mer and northwest of Bayeux in Colleville-sur-Mer

                Rhone American Cemetery and Memorial, Draguignan, Var

                Suresnes American Cemetery and Memorial (see above)

Italy           Florence American Cemetery and Memorial, 7½ miles south of
                Florence

                Sicily-Rome American Cemetery and Memorial, just east of Anzio at
                the north edge of Nettuno, 38 miles south of Rome

Luxembourg      Luxembourg American Cemetery and Memorial, Luxembourg

Netherlands     Netherlands American Cemetery and Memorial, Margraten

Philippines     Manila American Cemetery and Memorial, 6 miles southeast of
                Manila

Tunisia         North Africa American Cemetery and Memorial, 10 miles north-
                east of Tunis

Great Britain   Cambridge American Cemetery and Memorial, 3 miles west of
                Cambridge

terred from other European cemeteries into these six. No matter where the body was interred or was moved to, the GRS kept a card on each of the deceased.

During World War II, families had four choices of how they wanted their soldier's remains handled:

1. Leave the remains wherever they might be buried initially.
2. Have the remains buried in an overseas cemetery other than a military one established by the United States.
3. Have the remains buried in an American military cemetery overseas.
4. Have the remains returned to the United States.

For soldiers who died overseas during World War I or World War II, records of their deaths and burials are part of Record Group 92, Records of the Office of the Quartermaster General. (For detailed descriptions of the many records in this record group, go to <www.nara.gov/guide/rg092.html>. Scroll down to the grouping under 92.9 Records of Graves Registration Organizations, 1917–1954.) The records for World War I, 92.9.1 Records of the Graves Registration Service, have not been microfilmed, but they are arranged alphabetically by surname. You can request a search by mail by providing the name of the soldier. If the name is common, also note the unit or other identifying information, such as the date of death, names of immediate family members, and the last place of residence in the United States. Write to the Military Textual Reference Branch (NWCTM), National Archives, 8601 Adelphi Road, College Park, MD 20740-6001. The records for World War II, 92.9.2 Records of the American Graves Registration Service, have been microfilmed on National Archives Microfilm Publication M1380.

During the Korean War, remains were initially shipped to a central mortuary in Japan, but all American dead were eventually returned to the United States.

## Gold Star Mothers

Mothers and widows who elected to leave their sons' or husbands' remains in Europe were entitled to make a pilgrimage to their loved ones' graves at the expense of the United States government, based on legislation passed in 1929. More than 17,000 women were eligible, and when the project ended in the fall of 1933, nearly 7,000 had taken advantage of the offer to visit the graves in Europe. The records of pilgrimages these Gold Star Mothers made are also in Record Group 92. The records are likewise arranged alphabetically by surname; but **there is a published roster of those who were eligible:** *List of Mothers and Widows of American Soldiers, Sailors, and Marines Entitled to Make a Pilgrimage to the War Cemeteries in Europe*, 71st Cong. 2d sess., House Document No. 140 (Washington, DC: Government Printing Office, 1930). To find a copy, contact a Federal Depository Library, which may be part of a major university or public library. You can also write to the National Archives address above with the name of the widow or mother, the name of the solider, and the city and state in which they lived.

**Printed Source**

### American Battle Monuments Commission

The American Battle Monuments Commission (ABMC), Pulaski Building, Room 5127, 20 Massachusetts Avenue NW, Washington, DC 20314-0001, was created in 1923 by Congress to commemorate the services of the American Armed Forces. The ABMC will provide the name, location, and general information about the cemetery in which a soldier overseas was buried; the plot, row, and grave number if appropriate; a black-and-white photograph of the headstone and section of the Tablets of the Missing on which the serviceman's name is engraved; and arrangements for floral decorations of the grave. Or visit the ABMC Web site <www.abmc.gov>, which maintains a searchable database of WWI, WWII, and Korean War dead. Also see *American Battle Monuments: A Guide to Military Cemeteries and Monuments Maintained by the American Battle Monuments Commission*, edited by Elizabeth Nishiura, for further information on World War I and World War II cemeteries overseas where American soldiers are buried.

## VIRTUAL CEMETERIES, OBITUARIES, AND FUNERAL HOMES

A growing number of cemetery transcriptions, obituaries, and funeral home records are on the Internet, so do not consider the following list complete or comprehensive. **For more sites than you ever dreamed possible, start with Cyndi's List at <www.cyndislist.com/cemetery.htm>.** There you'll find general resources; how-to articles about cemetery research; links to publications, software, and supplies; locality-specific links; and more. Also try searching in an Internet search engine under the keywords "cemetery," "cemeteries," "obituary," "obituaries," and "funeral homes."

**Internet Source**

### African American Cemeteries Online

www.prairiebluff.com/aacemetery/
This ongoing project is to record African-American cemeteries in all fifty states. As of this writing, more than half of the states have entries of some of their cemeteries.

### Cemeteries From the U.S. Civil War Center

www.cwc.lsu.edu/cwc/links/hist.htm#Cemeteries
On this site, you'll find links to Civil War cemeteries, parks, forts, and so forth. Its goal is to compile a list of all Civil War–related links on the Internet, so let the site know of other links that aren't listed here. When you click on a link for a cemetery, you might get a transcription of gravestones, or you'll be linked to the cemetery's home page.

### Cemeteries, Graveyards, Burying Grounds

www.potifos.com/cemeteries.html
Here are more than one hundred links relating to cemetery preservation, ceme-

tery lists and directories, state-by-state sources, online discussion groups, organizations and publications, worldwide sources, and more.

### Cemetery Junction

www.cemeteryjunction.com

This site has online directories of cemeteries, obituaries, and funeral homes. There are nearly 30,000 cemeteries listed in the United States cemeteries directory, which gives addresses, a map, and links to transcriptions for some listings. You'll also find nearly 20,000 links to family cemeteries, searchable by surname. The U.S. Obituary Sources has nearly 600 links, and the U.S. Obituary Citations has more than 25,000 listings in its Regional Obituary Indexing Project. You'll also find some Australian cemeteries on this site.

### Cemetery Records Online

http://interment.net

Interment.net publishes cemetery records and other materials relating to cemeteries. Like the other sites, it relies on the contributions of genealogists and researchers to submit cemetery transcriptions, which currently amount to more than two million records from nearly 4,000 cemeteries across the globe. Steve Johnson, who owns the site, also publishes "The Cemetery Column" online with information and advice on cemetery research. You'll find information on cemeteries in the United States, Canada, Australia, New Zealand, Ireland, and the United Kingdom.

### Cemetery Photos

www.rootsweb.com/~cemphoto/

Part of the RootsWeb network, this site connects you with someone who can help you get a photograph of your ancestor's tombstone. If there isn't a person available in the locality you need, you can place a query to find someone. There are photos already online that you can view, or you can submit photos you have. You'll also find a mailing list, a chat room, tips on taking tombstone photographs, and links to member pages that have cemetery photos.

### City of the Silent

www.alsirat.com/silence/index.html

City of the Silent claims to be the Web's "most extensive cemetery site." Here you can find information on cemetery symbols, epitaphs, folklore and folk art, tombstone rubbings, cemeteries as culture, cemeteries through time, and much more. There are also links to other death-related sites.

### FinalThoughts

www.finalthoughts.com

While there are no cemetery transcripts or links on this site, there is a genealogy link that offers a few articles. Basically, this site is for final needs, but what is unique is that as a member you can archive e-mail messages about your final wishes and feelings. The messages will be sent to your family after your demise.

And you needn't forewarn your relatives that you've signed up for this service. It can be a total surprise, although someone will have to notify FinalThoughts when it's time to send the e-mails. Think of the treat your family will get after they get home from your funeral and check their e-mail. It's like being able to speak from the grave! You didn't know there was e-mail service in the Great Beyond, did you? Oh, if only our ancestors had had this opportunity.

## Find a Grave

www.findagrave.com/index.html
Find a Grave lists more than 2.5 million names in nearly 30,000 cemeteries. Whether you're looking for the grave of a famous person or Aunt Flo, this is the site to check. This site also encourages visitors to add burial records.

## funeralCENTRAL

www.funeralcentral.com
Partnered with the Federation of Genealogical Societies, funeralCENTRAL publishes funeral notices similar to those submitted by funeral homes to newspapers. It's a free service, but the funeral home must send the notice for inclusion in the database. For a fee you can create a memorial by adding family photographs and stories.

## Funeral Net

www.funeralnet.com
From this site, you can locate cemeteries and funeral homes, as well as search for obituaries. While the database of funeral homes was compiled from *The National Yellow Book of Funeral Directors*, the cemetery and obituary database is incomplete. When I entered the localities for cemeteries in eastern Colorado I knew existed, I didn't get any hits. I also entered names of two people who had died recently, both of whom had obituaries in our local newspaper, and neither of them were in the database. If you click on the "genealogy" link from this site, you'll be shown a window with the Ancestry.com search engine.

## Genealogy Cemetery Resources

www.geneasearch.com/cemeteries.htm
This site links to cemetery Web sites that include transcriptions and directions and some sites with photographs.

## Haunted Cemeteries

www.zerotime.com/ghosts/cemet.htm
There are no transcriptions at this site—just descriptions of haunted cemeteries and who is believed to haunt them. If your ancestors happen to be buried in any of these graveyards or your travels take you to where these cemeteries are located, you may want to check out the hauntings for yourself.

### Headstone Hunter

www.headstonehunter.com

This is a free service for genealogists searching for cemetery headstone photographs. You can post requests for photos or volunteer to take photos.

### Obituary Central

www.obitcentral.com/obitsearch

The goal of Obituary Central is to locate, categorize, and present obituaries online. The site's staff obtains obituaries from contributions and from elsewhere on the Web. You'll find an Obituary Links Page arranged by state and county with thousands of links to online obituaries, cemetery transcriptions, and death notices. In the Obituary Archive Search Engine, you can check a vast collection through a surname search. You'll also find on this site Canadian Obituary Links, a Family Surname Obituary Archive, current obituaries, and more.

### Obituary Daily Times

www.rootsweb.com/~obituary/

This massive obituary database lists not only newspapers that are being indexed, but those that are in need of indexers. In addition to the database, if there is a Web site for the newspaper, there will be a link to it. While this is an extensive database, the obituaries are not online. The database will give you the pertinent information so that you can request a copy of the obituary.

### Obituary Lookups

http://freepages.genealogy.rootsweb.com/~obitl/

Staffed solely by volunteers, the Obit-Lookups-L is a community of researchers from all over the world who are willing to look up obituaries for free. Go to this site's home page for instructions on how to make a request or how to become a volunteer.

### Online Searchable Death Indexes for the USA

www.germanroots.com/deathrecords.html or

http://home.att.net/~wee-monster/deathrecords.html

This collection of links is to online death indexes and databases from all over the country. These include obituary indexes, cemetery databases, the Social Security Death Index, and links to smaller death indexes at the state and county level. It's updated frequently, so if you don't find your area of interest, keep trying.

### Resting Places of United States Colored Troops

www.coax.net/people/lwf/cem_usct.htm

An ongoing project, this site is compiling a list and links to cemeteries where African-American troops are buried.

### Saving Graves

www.savinggraves.com

This site is dedicated to the protection, restoration, and preservation of endangered cemeteries worldwide. On Saving Graves, you'll find Endangered Cemeteries Reports and learn about events and volunteer programs. It also reports on the cemetery status and laws of each state, gives online records, and tells how you can help preserve your local cemetery. This site is compiling the WPA Cemetery Index Project (see Cemetery Transcriptions on page 57.)

## Tomb With a View

http://members.aol/TombView/twav.html

*Tomb With a View* is a quarterly newsletter for cemetery and gravestone buffs. The newsletter covers cemetery art, history, heritage, social customs, and preservation. You'll also find book reviews, unusual epitaphs, and lots of fascinating facts. A few articles are online, as well as the contents of the current and past issues, but the newsletter is available by traditional mail subscription only. You can subscribe online, or write to *Tomb With a View*, P.O. Box 24810, Lyndhurst, OH 44124-0810.

## Tombstone Transcription Project

www.rootsweb.com/~cemetery/

This is another site that is part of the RootsWeb/USGenWeb network. The Tombstone Transcription Project organizes volunteers who will transcribe tombstone inscriptions in their area for publication on this site. To search the database, which is arranged by state and county, go to View Registry.

## Tombstone Traveller's Guide

http://home.flash.net/~leimer/

You won't find cemetery transcriptions or directories on this site, but you'll find some interesting trivia and cemetery photographs. Check here for Deathly Movies, Deadly Superstitions, Historic Graveyards, Tombstone Mysteries, and other interesting tidbits.

## Tombstones and Monumental Inscriptions

http://gye.future.easyspace.com

On this site you'll find photographs of churches, church graveyards, cemeteries, and tombstones. This is another place to look for tombstone transcriptions or to post any you've done.

## Virtual Cemetery

www.genealogy.com/vcem_welcome.html

Virtual Cemetery is similar to other sites in that you'll find a collection of tombstone photographs and transcriptions. This site accepts and welcomes contributions. At Virtual Cemetery, you can help others searching for information, create an online memorial for your ancestors, and post your tombstone photos online.

## Woodmen of the World Gravestones

www.woodmen.com

Woodmen of the World is a century-old fraternal organization where members could get discounts on headstones and monuments. These markers vary in size and shape, but most resemble tree stumps or stacks of cut wood. Some are quite elaborate, others simple stone markers. Usually they include the insignia of the organization. To find out more about this organization and the grave markers, visit this site. (See chapter five for more information on Woodmen of the World markers and insignia.)

### Yahoo's Cemetery Listings

http://dir.yahoo.com/Society_and_Culture/Death_and_Dying/Cemeteries
Here is yet another site with about fifteen links to cemeteries and cemetery studies. It's not nearly as extensive as Cyndi's List, but you may find something listed here that isn't yet on Cyndi's.

## WHAT'S NEXT?

Through the sources listed in this chapter, you should be able to locate most of your ancestors' graves, assuming a headstone still marks the spot, or locate the cemetery, assuming there is a record of the burial. As mentioned earlier, few people are lucky enough to find final resting places for all of their ancestors. If you're still having problems and are getting rather desperate, there is one final method for locating an ancestor's grave: If you know where he or she was buried, but there's no marker, then run right out and get yourself a Ground Penetrating Radar system. They only cost in the tens of thousands of dollars, but you've already spent that on genealogy anyway, right? One of these nifty devices can detect disturbed earth, defining its dimensions (width, length, and depth). A grave less than four feet long is very likely a child's grave. One five feet or more in length is an adult grave. Between four and five feet is anybody's guess. The problem, of course, is identifying the body beneath. But before you get your shovel out of the car, go back and reread Grave Openings and Transfers on page 63.

Once you find your ancestor's final resting place, you'll want to plan a trip to the cemetery. But before you go, there are some things you should know about cemeteries.

# THREE

# Searching a Cemetery

*The graveyards are full of people the world could not do without.*

—*Elbert Hubbard*

After locating the cemetery or cemeteries in which your ancestors were buried, at some point you should visit the place and see the gravestones in person. But before you jump into the car, there are a few tips that will help make your visit more pleasant and productive.

Perhaps the best time of year to make a field trip to a cemetery is in the early spring, after the snow and freezing winter rain are no longer a hindrance, yet before the weeds become overgrown. And before the snakes have come out of hibernation.

Cemeteries are wonderful places to get chiggers, ticks, bug bites, poison ivy rashes, and sunburns, so **wear protective clothing, sturdy running/tennis shoes or boots, and a hat, and bring along bug repellent and sunscreen.** (The cemetery is not the place to stop if you are dressed in your Sunday best, complete with high heels—unless you want to help aerate the grounds.) My husband, Steve, and I nicknamed one overgrown cemetery in Missouri the "tick cemetery," since it

Tip

## TICK REMOVAL

If you're not familiar with tick removal, the one thing you don't want to do is pull it out. The tick's body will separate from its head, and its little head will stay burrowed in your skin. Dowse the tick in oil—any kind will do from baby oil to cooking oil to motor oil—and it will begin to suffocate and pull itself out. When you hear it take a gasp of air, remove the creature with tweezers.

was infested with them. I escaped tick-free, but both Steve and my daughter, Laurie, were not so lucky. Make sure you do a tick check as soon as you get home. Ticks love to find warm little crevices of your skin to burrow into, such as under arms, bras, socks, waistbands, and hats.

**Warning**

**As you walk through the cemetery, watch for uneven ground, since graves tend to sink.** When Laurie was three or four, I took her for her first of many cemetery outings. She was walking behind me, when all of a sudden I heard her call out for me. She had fallen into a sunken grave. Laurie was OK and continues with her therapy. Her therapist assures me that she still has a good chance of leading a normal life.

If there is a cemetery caretaker's office, be sure to stop in and ask if there is a map or any literature about the cemetery. If you plan to do any headstone rubbings (see chapter four), ask the caretaker's permission. In large cemeteries it may be next to impossible to find your ancestor's grave without a map and knowing the section and plot in which the person was buried. Additionally, the cemetery record might give you information you didn't have from other records (see chapter two).

## CEMETERY SAFETY

It is never a good idea to go into a cemetery alone. Even if your partner doesn't enjoy walking amongst the dead, at least having another living person in the near vicinity is valuable protection. I have heard stories of individuals breaking an ankle or leg, falling down, or encountering wild animals (and the occasional strange human being) lurking in cemeteries. Better safe than sorry.

I have had only one occasion (it only takes once) when I went to a cemetery alone. I had taken my dog with me for company, and I had him tied on a rope to a nearby tree, when he started to growl and the hair on his back stood up. I couldn't see what he was upset about but untied him and held his rope. He is a 105-pound Akita-Shepard mix, so he's pretty intimidating. After several minutes, I saw an individual approaching from under an overgrown bush wearing camouflage gear. Since I was out in the middle of nowhere with my purse and camera gear, I felt very endangered. I instructed the individual to stop, which of course he ignored, so I threatened to let the dog go. Since the dog was being pretty vocal and pulling at the rope, I knew he would protect me, or at least keep the guy busy while I could get to my car and cell phone. The man obviously did not want to take on my dog and quickly left. I retreated to my car, having learned a valuable lesson due to my carelessness. I never go into cemeteries now alone or without my cell phone. Someone was obviously watching over me since it had been the first time I had ever taken the dog with me. He earned his treats that day!

—Marcia Melnyk, reprinted with permission from *The Genealogist's Question & Answer Book* (Cincinnati: Betterway Books, 2002).

# SURVEYING THE BONE YARD

You need to consider many elements when researching in a cemetery. Don't just rush in to find your ancestor's grave, photograph the headstone, then leave. Look around. This is your ancestor's final resting place. You will never be closer to your ancestor than right at this moment. What does the cemetery look like? Take a few pictures of the overall cemetery and of the gateway into the graveyard. Stroll among the graves. Look for the oldest section. Feel the different textures of the markers. Read some of the inscriptions. Take your time.

## Types of Cemeteries

What kind of cemetery is it? I bet you didn't know that there are eight different classifications of cemeteries, according to Kenneth T. Jackson and Camilo José Vergara's *Silent Cities: The Evolution of the American Cemetery*. I've added a ninth.

1. **Church graveyard.** These were our country's first cemeteries. In Europe, the elite were buried inside the church under the stone floor or in the church burial yard. This tradition of church burial—including some interments under the church floor—was carried to America. (See figure 3-1 below.) David Charles Sloane in *The Last Great Necessity: Cemeteries in American History* (page 23) reports that in 1823, "there were over 570 vaults underneath New York City

**Definitions**

The word "cemetery" was popular in the early 1830s, after several garden cemeteries opened. Its origins are Greek, meaning *sleeping chamber*. In this book, the words "cemetery," "burial ground," and "graveyard" are used interchangeably.

**Figure 3-1** Reformed Dutch Church and Cemetery, a good example of a church graveyard, Locust Valley, New York. *Collection of the author.*

**Warning**

---

### STAY OUT OF FARMERS' FIELDS!

My parents and I were taking a short trip to the Midwest when I informed them we were taking a little detour to see the condition of the grave site of my great-great-grandfather and grandmother, Henry and Eve George, buried in the Farmer's Valley Cemetery in eastern Nebraska. When we arrived at the location, a sign proclaimed "No Trespassing!" Being a rancher's daughter and remembering days of work when careless people left gates open and let cattle out, I was certainly going to obey this order. I spotted a farm just over the rise, however, so decided to go and see if this man would kindly give me permission to visit the little cemetery. I politely asked the question to a somewhat cantankerous gentleman. He looked me over carefully, looked my parents over, and then checked the license plate of our car. After careful consideration, he reluctantly gave his permission with the additional comment, "You're from Wyoming, so I guess it will be okay."

I was a little curious about this statement and just had to ask if he was from Wyoming, or if he knew people from there in order to trust us with his property.

"Heavens no!" he replied, "I'm not from Wyoming, but I don't think you would be the type to mess with the marijuana!"

"Marijuana?" we shouted at once. We certainly did not want to get into that problem!

"Yup," he said. "It grows wild here and there, and those easterners and Californers come trooping around these farmlands to pick it and mess up my corn crops!"

We ardently promised not to touch anything in his field—not even a fat ear of corn. We thanked him and merrily went on our way. By the way, the old stones in the cemetery were in good shape, and the photos turned out quite well.

—Sharon Lass Field

---

Churches." When the church graveyard became too crowded and the odor from the decomposing bodies buried under the church floor became overwhelming and unsanitary, town cemeteries were born. Property usually on the outskirts of town was set aside for the graveyard. These early church and town graveyards probably won't be laid out in neat rows like later cemeteries. Grave placement tended to be haphazard.

2. **Family burial plots.** Although called "family cemeteries," neighbors and relatives by marriage were also buried in these graveyards. Family burial grounds are most common in the South, where plantation living made it impractical to transport a body miles into town for a church yard burial. Burial grounds were on a person's property, usually located in an orchard or a garden, often on a high point of the land. They may be difficult to locate today if the cemetery

hasn't been maintained and is not well known among the community. Some genealogical societies have a cemetery committee, that not only transcribes tombstones in local cemeteries, but also attempts to locate and document family burial grounds. So for hard-to-find grave sites, check with the local genealogical society and talk with old-timers in the area. Some family plots, however, might have buildings over them now, or as one genealogist found, the family burial plot was at the end of a major airport's runway. She had to get permission from airport authorities to set foot on the land and visit her ancestors' graves.

3. **Country cemetery.** These are the ones you see as you drive along the highways of America. (See figure 3-2 below.) Sometimes they are on the edge of town; sometimes they are within a mile or two of the town. When possible, these cemeteries were set upon a hill to protect the graves from floods. They are usually not very large, making them easy to search, and they often contain homemade or mail-order markers (see figure 3-3 on page 86 and also chapter one). Rarely will you find large monuments or mausoleums. Perhaps the most famous of the country graveyards is the fictional one in Grover's Corner, New Hampshire, located on a "windy hilltop" in Thornton Wilder's *Our Town*.

**Figure 3-2** Ramah Cemetery, a country cemetery, in Ramah, Colorado.
*Collection of the author.*

4. **Garden cemetery.** As Americans' attitudes toward death changed from the grim reality of death toward finding beauty in death—for example, using makeup on the deceased and making loved ones look lifelike—cemeteries began to take on a more pleasingly aesthetic look. The garden-type cemetery replaced the graveyard and church yard, and the word "cemetery" replaced the terms "graveyard" and "burying ground." The first of its kind, in 1831, was Mount Auburn Cemetery in Cambridge, Massachusetts. These cemeteries look like parks with pathways, ponds, trees, foliage, and benches (see figure 3-4 on page 86). Before there were public parks, this was where people went on Sunday afternoons to picnic, contemplate, make love, and take afternoon strolls. Even the names of cemeteries started to emphasize beauty and natural spaces: Laurel Hill (Pennsylvania, 1836), Green-Wood (New York, 1838), Spring Grove (Ohio,

**Figure 3-3** Homemade carving on purchased marker, often seen in country cemeteries. Thomas Kipp stone, 1782. East Hillside Cemetery, Glen Head, New York.

*Collection of the author.*

1845). These are large cemeteries, and you will likely need to visit the cemetery office to find out where your ancestor was buried. Usually the office will give you a map and point out the section you need to find.

**Figure 3-4** Spring Grove Cemetery, Cincinnati, Ohio. Garden cemeteries such as this became popular in the 1830s and 1840s.

*Collection of the author.*

5. **Urban cemetery.** These city cemeteries might look like a "stone yard" with their rows and rows of tombstones, straight paths, and little foliage. They, too, can be fairly large, requiring you to check with the office for grave location. Urban cemeteries are often "public" cemeteries that are run by the city. (See figure 3-5 on page 87.)

6. **Veterans cemetery.** These are for the honorably discharged and their families. There are 119 national veterans cemeteries; Arlington National Cemetery is

**Figure 3-5** Evergreen Cemetery, Colorado Springs, Colorado. This photo depicts an urban cemetery, but Evergreen is interesting because it ranges from urban to garden cemetery, and includes a section that resembles a memorial park, fraternal sections, veterans sections, and a potter's field.
*Collection of the author.*

**Figure 3-6** Veterans' section, Evergreen Cemetery, Colorado Springs, Colorado.
*Collection of the author.*

the best known. (See chapter two for more information on veterans cemeteries.)

7. **Memorial park or lawn-park cemetery.** These are flat, grassy lawns with barely any visible evidence that people were buried there—and that is their purpose: to eliminate suggestions of death (see figure 3-7 on page 88). There are no grave mounds, and the headstones are flat and flush with the ground for easier mowing. The markers contain the name of the deceased and usually just a birth and death year. There's typically nothing to offer details on family relationships or to show personalities of the deceased. Occasionally, you'll find "Father" or "Mother" also carved, but that is usually the extent of it. The first of this kind of cemetery was established in 1917 in Southern California, known today as Forest Lawn. The goal was to give the cemetery a more parklike landscape. It was not until after World War II that memorial parks became popular and were established across the country.

8. **Potter's field.** This is where the county or city buries the poor, the unknown, and the unwanted, also criminals, suicides, and illegitimate babies. Sometimes there are mass graves; individual graves will either have no marker

**Quotes**

We are the citizens of the Trinity pit, dear reader: the murderers and drunkards, the prostitutes and unbaptized babies of Sunderland; we are those you would not consecrate, those you buried at midnight, those you have forgotten.

—Sheri Holman's
*The Dress Lodger*

or a temporary marker placed by the funeral home or cemetery. (See figures 3-8 and 3-9.)

9. **Pet cemetery.** While in most states pets cannot be buried with people, people (their cremains) have been buried in pet cemeteries with their faithful companions. (See figures 3-10 and 3-11.) **If you're not having any luck finding your ancestors in the people cemetery, then try the pet cemetery.** Start online with Yahoo's pet cemetery links: <http://dir.yahoo.com/Business_and_Economy/Shopping_and_Services/Funerals/Pets/Cemeteries/>, then try entering the keywords "pet cemeteries" into your favorite search engine. Hartsdale Pet Cemetery and Crematory boasts being "America's first and most prestigious pet burial grounds." Established by veterinarian Samuel Johnson on his apple orchard in 1896, this cemetery is the final resting place of nearly seventy thousand pets owned by everyday citizens and renowned people, such as pop singer Diana Ross.

Tip

## Grave Orientation and Decoration

As you'll read more about in chapter six, one of the customs in many cemeteries is that of orienting the graves on an east-west axis. The inscription on the headstone might face east or west; however, many face west so that visitors are not standing on the grave to read the inscription. But inscriptions can be on all

**Figure 3-9** Temporary funeral home marker from Love Funeral Home, Limon, Colorado, marking the grave of "Unknown," Simla Cemetery, Simla, Colorado. *Collection of author.*

**Figure 3-10** Hartsdale Pet Cemetery, Hartsdale, New York. *Courtesy of Suzanne Mc-Vetty.*

sides of a marker, so check the back and the sides. If there is a footstone to the west of the grave, then it's obvious in which direction the body was placed. The body is laid with its head to the east and feet to the west, so that it will rise up facing east. Since the forces of our weather patterns tend to go from west to east, that leaves many of these markers, especially marble, eroded and no longer readable.

It's common today to find graves decorated with artificial flowers (see figure 3-12 on page 90), and around Memorial and Veterans Days you'll also find little U.S. flags. Some organizations place a metal insignia marker next to the grave, such as the National Society, Daughters of the American Revolution and the Veterans of Foreign Wars. You may also find toys and other holiday decorations, especially on children's graves. African Americans and some Na-

tive American tribes leave broken dishes and pottery on a grave to symbolize the shattered life. These items are usually ones the deceased used right before death and were broken at the grave site. Lanterns and lightbulbs may also adorn graves to light the way into the afterlife. Shells are another common grave decoration, especially in coastal states. While all types of shells are used, the conch shell in particular is thought to represent the female reproductive tract, ensuring rebirth in the afterlife. Notes to the deceased and food might also decorate the grave.

**Figure 3-12** Grave marker of "Lizbeth," a.k.a. Lizzie Borden, 1927, Fall River, Massachusetts. Flowers and notes typically surround her grave, even today.

*Collection of the author.*

## Types of Foliage and Landscaping

Rosebushes, where climate allows, commonly mark graves. The rose is symbolic of motherhood and beauty. You may even find your ancestors buried in cemeteries with the word "rose" in the names. Lilies and irises are also popular blooming flowers. Evergreen bushes and trees are perhaps the most common foliage planted around graves. Artificial flowers—especially faded plastic ones—litter most graves.

Graveyards of the seventeenth and eighteenth centuries, while simple and without any particular landscaping, may be fairly crowded and have haphazard rows of graves. There will be little, if any, foliage other than natural grasses. When rural and garden cemeteries became popular in the early 1800s, more foliage and a landscaping pattern were used. Some cemeteries may be elaborately landscaped, from gates to foliage to pathways to small lakes.

### Mounding and Scraping

Mounding—to give the appearance of a fresh burial—and scraping a grave—keeping it free from grass—are customs in some parts of the country, but are most prominent in the South. This tradition stems from the belief that it was disrespectful for grass to grow on a grave. Other more practical reasons were to stifle grass fires or to prevent livestock from grazing on the grave if there was no fence.

### False Crypts, Table Tombs, Grave Houses, and Oven Crypts

False crypts (also known as "chest tombs," "box tombs," "stonebox graves," or simply "tombs" or "crypts") look like an above-ground tomb. The crypt is usually an enclosed base made of brick or stone, on top of which is an inscribed stone slab. The body, however, is interred underground. (See figure 3-13.)

**Figure 3-13** False crypt, Trinity Churchyard, Manhattan. *Collection of the author.*

A flat slab or ledger slab was placed flush to the ground or it rested on a low brick base. This stone slab over a grave is called a "wolf stone"; its purpose was to prevent wolves and other animals from digging up the grave.

A tabletop tomb looks like a stone table (see figure 3-14 on page 92). It consists of an inscribed slab supported by four to six legs. You can find these dating back to colonial times.

Grave houses are roofed structures that are either enclosed with wooden

**Figure 3-14** Tabletops, North Burial Ground, Providence, Rhode Island.
*Collection of the author.*

pickets or partially enclosed. False crypts, table tombs, and grave houses were meant to protect graves from animals, vandals, and the elements.

Popular in New Orleans cemeteries is the "oven crypt," so called because it looks like a bread oven in a wall. These space-efficient vaults are stacked one on top of another. The coffin is slid inside, and because of the heat and humidity in the area, these oven crypts provide a slow means of decomposing the body. Within a year, only bones are left. Due to flooding and the high water level, there is only above-ground entombment in New Orleans. Cemetery space is limited, so when a crypt is needed, the coffin is removed, the bones are pushed to the back of the vault, and another coffin is inserted. On the vault's marker, there might be several generations of names.

### Mausoleums

If your ancestors were entombed in a family mausoleum, you can be fairly confident they had some bucks. Sometimes the deceased was cremated, and the urn was put in the mausoleum; more commonly, caskets were placed inside. If the mausoleum door is locked, see if the cemetery caretaker has a key, but the only key may be lost or with family members. Some mausoleums have glass doors so you can see inside, where there may be photographs or personal items once belonging to those entombed. See figure 7-6 on page 181. I visited one cemetery where the glass doors were smoked, so you had to press your face against the doors to see inside. A few inches from my face and looking back at me was a life-sized statue of the deceased. Now don't tell me the guy didn't have a sense of humor. In some coastal localities, such as New Orleans, underground burial is practically unheard of because of the water level. The dead are entombed in family vaults, benevolent society mausoleums, or crypts.

## The Cemetery Community

Your first inclination to get a feel for the community your ancestors lived in may be to turn to the census, the newspaper, or a county history. **Spending some time in your ancestor's cemetery community, however, can give you an equally good glimpse of a time and place.** Used in conjunction with census records, newspapers, and county histories, the aspects you'll find in the cemetery will add to

**Notes**

your appreciation. Here is an example from my cemetery study, *Communities at Rest: An Inventory and Field Study of Five Eastern Colorado Cemeteries*, page 2:

> Many of the surnames inscribed on the tombstones in the vicinity of Calhan and Ramah, Colorado, are of European origin, specifically from the Austro-Hungarian Empire. In the 1920 federal census for Colorado, El Paso County, some of the population listed their origins as Austrian, Slovakian, or Czechoslovakian. *The History of Calhan and Vicinity, 1888–1988*, by Larry King (Simla, Colo.: Gaddy Printing Co., 1987), gave more specific place names in the section devoted to family histories.
>
> Most of these ethnics arrived in America during the peak years of immigration between 1880 and 1920. After arrival, some worked their way to Colorado by way of the Pennsylvania coal and steel mines. Once in Colorado, some worked as laborers on the railroad being built between Limon and Colorado Springs. By 1920, almost all were involved in farming or ranching and owned their own acreage. In order to obtain land under the Homestead Act, these immigrants had to have filed a declaration of intent for citizenship; as the 1920 census reveals, the majority followed through on their intent and became naturalized citizens.
>
> The predominant religion among this immigrant group was Orthodox, as evidence by the frequent use of the Orthodox cross on their grave markers.

By surveying the cemetery and reading all the gravestones (for small cemeteries and graveyards), or a good number surrounding your ancestors' graves, you might be able to determine aspects such as the following.

- **Migration patterns.** On some headstones, you may find where people in the community originated, such as places of birth or evidence that a person moved to the area from another state or country.
- **Family groupings.** In some cemeteries, you may find family plots conveniently marked by fencing or concrete curbing around the section. In others, you'll have to note those buried in front, behind, and to the sides of your ancestors. Even if the names aren't familiar to you now, still record the inscriptions on these markers. Further research might reveal a connection. Another clue to family relationships is similar-looking stones placed around the same time period.
- **Ethnicity.** A search of a Colorado cemetery near Steamboat Springs revealed a number of different ethnic groups, from Chinese to Italian to Spanish. This was an old mining town that drew a number of people of different origins to work in the mines.
- **Epidemics.** If you see a lot of markers with a death year of 1918, for example, you can infer that these people probably died in the Spanish influenza epidemic of that year. (For a list of epidemics in this country, see Appendix B.)
- **Disasters.** Floods, hurricanes, tornadoes, earthquakes, fires, mining accidents, and other tragedies often claim the lives of large numbers of people. Oftentimes, you'll find carved on some of the victims' markers what the

---

## "A DEAD WHAT?"

One Friday afternoon a few years ago I was at Mount Zion Cemetery, a large Jewish cemetery in Maspeth (Queens), New York. Knowing that Mount Zion's gates are locked at 5:00 P.M. and that I was far from the entrance, I finished my work at 4:30 and was prepared to leave. But my car wasn't: The battery had died! Would I have to abandon my car for the weekend (gates remain closed on Saturday, in observance of the Sabbath), walk half a mile, scale a barbed-wire fence, and find an alternate way back to my home, thirty-five miles east? Fortunately I had with me a newly acquired cell phone and was able to call the cemetery office to plead for an extension on gate closing, and the Auto Club for a battery boost. The Auto Club's response: "You're at the cemetery with a dead what?"

—Renee Steinig

catastrophe was. If not, and there are a number of stones with the same death date, check the local newspaper to see what was going on that caused so many deaths. (See Appendix B.)

- **Occupations and trades.** You may be able to get a sense of the types of work people did in the community. While the census would give you the best feel for this, you may get a sense of people's businesses and trades by looking at the artwork and the epitaphs.

- **Life expectancy.** On a notepad, take a random sampling of about three dozen markers for adults (those who were at least twenty-one years old when they died). Write just the birth and death years and sort by sex. Total the ages for both men and women, then divide that number by the number of individuals for each sex. That will give you the average age at death for men and women of the community. Ideally, you would need to do the whole cemetery to get a more accurate life expectancy, but this random sampling will get you in the ballpark.

- **Religion.** Each religion has its own symbol (see Appendix A). By noting the symbols you see carved on headstones, you can determine what the predominant religions were in an area. There may also be separate sections set aside for different religions.

- **Organizational membership.** Members of fraternal organizations and other societies, such as the Masons, often had that organization's symbol carved on the headstone. Survey the cemetery for clues of organizational participation in the community. There may be a separate section set aside for the organization.

- **Economy of the community.** The overall cemetery can tell you something about the community's economy. If there are a lot of elaborately carved markers and mausoleums, then it's a well-off community. If you find rocks instead of markers, a lot of homemade markers, or the funeral home temporary marker still in place after many years, then the area is (or was) economically depressed.

## ANALYZING THE HEADSTONE

*Let's talk of graves, of worms, and epitaphs,*
*Make dust our paper, and with rainy eyes*
*Write sorrow on the bosom of the earth.*
—*William Shakespeare,* Richard II, *Act 3, Scene 2, lines 145–147*

Now let's look at the headstone and footstone. Each marker is unique in its information. Here are some of the items you might find on an ancestor's tombstone:

- name of the deceased
- age at death
- birth date
- birthplace
- death date
- death place
- artwork (see chapter five)
- verse or epitaph (see chapter five)
- place of origin
- relationships
- minibiography
- marriage information
- migration information
- immigration information

**Internet Source**

**BIRTHDATE CALCULATORS**

Two sites will help you convert the death information on a tombstone to a date of birth: <www.lon gislandgenealogy.com/ birth.html> and <www.oliv etreegenealogy.com/ misc/birthcalc.shtml>.

Footstones may have no engraving, or they may display the carved initials of the deceased. Some may be sunken into the ground so that they are no longer visible.

**Realize, too, that a marker does not always designate that remains are there below ground.** The marker could be merely a memorial, while the loved one's remains were never recovered or were buried elsewhere. Cemetery records, if they exist, should reveal this information. Watch for clues on headstones, such as "Sacred to the Memory of. . . ." This is not a surefire indicator, of course, since memorial stones can mark a grave, too, but as you'll see in chapter five, surviving relatives chose certain phrases, epitaphs, and art for a reason.

Unfortunately, vandals, weathering, pollution, and sometimes other genealogists are a gravestone's worst enemies. Weathering is a natural decaying process that affects many surfaces. When water gets into the cracks of a headstone and freezes, it expands, causing stress on the marker. This weakens the stone and makes it more prone to other hazards. Lichen and moss, fungal plants that grow on solid surfaces such as rock, attach to headstones and spread, further weakening the stone. The geographic areas with the worst graveyard deterioration from pollution are in the Ohio River Valley, the Delaware Valley, and

**Reminder**

**Step By Step**

---

# ESTIMATING A BIRTH DATE FROM A TOMBSTONE INSCRIPTION
## OR
# WHY DIDN'T THEY TEACH ME THIS KIND OF MATH IN SCHOOL?

### Example #1

Let's say the ancestor's death date is recorded on the tombstone as 25 May 1842, age 36 years, 2 months, and 10 days. Here's a formula for calculating the probable date of birth:

| 1842 (year of death) | 5th month (May) | 25th day |
|---|---|---|
| −36 years old | −2 months | −10 days |
| 1806 | 3rd month | 15th day |

The ancestor was born probably on 15 March 1806.

### Example #2

Now let's suppose the ancestor's death date is recorded on the headstone as 25 May 1842, but is age 60 years, 8 months, and 5 days. Follow the same formula, but now you'll have to "borrow" some months to get the answer.

| 1842 (year of death) | 5th month (May) | 25th day |
|---|---|---|
| −60 years | −8 months | −5 days |

Work the problem from left to right as you would any math problem. Here, you will need to borrow 12 months from 1842, so instead of 5 months, it becomes 17 months.

1 (borrowing 12 months) 5 + 12 = 17

| 1842̶ | 5̶th month (May) | 25th day |
|---|---|---|
| −60 years | −8 months | −5 days |
| 1781 | 9 | 20 |

The ancestor was born probably on 20 September 1781.

### Example #3

Now let's make it a little harder. The ancestor's death date on the tombstone is 25 May 1842, age 45 years, 8 months, and 28 days. This time, you also need to borrow days from a full month. But several months have 30 days, and some have 31, not to mention February. Borrow the number of days in a month from the month given: May has 31 days, so you will borrow 31 days. Then you will have to borrow 12 months from 1842.

| 1 | 12 mo + 4 = 16 | 31 days + 25 = 56 |
|---|---|---|
| 1842̶ | 5̶th month | 2̶5̶th day |

So, your math problem is now:

| 1841 year | 16 months | 56 days |
|---|---|---|
| −45 | −8 | −28 |
| 1796 | 8 | 28 |

The ancestor was born probably on 28 August 1796.

**Figure 3-15** Three field stones with initials, East Hillside Cemetery, Glen Head, New York.
*Collection of the author.*

most urban areas. Industrial and urban air pollution cause erosion especially on marble headstones. While acid rain is an enemy of gravestones, it tends to dissolve only a thin surface layer. Sulfur dioxide gas, which is released by burning high-sulfur coal, is the real enemy because it forces stones apart. Serious deterioration happened primarily between 1930 and 1960, before pollution controls were imposed on industries.

And then there are the unenlightened genealogists, cemetery buffs, and descendants: those who use wire-bristled brushes or chemicals to clean the stone; those who leave crayon or rubbing wax marks because they weren't careful; those who let their children run rampant in the cemetery, accidentally knocking down, chipping, or breaking ancient markers; those who use colored chalk on a marble stone, permanently staining it blue or some other color. If you think I'm making any of this up, think again. I've seen this kind of damage to stones, and it makes me want to cry. This isn't intentional vandalism, either. These are people who simply aren't careful and who think that stone is impervious. They're wrong—dead wrong.

## Types of Markers

What kind of gravestone marks your ancestor's grave? Though parts of the inscription may be weathered and unreadable (usually the dates, naturally), or it may have sunk into the ground so that you cannot read the death date, you can still get an idea of when the stone was placed by the composition of the stone and the type of lettering. **By identifying the composition of the stone, you can also tell if it is a replacement marker.** A granite stone with a death date prior to 1880, for example, is not the original marker.

**Tip**

Before the 1650s      Graves were marked with either wood or field stones, that is, uncarved, rough-cut rocks and boulders. If anything was cut into the stone, it was generally the initials of the deceased and perhaps the year of death. You can find field-stone markers dating into the 1700s, as well.

1660s–1850s      Tombstones were made from sedimentary rock, such as red or brown sandstone or limestone, and dark

**Case Study**

## ANALYZING A HEADSTONE INSCRIPTION[1]

Be aware that stonecutters did make mistakes. Just because it's carved in stone doesn't mean it's accurate. It was too costly to correct a mistake.

When I visited my great-grandmother's grave and that of her twin sister, I dutifully took a photograph of the marker and copied down the inscription:

MARY CLARK
1871+1907
TWIN
DELIA NORRIS
1871–1929

As I did more research on the twins, I found out that not only was this not the original stone, but the dates were completely wrong.

Several discrepancies exist for the dates Delia and Mary were born and died, but based on the following evidence, I believe that the twins were born probably in April 1860, perhaps on the 29th day of that month. Delia died on 19 April 1925, and Mary died on 28 April 1908.

According to the information on Delia's death certificate, she was born on 29 April 1867.[2] This appears incorrect based on other sources. The age at death given on this record—57 years, 11 months, and 21 days—does calculate to the birth date given; but no doubt her age was calculated from her death date minus the birth date supplied by the informant, Delia's second-eldest daughter, Margaret Merritt. It is doubtful that Margaret would have known her mother's precise age in years, months, and days. Additionally, birthdays were not the celebrated occasions they are today. Some people had no idea how old they were nor exactly when they were born. Perhaps Margaret knew the day and month her mother and family acknowledged Delia's birthday, but not the exact year and certainly not her precise age.

Delia and Mary's joint tombstone incorrectly recorded a birth year of 1871;[3] however, this stone was placed sometime between 1934 and 1985, long after their deaths. According to *Connecticut Headstone Inscriptions*[4] for New Catholic Cemetery,[5] there was only a headstone for Delia in December 1934 when that transcription was made, and at that time, the marker showed Delia "died Apr. 19, 1925, age 57 yrs., 11 mos., 21 das." The death date and age at death on this original stone, not surprisingly, match the death certificate. When I visited St. Mary's Cemetery in September 1985, there was a joint, polished gray granite flat marker which read, "Mary Clark / 1871+1907 / TWIN / Delia Norris / 1871—1929." Delia did not die in 1929, as the newer marker indicated.

On the birth records of all seven of Delia's children, her year of birth calculates to between 1858 and 1861. Likewise, on the birth records for Mary's two sons, her age calculates to a birth year of about 1859.[6]

More convincing, however, is the one and only census on which both twins were enumerated. The 1900 federal census[7] recorded Mary's birth as April 1860. Two pages away, Delia was recorded with the same age, birth month, and year (and it was likely the enumerator interviewed them independently).[8] Given the age calculations on the children's birth records and this data, the census appears to be the most reliable source in this case.

Mary's death date was given in the estate file of her husband, James Clark, initially filed 20 March 1899, with papers dating from and beyond June–August 1908, the year Mary died.[9] Because Mary died leaving a minor child with no guardian, and the estate of her husband had not yet been settled by the time of her death, the court was swift in acting on Mary's behalf, assigning an administrator and a guardian for her child. This document, dated 24 June 1908, recorded Mary's death date as 28 April 1908, which was confirmed by her death certificate.[10] The new headstone inscription, however, showed a death year of 1907.

Thus, the new headstone, placed after December 1934 and before September 1985 contains errors in both the birth and death years for the twins.

---

[1]This case study is reprinted from Sharon DeBartolo Carmack, *My Wild Irish Rose: The Life of Rose (Norris) (O'Connor) Fitzhugh and her mother, Delia (Gordon) Norris* (Boston: Newbury Street Press, 2001), 57–59.

[2]Death certificate, Town Clerk's Office, Greenwich, Conn.

[3]Tombstone inscription, St. Mary's Cemetery, North Street, Greenwich, Conn., initially viewed and photographed by the author September 1985 and on subsequent visits. Delia and Mary's marker is along the West Putnam fence, third row from the fence, behind the "circle," which lies between sections 1 and 4.

[4]New Catholic Cemetery, Section 3, Charles R. Hale Collection, (Hartford, Conn.: Connecticut State Library, 1937), 109. The author called St. Mary's Cemetery in March 2001 to see if they had a record of the new stone being placed, but they did not. Phone calls to two monument makers who handle the majority of business for St. Mary's Cemetery were also fruitless. According to Carl at DeLia Monuments, the original owner did not keep good records and did not leave them with the new owners; Douglas at Rye Monument said they had a fire in 1985 and lost all of their records.

[5]According to Rob Hannigan, development manager for the Catholic Diocese in Bridgeport, Conn., St. Mary's Cemetery in Greenwich was established in 1899 and was originally known as New Catholic Cemetery. The ledger books for this cemetery date back only to 1934.

[6]See Carmack, *My Wild Irish Rose*, for complete information.

[7]1900 federal census, Connecticut, Fairfield Co., Greenwich, ED 72, sheets 23A and 25A, #423–510.

[8]Both women had small children at home and were without occupations, so I am making the assumption that they were both at home when the enumerator came and that Delia and Mary supplied the information.

[9]Greenwich Probate District 26:416, Connecticut State Library, Hartford, Conn.

[10]Death certificate #19506, State of New York, Department of Health, Bureau of Vital Statistics.

slate. Sandstone and limestone weather easily. (See figure 3-16.) Slate is more resistant to weathering and pollution and shows less wear despite being exposed to the sun and severe weather. Slate does flake and peel easily, however. Inscriptions were carved in Roman lettering. Wooden markers or crosses were also used.

**Figure 3-16** Red sandstone with chipping and flaking, Andrew James stone, East Hillside Cemetery, Glen Head, New York. *Collection of the author.*

**Figure 3-17** Anne Luister stone, 1825, example of italic and Roman lettering, East Hillside Cemetery, Glen Head, New York.

*Collection of the author.*

About 1800–1850s    A grayish-blue slate came into use. Inscriptions started appearing in italic script lettering. Unfortunately, italic script weathers badly, and hairline strokes practically have disappeared, so the numbers 1, 7, and 4 may all look like a 1; the numbers 3, 8, and 9 might be difficult to distinguish. In the 1840s, Roman lettering returned in popularity, perhaps because italic script was more difficult to carve. (See figure 3-17.)

1830s–1880s    Marble became popular, although its use can be dated back to the late 1700s. Marble is especially prone to

## NEW GRAVE MARKERS VS. OLD GRAVE MARKERS

Note that the original stone, below right, carried a symbol not reproduced on the new stone, on the left. The symbol on this stone is the Three Legs of Man. It was adopted in the thirteenth century as the armorial bearings of the native kings of the Isle of Man. The Isle of Man lies in the middle of the British Isles, in the Irish Sea between England, Scotland, Wales, and Ireland. The symbol is still used today on the Isle of Man flag. Indeed, according to the International Genealogical Index and the Ancestral File, Catherine was born in Peel, Kirk German, Isle of Man. This is an important clue to her origins that would be lost if the original stone had not been left when the new stone was placed. Likewise, if a cemetery transcriber failed to note the symbol, and you were relying solely on the published or online transcriptions of headstones in this cemetery, you'd miss the clue.

**Figure 3-18** New marker with old date. Granite makers, especially flat ones flush with the ground, were not in use in 1850 when Catherine Killip died. Fortunately, the original stone is still in place in front of the granite marker. Do you see a mistake in the new stone? The original claimed Catherine was ''aged 37 years''; the new marker has her ''aged 57 years.'' Salt Lake City, Utah, Cemetery.

*Collection of the author.*

staining and weathering, and it dissolves easily in acid-rain pollution. This breakdown in marble leaves inscriptions unreadable and causes a dullness to appear on the polished surface, followed by a roughened texture that eventually becomes pitted and grooved. In the early 1850s, the use of photographs (daguerreotypes) secured to tombstones began (see Photographs on Markers on page 102). The vast majority of these graven images portrayed the deceased alive, but some were postmortem photographs.

1880s–1910s    Soft, gray granite and cast-metal markers began being

**For More Info**

For more information, see Sharon DeBartolo Carmack, ''Carved in Stone: Composition and Durability of Stone Gravemarkers.''

used. Raised lettering on granite became popular. This soft granite weathers somewhat and is prone to lichen and moss. In the early 1900s, sandblasting replaced stone carving by hammer and chisel.

1920s–present      Granite is the most popular marker and is often polished. This polished granite appears to be durable enough to withstand elements like pollution, weathering, lichen, and moss.

## Photographs on Markers

The precursor to memorial photographs on grave markers was portraits of the deceased carved into the stone, usually as a cameo portraiture with wings, indicating that the deceased had gone to heaven. The earliest known carved portrait was cut in 1744. As soon as photography was invented with the daguerreotype in the 1840s, photographers began thinking of ways to secure photographic portraits onto gravestones. (See figure 3-19 for an example.) Daguerreotypes on tombstones were images taken of the deceased when alive; postmortem images were rarely used, unless it was an infant or child who had not had the opportunity to have a photograph taken before he or she died. The first known patent for a memorial tombstone photograph was in 1851 by Solon Jenkins Jr. of West Cambridge, Massachusetts. Some of the early patents show the photograph in a locket-type setting on the marker; visiting family members had to slide aside the protective covering to view the photograph.

**Figure 3-19** Anna and James Gage stone, 1928, Lake Cemetery, Lamar, Kansas. *Collection of the author.*

Few nineteenth-century photographs on tombstones still exist, although the number of patents, advertisements, and articles in photographic magazines of the time suggest it was a popular custom. You are more likely to find headstone porcelain or ceramic photographs taken in the twentieth century.

Some cemeteries have rules against placing memorial photographs on grave markers. Because a portrait can be damaged and destroyed easily or removed by vandals, it leaves an unsightly cavity in the headstone. And you can imagine how upsetting it is to finally find an ancestor's marker, only to find the photograph missing. This happened to me. I had never seen a picture of my great-great grandmother Isabella (Veneto) Vallarelli, who had immigrated to America

**Figure 3-20** Isabella Vallare-lli stone, 1921, missing photograph. St. Mary's Cemetery, Rye, New York. *Collection of the author.*

from Italy at the age of sixty-three in 1916. On the passenger list, she was described as being only four feet tall. She died in 1921 and was buried in St. Mary's Cemetery, Rye, New York. When I visited the cemetery a few years ago to see her grave, I was heartbroken to see an empty oval where her photograph had once appeared (see figure 3-20 above). I checked with the cemetery office, but they said the old porcelain photos often come loose and fall off. They had a box full of them, in fact, many of them broken, but there would be no way to identify them unless you knew what the person looked like.

## Types of Veterans' Markers

Prior to and during the Civil War, most soldiers' markers were nothing more than rounded-at-the-top wooden boards with carved inscriptions. These were not durable and had a life expectancy of only five years. Not until 1865, when more than 100,000 soldiers were buried in the national cemeteries, did the government give serious consideration to abandoning the use of wooden markers. A seven-year debate arose over whether the graves should be marked with marble or galvanized iron coated with zinc. By 1873, marble had won out. Following is a chronology of the size and shape of veterans' markers as they changed over the years.

| | |
|---|---|
| 1873 | Referred to as the Civil War–type marker, this was used in national cemeteries (see figure 3-21). For the known dead, markers were made of polished marble (or durable stone) four inches thick, ten inches wide, and twelve |

inches high above the ground, and the tops were slightly rounded. The number of grave, rank, name of soldier, and name of state were carved on the front in a sunken shield. These markers were furnished for members of the Union Army only. For the unknown dead, markers were made of polished marble (or durable stone), six inches square and thirty inches long. The number of the grave was cut on the top. Stones were also furnished for the unmarked graves of eligible deceased soldiers of the Revolutionary War, the War of 1812, the Mexican War, and the Indian Campaigns.

1879     Congress authorized furnishing stones for unmarked graves of veterans in private cemeteries.

**Figure 3-21** John Somervill, Private, Co. A, 25 Indiana Inf[antry], Civil War Union marker, Evergreen Cemetery, Colorado Springs, Colorado. *Collection of the author.*

1899     For Spanish-American War veterans, markers were the same design as Civil War markers, but the words "Spanish-American War" appeared.

1903     Stone size changed to thirty-nine inches high, twelve inches wide, and four inches thick. In October of that year, the use of stone blocks for marking unknown graves in national cemeteries was discontinued. Graves were marked with the same design as those for the known dead.

1904     Congress authorized headstones for unmarked graves of civilians buried in post cemeteries.

1906     Headstones were furnished for the graves of Confederates who died, primarily in Union prison camps, and were buried in federal cemeteries. Congress adopted the same size and material for Confederate headstones as was used for Union soldiers, but the top was pointed instead of rounded, and the shield was omitted. (Lore has it that the pointed top was to prevent the "damn Yankees" from sitting on Confederate headstones.)

ca. 1918    A new headstone known as the "General" type was designed for veterans' graves, except those veterans of the Civil and Spanish-American wars. Made from American white marble, the stone was slightly rounded at the top, forty-two inches long, thirteen inches wide, and four inches thick. The inscription included the name of the soldier, rank, regiment, division, date of death, and the state from which the soldier came. Religious emblems were adopted for use only on the General-type headstone. The choices were limited to the Latin Cross for Christians or the Star of David for Jews.

## ZOMBIES IN THE CEMETERY

Walking through old cemeteries never bothered me as Mom was into genealogy long before it was popular. I always found something poignant in the crumbling, moss-covered headstones in the older parts of the cemetery.

One Halloween, I discovered a pre-Civil War section of a cemetery while visiting family in Illinois. Korkie, my grandfather's little black dog, was patient with me as I meandered down the old gravel lane leading to the river. I was supposed to be exercising him rather than reading headstones. The artistry of one headstone caught my eye and I stopped to take a closer look. I slid on the loose gravel and didn't stop until I ended up in a storm drain large enough to drain a lake. The sun was just setting as I painfully pulled myself out of the dark hole. Korkie, frantic from my sudden disappearance, was doing his best to help me out by alternately tugging on my sleeve and barking excitedly. I must have looked a sight coming out of that hole, dressed entirely in gray and covered with abrasions and rotting vegetation. Only the taillights of the passing car were visible through the dust and flying gravel by the time I drew enough breath to call for help. I managed to get back to my uncle's house just after dark and before the family launched a search party. We all had a good giggle about my underground adventure that night.

The next morning, our giggles turned into guffaws when the news reported that some local teenagers from prominent families had been arrested for speeding. All were hysterical at the time of the arrest. They were claiming to have witnessed a zombie rising out of a grave in the old cemetery.

—Debbie Randolph

**Figure 3-22** Civil War Confederate marker, unknown citizen, CSA, Confederate Cemetery, Vicksburg, Mississippi. *Collection of the author.*

| | |
|---|---|
| 1929 | Congress authorized the Confederate marker for graves in private cemeteries. |
| 1930 | The inscription of the Confederate Cross of Honor was authorized. The symbol was carved in a small circle on the front of the stone above the standard inscription of the soldier's name, rank, company, and regiment. |
| 1936 | The flat marble marker was approved for cemeteries allowing only that type of marker. The size was twenty-four inches in length, twelve inches in width, and four inches deep. The marker was placed flush to the ground, with the inscription placed parallel to the greatest dimension of the marker. The inscription included name, state, rank, organization, date of death, and a religious emblem above the inscription. |
| 1939 | The flat granite marker was approved. The size was |

**Figure 3-23** Victor L. Insley flat, bronze marker, 1999, Memorial Gardens, Colorado Springs, Colorado. *Collection of the author.*

twenty-four inches in length, twelve inches in width, and four inches deep. The marker was placed flush to the ground, with the inscription placed parallel to the greatest dimension of the marker. The inscription included name, state, rank, organization, date of death, and a religious emblem above the inscription.

1940    The flat bronze marker was approved. The size was twenty-four inches in length, twelve inches in width, and three-sixteenths of an inch thick with raised lettering. The marker was placed flush to the ground, with the inscription placed parallel to the greatest dimension of the marker. The inscription included name, state, rank, organization, date of death, and a religious emblem above the inscription. (See figure 3-23.)

1941    Granite markers were approved for all soldiers of any war. (See figure 3-24.)

**Figure 3-24** Raymond William Marion granite marker, 1999, Evergreen Cemetery, Colorado Springs, Colorado. *Collection of the author.*

1944    The date of birth was added as part of the inscription.

1945    The words "World War I" or "World War II" were added as part of the inscription as shown in figure 3-25.

1947    The use of granite was discontinued because of cost.

1948    The flat granite marker was approved for use in national cemeteries in Hawaii and Puerto Rico. The thickness reduced to three inches.

**Figure 3-25** Ed Golden
World War I marker,
1965, Evergreen Ceme-
tery, Colorado Springs,
Colorado.
*Collection of the author.*

| 1951 | The flat granite marker was approved for use in the new Williamette National Cemetery in Portland, Oregon. Also in this year, the Buddhist emblem was approved as part of the inscription. In late 1951, the word "Korea" was approved for those who died in Korea or whose death was attributable to service in Korea. |
|---|---|
| 1954 | The word "Korea" was approved for those who served within the areas of military operations in the Korean Theater between 27 June 1950 and 27 July 1954. |
| 1964 | The word "Vietnam" was approved for those who died in Vietnam or whose death was attributable to service in Vietnam for the duration of current military activities in Vietnam or until such time as the military activities were given an official designation. The inclusion of the word "Vietnam" was retroactive to 1954. The word "Korea" was approved on headstones of all military personnel and veterans who were on active duty during the period of 27 June 1950 through 27 July 1954, and on markers for active duty decedents who lost their lives in Korea or adjacent waters as a result of hostile action subsequent to the 1953 Armistice. |

| 1983 | The words "Lebanon" or "Grenada" were authorized for those killed as a result of those military actions. |
| 1990 | The words "Panama" and "Persian Gulf" were authorized for those killed in action. |

## Roadside Memorials

*They're numerous enough to notice. Infrequent enough to startle at seeing.*
—*ChrisTina Leimer, The Tombstone Traveller's Guide,*
*www.flash.net/~leimer/spont.html*

There is a growing custom of placing crosses or memorials along the roadside to mark where someone died. The origins of this custom are uncertain. Some believe it stems from Mexican burial traditions. As the casket was carried from the church to the cemetery (*camposanto*), the family marked the spots along the path where the pallbearers stopped to rest. You can find roadside memorials in practically every state and in many foreign countries.

In America, most roadside memorials are simple—white crosses, made from wood, plastic, or metal. Marked on the cross is the name of the deceased or the person's initials and a death date. Many are decorated with artificial flowers, ribbons, balloons, notes, or items held special by the deceased. (See figure 3-26.) Sometimes loved ones even place a photograph by the cross. Some crosses

**Internet Source**

For more information on veterans' stones, see <www.cem.va.gov/hmhist.htm>.

**Figure 3-26** Patricia A. Everett and Terry A. Shank roadside memorial, Templeton Gap Road between Woodmen Road and Powers Boulevard, Colorado Springs, Colorado.
*Collection of the author.*

are not marked at all; only the family, friends, and community know who the cross memorializes. These memorials are usually placed shortly after death, helping family and friends begin the grieving process even before the funeral.

In many states, legislation is underway that would outlaw these roadside markers. Transportation officials believe the memorials distract drivers, cause traffic hazards, and inhibit road maintenance. The public outcry, however, may keep this tradition going, and some states will no doubt create regulations for placing roadside crosses and memorials.

## WHAT'S NEXT?

Now that you know what to look for in the cemetery and know what you're looking at, let's talk about how you can bring home your ancestor's tombstone—legally!

# FOUR

# Bringing Home a Tombstone—Legally!

*Just be content to do a rubbing . . . or else copy the engraved information on your clipboard. And if the name is spelled funny . . . for goodness sake, don't try to chisel a correction. It is probably considered sacrilegious at the very least to chip away, carve your initials, or otherwise mess around defacing grave markers.*

—Laverne Galeener-Moore, *Collecting Dead Relatives*

L ike your research trip to the library or courthouse, you need to be prepared for your trip to your ancestor's final resting place, taking along your "cemetery tools," so you can bring home a replica of your ancestor's grave marker. (Bringing home the actual marker is considered larceny in most states, so I don't recommend it.) I keep a well-stocked, dedicated tote bag just for such excursions to the cemetery, since one never knows when one will have to make an emergency trip to the graveyard.

## YOUR CEMETERY EQUIPMENT

If possible, use a tote bag that is (1) brightly colored, so you'll easily spot it at a distance if you set it down and wander off to look at stones, and (2) waterproof, because the ground may be damp or wet. Stock it with the following items:

- Notebook and pens or pencils. Always copy down the inscription, even though you may take a photograph or make a rubbing.
- Carpenter's apron. These have quite a few pockets that you can put some of your equipment in as you move from tombstone to tombstone.
- Gardener's knee pads. You'll be getting down and dirty to clear away overgrown weeds and grass that hamper your reading or photographing of the inscription.

- Garden shears to trim away the weeds and grass.
- Whisk broom to remove the trimmed weeds and grass and some of the dirt from the base of the stone.
- Sprayer bottle filled with water, rags, and a soft nylon-bristled brush (more on page 113).
- White chalk (not colored chalk; see page 115).
- Sunscreen. Remember to practice safe sun!
- Bug repellent. Deep Woods Off is *the* cologne of true genealogists.
- Camera and accessories (see page 115).
- Rubbing equipment (see page 119).
- Casting equipment (see page 122).
- Wet wipes. You'll want to wipe off your hands before you eat.
- Lunch or snacks (see picnicking in chapter nine).

You'll probably think of other items to bring. Marcia Melnyk, author of *The Genealogist's Question & Answer Book*, takes a bright orange ball cap to wear. This is part of her "I'm not a deer" garb. She also brings a retractable fifty-foot measuring tape to measure stones and the distances between stones.

Notes

## TAKING NOTES AND TRANSCRIBING MARKERS

When you locate your ancestor's grave, copy the marker's inscription. **Here are some other items you should note:**

- What type of cemetery is it (see chapter three)?
- What is the location of the cemetery? If it is a rural or family burial plot, record in your notes the directions to the cemetery, in case you or another researcher wants to return. If possible, give the location according to township, section, and range, or other land description, and certainly record the directions you took to get there. If you're into gizmos and gadgets, get a Global Positioning System (GPS) for your PalmPilot to track the cemetery's position according to latitude and longitude coordinates. For more on GPS, see Steve Paul Johnson's article "Using a GPS Device" at www.interment.net/column/records/gps/index.htm.
- What is the location of the grave from the entrance? You'll want to be able to find it again or tell others how to get there. If there is no map, create directions based on the entrance into the cemetery. "From the gate, walk left (or south) along the first row. The gravestone is six stones from the entrance."
- Is there a cemetery map that gives sections and plot numbers? If so, mark the location on a copy of the map and keep it in your files.
- How are the graves oriented? On an east-west axis? Haphazardly? In neat rows?
- Was your ancestor buried in a particular section of the cemetery? For example, a section reserved for a religious group, for veterans, for members of a fraternal organization, or with other disaster victims.
- Who's buried around your ancestor? Note the names of the people buried

not just to the sides of your ancestor, but also in front and in back. Later research may reveal that they were relatives.

- What kinds of decoration and foliage appear on or around your ancestor's grave? Is the grave scraped or mounded (see chapter three)?
- Is there a false crypt or grave house (see chapter three)?
- What kind of artwork was carved on the stone? These symbols have different meanings (see chapter five and Appendix A).
- What is the shape of the marker, and what is it made of? Marble? Granite? Slate? Limestone? If the stone is granite and the death date is 1789, then this isn't the original stone. Granite wasn't used until the 1880s (see chapter three).
- What kind of inscription was carved on the stone? Only a name and dates? Does the epitaph or poetry speak of the dead, or is it a farewell message?

## Transcribing the Stone

What is carved on your ancestor's marker? Copy the entire inscription, exactly as it was carved, including any artwork. **Remember, you are creating a source document that other researchers will use, too.** (For more on transcribing stones, see chapter eight.) Copy any abbreviations, but don't interject your own. Five years from now, you won't remember if that shorthand was yours or on the actual stone. Put any information you add or question in brackets. For instance, you might only be able to read a few letters in a name, but you are guessing at the rest: Willi[am?]. Here are two examples of how to make a transcription of a marker:

**Reminder**

McCue

|   Son   |   Mother   |
|---------|------------|
| John R. |    Jane    |
| 1914–1946 | 1895–1948 |

The example above is meant to replicate the information carved and the placement of the lettering. Or, you can use slashes to indicate line breaks:

McCue
Son / John R. / 1914–1946
Mother / Jane / 1895–1948
[son's inscription to the left; mother's to the right as you face the stone]

## TAKING PHOTOGRAPHS

Before you take a photograph of the stone, it may need some light cleaning. Lichen and moss love to attach to tombstones, and birds find them irresistible to perch and poop on, making the inscriptions harder to read and unattractive to photograph. Spray the stone with plain water, distilled if available. Use a soft nylon or plastic brush to *lightly* loosen the debris, then *gently* rub it away with your rag. If what you are trying to remove does not come off with this gentle, light cleaning, then leave it alone. Algae, lichen, and fungi can stain stones, and this cannot be removed safely. **Do not use any types of cleansers or chemicals to try and clean a stone, as this can cause permanent damage.** Remember, tombstones are historical artifacts; some have been around since the 1600s. Just because they are made from stone doesn't mean they're durable.

## A WORD OF GRAVE CAUTION

You *must* be able to distinguish between a stable and unstable gravemarker before you attempt to make a rubbing or gently clean away any debris. When in doubt, *don't*. And it's best to get permission before doing a rubbing. In some states, such as Massachusetts, it's prohibited. As with historical documents, tombstones are artifacts that must be treated with respect and care. You do not want to do anything that will damage the stone or to deprive future generations from enjoying and appreciating a cemetery as much as we do.

Some stones may already be flaking, crumbling, or chipping, in which case, *do not do anything to the stone.* Acid-based compounds, like vinegar, can eat away marble. Many genealogists, myself included, used to use shaving cream to clean the stone and bring out the image; however, gravestone preservationists caution that shaving cream has a low pH, which means it is acidic, and over time will harm the stone. While you may not think there are any particularly

**Figure 4-1** Marker photographed without chalk; marker photographed after light coating of chalk. Ella Foster marker, 1893, Evergreen Cemetery, Colorado Springs, Colorado.

*Collection of the author.*

## SECOND THOUGHTS ABOUT USING CHALK

Concerning the use of "sidewalk" chalk, I looked into this type of chalk in some detail last year when someone questioned me about it. I discovered that molded chalk is made of plaster of paris, which is defined as quick-setting gypsum plaster consisting of a fine white powder (calcium sulfate hemihydrate) that hardens when moistened and allowed to dry. Sidewalk chalk, on the other hand, while similar in appearance, is much harder than regular chalk and in fact will actually scratch a typical chalkboard if used on one.

I went so far as to buy a package of Crayola sidewalk chalk and several other brands and experimented with them using an old blackboard. Without my rubbing hard, they did scratch the blackboard. Granted, this was done not using a full side, rubbing smoothly as you would on a gravestone, but the flat end. As a result of this, I've taken the position of not recommending the use of sidewalk chalk.

—William Spurlock, founder of Saving Graves <www.savingsgraves.com>

harmful ingredients in whipped cream, sour cream, ice cream, or any other kind of cream, don't use these on gravestones as a means to enhance the carving! Save them for lunch. What about dusting the headstone with talcum powder, flour, or cornstarch, you may ask? While probably not directly harmful to the stone, powdery substances are messy and don't work all that well. And, remember, flour and water can make paste. So whether you leave the flour for the next rain to clean away or use a sprayer bottle to clean away the flour yourself, this combination is not something you want glued to a tombstone or left on the ground around it. If you absolutely must use something to bring out the image, use a fine layer of white chalk—and only white—and rub it gently on the stone. (See figure 4-1.) **Colored chalk can stain the stone.** Once again, only use chalk on the most durable and stable of headstones. If in doubt, don't!

After you have photographed a chalked stone, use your sprayer bottle of water to clean off the chalk residue. Rain will eventually clean off the chalk, but if there happens to be a drought that year, it'll be a long time before the stone gets cleaned. It is always best to leave the stone in the same, or better, condition as you found it.

To photograph tombstones, you will need the following items:
- camera and film
- sprayer bottle with water
- plastic or nylon brush (never wire)
- rags
- mirror (preferably portrait-sized)
- white chalk

Bring a camera with a focusable lens, zoom lens, and a flash. It's far easier to

**Warning**

hold a camera than to use a tripod. Cameras with a fixed focus generally do not allow you to get shots of headstones in which you can read the inscription clearly. Professional photographers recommend you use black-and-white film because it captures better detail and textures, and it has a much longer life than color film.

**Tip**

**Use zoom or magnifying lenses to take close-up shots of any photographs you find secured to the headstones.** When I found my great-grandparents' headstone, there were photographs mounted on the stone. (See figures 4-2a below and 4-2b on page 117.) These were the only photographs I thought existed at the time, so I took close-up photographs of the images. I then had the photos enlarged and framed.

**Figure 4-2a** Ebetino family marker with photographic tiles, St. Mary's Cemetery, Rye, New York. *Collection of the author.*

Sometimes using the flash and taking the picture from an angle will have the same reflective quality as using a mirror (see pages 117 and 118). On the other hand, a direct flash on a polished granite stone may have the undesired effect of washing it out or giving you a "hot spot" on the picture. If I'm unsure how a photograph will turn out, I take several shots: one with a flash, one without; one at an angle, one head-on. This is especially true if I've come a long distance and may never be back to that cemetery again. Better to waste some film than end up with photographs that are useless.

**Tip**

**Photographs turn out better if you take them on a slightly overcast day.** In many cemeteries, graves lie on an east-west axis (which is a natural compass if you happen to be lost). If the inscriptions are on the east side of the stone, take photographs during midmorning when the sun is just above your head and shoulders enough so you don't cast a shadow on the stone; however, if the inscriptions are on the west side of the stone, the early and midmorning sun will be shinning in your eyes and in the camera lens. Similarly, late afternoon sun causes the same problems in reverse. Therefore, try to plan your cemetery trip for midday when the sun is directly overhead.

**Figure 4-2b** Using magnifying lenses, take close-up shots of the photographs. Photograph of Angelina (Vallarelli) Ebetino. *Collection of the author.*

The reflection of a mirror will help light up the stone for a better photograph, but you will need an assistant to hold the mirror while you take the photograph. Hold the mirror so that it faces the inscription of the headstone, then tilt or angle the mirror to catch the sun and reflect it onto the marker. It will light up the image. (See figure 4-3 on page 118.) The reflection might be overpowering, however, and a mirror can be difficult to travel with, so here are some alternatives that you can conveniently pack and that will cast a softer light reflection:

- A piece of cardboard wrapped in aluminum foil, shiny side out.
- Car windshield sun reflectors. There are shiny silver ones that fold into a circle or roll up.
- A photographer's reflectors. These are also portable and fold into a circle.

Sometimes, just wetting the stone with water may bring out the inscription, especially if it's a granite or sandstone marker.

Tombstones are best photographed at eye level, rather than aiming the camera down from a standing position. This means squatting, kneeling, sitting, and even lying flat on your belly to get some of the smaller markers. This is another reason you'll want to wear jeans and protective clothing.

Even though you are photographing tombstones, it's wise to also make a written record of the inscription. Sometimes the photo doesn't turn out, or worse, like a friend of mine discovered after taking a whole roll and getting home, there is no film in the camera! If Marcia Melnyk, author of *The Genealogist's Question & Answer Book*, has traveled a distance to get to the cemetery, she takes her film to a one-hour processing place before she leaves the area. If any pictures need to be retaken, she can do it before she leaves the area. "Noth-

**Figure 4-3 a, b, & c** Hold the mirror so it captures the sun and reflects on the marker. Experiment with different angles so the reflection isn't overly harsh and washes out your photograph. John and Elizabeth (Lehmann) Schmutz marker, St. George, Utah, City Cemetery.
*Photographs courtesy of The Studio, Hurricane, Utah.*

ing is more disappointing," she says, "than to get home and find out that the pictures did not come out." Of course, if you are using a digital camera, you can tell right away whether or not your photographs are good ones. If you own a video camera, take advantage of the audio feature and read aloud the inscription as you film the stone.

**Warning**

## MAKING A TOMBSTONE RUBBING

Remember when you were in elementary school and you put a leaf or penny under a piece of paper, then rubbed the crayon on top of the paper? An image of the leaf or penny magically appeared on the sheet. That's exactly the same concept you'll use when making a tombstone rubbing. But, once again, **if the stone appears or feels unstable or is cracked and weakened,** *do not attempt to do a rubbing.*

Before you begin, always check with the cemetery sexton, superintendent, or caretaker to see if rubbings are allowed. In some states, such as Massachusetts, they are prohibited. I can think of a lot of reasons to end up in jail, but I'm sure getting picked up for making illegal tombstone rubbings is not one you considered.

Here's what you'll need for making a tombstone rubbing:

- rubbing wax or jumbo crayons (or ask your local home improvement center for one of the black crayons they use to mark lumber)
- scissors
- masking tape or a partner
- nonfusible, medium- to heavy-weight interfacing fabric (Pellon is one brand name)

Supplies

## WHERE TO BUY RUBBING SUPPLIES

To order books, novelty items, and rubbing supplies:

Association for Gravestone Studies
   278 Main St., Suite 207
   Greenfield, MA 01301
   E-mail: info@gravestonestudies.org
   Web site: www.gravestonestudies.org

Center for Thanatology
   391 Atlantic Ave.
   Brooklyn, NY 11217-1701
   Phone: (718) 858-3026
   E-mail: rhalporn@pipeline.com
   Web site: www.thanatology.org

Oldstone Enterprises
   1 Deangelo Dr.
   Bedford, MA 01730
   Phone: (781) 271-0480
   Fax: (781) 271-0499

Many people use large sheets of butcher paper or even white shelf paper or wallpaper to make rubbings. Kathleen Hinckley, a professional genealogist in Denver, uses interfacing fabric, and I've found that this works much better than paper. Paper tears and creases, and it is harder to manage if you're traveling. Interfacing can be folded in your suitcase, it doesn't tear, and you can iron it when you get home.

**Figure 4-4 a.** The grave of Sena Martin, wife of D.J. Martin, Evergreen Cemetery, Colorado Springs, Colorado. *©2001 Susan Rust.*

**b.** Cut off a piece of interfacing larger than the stone you want to rub. Either masking tape the interfacing to the back of the stone or have a companion hold the fabric tightly around the stone. *©2001 Susan Rust.*

**c.** Rub the side of the crayon (not the tip) or special rubbing wax over the fabric, and watch the image appear.
*©2001 Susan Rust.*

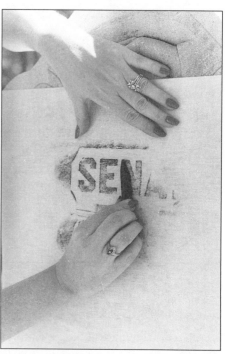

**d.** You can use jumbo crayons with the paper peeled off (give that job to a toddler, and it'll be done in half the time it'll take you).
*©2001 Susan Rust.*

**e.** If the fabric shifts, the image will be distorted, so keep the material taut.
*©2001 Susan Rust.*

**f.** Your tombstone rubbing will be an exact replica of the stone. At home, iron to set the crayon or wax into the fabric. Your rubbing is now a family artifact and suitable for framing.
*©2001 Susan Rust.*

**Money Saver**

**Interfacing fabric is inexpensive (about $1.25 a yard) and may be purchased at any fabric store** (it's the stuff seamstresses use to make collars and cuffs stiff in shirts). I use the medium- to heavy-weight type that is *non*fusible. Fusible interfacing has little glue pellets that melt when you iron the interfacing to a piece of fabric instead of sewing it in. Buy interfacing in bulk, about ten yards at a time, to keep in your cemetery tote bag. If you take anyone with you to the cemetery, especially kids, they'll want to try making a rubbing, too, because it's so much fun. But please supervise children at all times, and make sure they do not get any crayon or wax on the tombstone.

Regardless of whether you use paper or fabric for your rubbings, make sure it covers the entire face of the stone and that your rubbing wax or crayon does not bleed through to the stone. Wrap the paper or fabric around the stone, and secure it on the back with masking tape or have a friend hold it taut. Do not use any other kind of adhesive tape other than masking tape, as other kinds of tape may leave a sticky residue on the stone. Then using rubbing wax or a crayon—never use inks, felt marking pens, or any other type of marker—go over the entire face of the fabric. The image of the stone will magically appear.

Remember to pick up any trash before you leave the cemetery. When you get the rubbing home, place it face up on your ironing board with an old towel over it. With a hot iron, press down on the towel rather than using a back-and-forth motion. This will heat the rubbing beneath it and set the crayon or wax into the fabric. Never put the rubbing face down on the ironing board cover and melt it with the iron that way; you'll end up with an unexpected ironing board decoration. Always put a towel between the rubbing and your iron. Take it from me, your spouse won't appreciate having a winged death head on the back of his dress shirt.

**Tombstone rubbings make great gifts for family members and can be displayed in your home.** They become as much of a family artifact to hand down as needlework and silver. Though she is not our ancestor, we have Lizzie Borden's tombstone rubbing framed and hanging in our living room along with her portrait. It's quite a conversation piece.

**Idea Generator**

## MAKING A CAST

For you artsy-craftsy types, you can also make a plaster of paris cast, an exact replica of your ancestor's tombstone. Before you try this, however, let me caution you that making a cast of a grave marker takes a lot of work and patience. It's a multistep process, and you will need a large worktable where you can leave the mold undisturbed for many hours while it dries and cures. **And remember, if the sturdiness of the stone is at all questionable, do not attempt to make a cast of it.** This project is only for the sturdiest of markers that have no flaking, chipping, or crumbling. For this project, here is what you will need. . . .

**Reminder**

*at the cemetery*
- heavy-duty aluminum foil
- masking tape or an assistant
- soft brush normally used to scrub under dirty fingernails
- pencils with erasers intact
- old toothbrushes, soft bristles

*at home*
- large worktable
- about seven to ten pounds of plaster of paris for a small tombstone
- large, preferably unused, plastic kitty litter box (buy a fresh one; Fluffy might need his) for mixing the plaster of paris
- metal trowel
- metal broad knife or putty knife
- spray paint, preferably the type that mimics the look of granite
- clear coat spray paint
- black indelible ink pen

See figure 4-5 on pages 123–125 for instructions on making the cast.

### Finishing the Cast

1. When you get home, set the foil cast on your worktable face (shiny side) down, so that the dull side is face up and the lettering appears backward.
2. Mix the plaster of paris in the clean, plastic kitty litter box according to the directions on the container.
3. With your trowel, begin filling the cast. Work quickly and distribute the plaster evenly, making it about one-quarter inch or more thick. You would

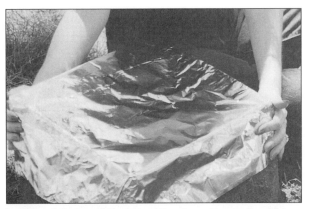

**b.** Wrap foil around the face of the stone. Secure the sides with masking tape, if necessary, or bring a friend to hold it in place. *©2001 Susan Rust.*

**Figure 4-5 a.** Use a sheet of heavy-duty aluminum foil, dull side to the face of the tombstone, several inches larger than the marker. *©2001 Susan Rust.*

**c.** Using the fingernail brush, make circular motions over the foil. *©2001 Susan Rust.*

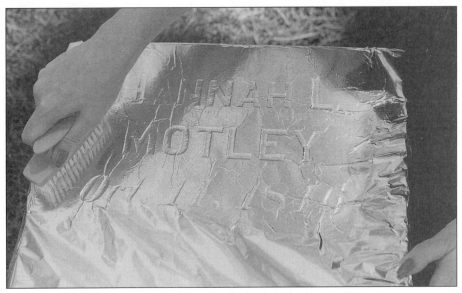

**d.** Make all moves gently; you don't want to rip the foil. The image will start to appear.
*©2001 Susan Rust.*

**e.** Using an old toothbrush, gently rub the bristles along each letter and number of the inscription, making the image even more defined. *©2001 Susan Rust.*

**f.** Now take the pencil with the intact eraser. Using the eraser, trace along the grooves to make the letters and numbers crisp. *©2001 Susan Rust.*

think the weight of the plaster would damage the foil cast you've made, but it holds up surprisingly well.

4. When you have filled the cast, use the trowel and putty knife to smooth out the top layer.
5. Let it dry overnight.
6. When the plaster is completely dry and set, remove the foil. Voila! You have an exact replica of your ancestor's tombstone.

You can leave the plaster cast as is, or you can paint it. Using the type of spray paint that mimics granite stone, paint the plaster replica, let dry, then apply a clear coat. Right away you will notice that the image might no longer be distinguishable. That's OK. Now take your black indelible ink pen and trace the lettering. That's it. You'll be so proud and will admire it lovingly when you show the family—until they ask, "So what are you going to do with it?"

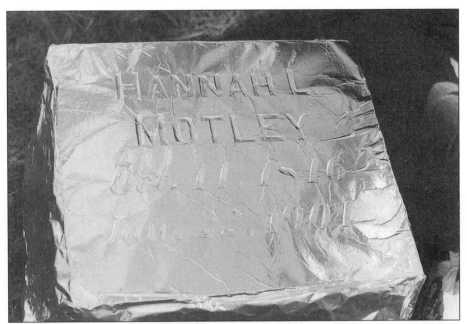

**g.** When finished and the image is clear, gently remove the foil. This is your cast. Place it flat in the trunk of your car so that nothing touches it. *©2001 Susan Rust.*

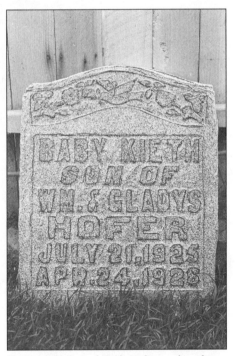

**Figure 4-6** Cast of Kieth Hofer marker, Evergreen Cemetery, Colorado Springs, Colorado. *Collection of the author.*

**Figure 4-7** Cast of Kieth Hofer marker after spray painting with granite-like paint, then outlining letters with a black indelible ink pen. Evergreen Cemetery, Colorado Springs, Colorado. *Collection of the author.*

**Figure 4-8** Cast of George Warner Murphy stone after painting inscription and artwork. Evergreen Cemetery, Colorado Springs, Colorado. *Collection of the author.*

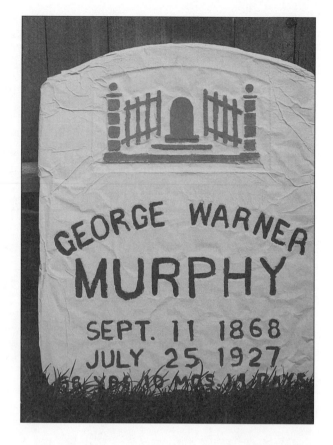

Whether you display it in your living room or set it in your yard for Halloween, you have brought home your ancestor's tombstone—and without getting arrested!

## WHAT'S NEXT?

Don't leave the cemetery just yet. There are still things to look for—clues about your ancestors that you don't want to miss!

# FIVE

# Cryptic Clues in the Bone Yard

*Over there—are the old stones,—1670, 1680. . . . Summer people walk*
*around there laughing at the funny words on the tombstones . . . it don't*
*do any harm.*

—*Thornton Wilder,* Our Town

About twelve years ago, I saw an announcement in the local newspaper that an art history professor was going to be presenting a talk at the university on Victorian tombstone art. That sounds interesting, I thought. It was a slide presentation of many headstones, mostly those from the West and Midwest, that filled the screen with carved handshakes, flowers, drapery, and other symbols. While the presentation was from the art historians' perspective, I wondered how this knowledge would benefit genealogists. I began checking out every library book I could find on the subject of funerary art and iconography. The more I researched the subject, the more I realized that this was an overlooked clue by most genealogists in their cemetery research. I visited cemeteries across the nation. Everywhere I went, I stopped in local cemeteries. On a vacation from Colorado Springs to Dallas, I don't think I missed a single graveyard. My family would groan every time I spotted another one. For U.S. regions I couldn't get to but had friends in, I enlisted their help, asking them to go to their local cemetery and take photographs of whatever looked interesting. By the time I put together my own version of a tombstone art lecture geared for genealogists, which I presented for the first time in 1991 at a national conference, my collection had grown to about one thousand slides and photographs of tombstones from all over the country and from all time periods. It has turned out to be a popular lecture topic.

While some symbols on headstones may seem obvious—a cross for one's faith, for example—others are rather cryptic—an inverted torch, for example (see figure 5-22 on page 142). When I give a *Reader's Digest* version of this lecture to school children and ask them to interpret certain symbols, their responses always tickle me. I show a seventeenth-century marker emblazoned with a skull and crossbones, and they immediately think the person was a pirate. When I say no, then they conclude that the person died from poisoning. Nope. 'Fraid not. It merely represented the earthly remains of the deceased—or so we think. We will never know with absolute certainty what our ancestors were trying to convey to the living through their tombstone art and symbols. Even some gravestone scholars disagree on interpretations. But we can make suppositions, based on our ancestors' attitudes toward death found in contemporary sources such as letters and diaries. So, if you find an interpretation different than what is presented in this book, that is why.

Why was it even necessary to "decorate" headstones with artwork? Scholars believe that one reason is many of our ancestors were illiterate and couldn't read the inscription and epitaph. However, everyone could see the symbol and understand its meaning.

Tip

Why is it important for genealogists to note and understand the artwork? Perhaps you have come across headstones that have sunk into the earth. The part that is now unreadable may be the death date, or perhaps the stone has weathered so badly that the vital information is no longer readable. Yet you can make out the name and the artwork, which was carved deeper. **By understanding the symbology of the artwork, you might be able to tell if the deceased was an adult or child, male or female.** From the art and symbols you might discover a religious preference, memberships in organizations, origins, perhaps an occupation, social and financial status in life, or even if the deceased had a sense of humor. (See figure 3-18 on page 101 for an example of how knowing the meaning of the symbol can aid in research. Pages 134–147 hold many examples of tombstone art commonly used in earlier eras.)

Although you'll find common art forms to a place and time period, artwork was not randomly chosen. Even though the living typically chose from stock motifs and epitaphs, the selected icon and verse would have meant something to the deceased or the descendants, thus sometimes giving us a glimpse into personalities and attitudes.

As mentioned in chapter two, most cemetery transcriptions, whether published with ink and paper or electronically, do not include what the grave marker looks like: how big it is, how it is shaped, or the type of art or symbols carved on it. These secondary sources are no different than any other, meaning, you need to seek out the original. By not knowing what art, if any, was carved on a stone, you may be missing a big clue in your genealogy. If you cannot visit the cemetery yourself, see if someone in the area can photograph the headstone for you. As noted in chapter two, you can find someone through the many Web sites offering such services.

## ART AND SYMBOLS

There are more than eight thousand religious and secular symbols, and hundreds of emblems to represent fraternal, civic, social, professional, or military

Observe the clasped hands!
Are they hands of farewell or greeting,
Hands that I helped or hands that helped me?
Would it not be well to carve a hand
With an inverted thumb, like Elagabalus?
And yonder is a broken chain,
The weakest-link idea perhaps—
But what was it?
And lambs, some lying down,
Others standing, as if listening to the shepherd—
Others bearing a cross, one foot lifted up—
Why not chisel a few shambles?
And fallen columns? Care the pedestal, please,
Or the foundations; let us see the cause of the fall.
And compasses and mathematical instruments,
In irony of the under tenants' ignorance
Of determinants and the calculus of variations.
And anchors, for those who never sailed.
And gates ajar—yes, so they were;
You left them open and stray goats entered your garden.
And an eye watching like one of the Arimaspi—
So did you—with one eye.
And angels blowing trumpets—you are heralded—
It is your horn and your angel and your family's estimate.
It is all very well, but for myself I know
I stirred certain vibrations in Spoon River
Which are my true epitaph, more lasting than stone.

—Percival Sharp in Edgar Lee Masters' *Spoon River Anthology*

affiliations. Obviously, it would be impossible to show photographs of them all in this book, but there is an extensive list of symbols in Appendix A. The illustrations shown in this chapter reflect the most popular funerary art.

According to Harriette Merrifield Forbes, author of *Gravestones of Early New England and the Men Who Made Them, 1653–1800* (page 114) and a pioneer in the field of gravestone studies, there are five categories of symbols during the colonial and early national periods in New England:

1. a recognition of the flight of time
2. the certainty of death and warnings to the living
3. the occupation of the deceased or his station in life
4. the Christian life
5. the resurrection of the body and the activities of the redeemed soul

Throughout the seventeenth and eighteenth centuries, New England cemetery iconography represented the reality of death: skull and crossbones, winged death head, skeletons. In colonial Tidewater Virginia, however, status was more important than signs of mortality. Those entitled to coats of arms would have them carved on their grave markers. The majority of markers in colonial Virginia do not display artwork, but when art was used, the next most common motif after the coat of arms was the skull and crossbones.

Beginning in the early 1800s and into the 1900s, attitudes toward death changed, and the winged death head was replaced by symbols depicting mourning, hope, and the resurrection as represented by the winged cherub, soul effigy, and willows and urns. This transition no doubt stemmed from the Great Awakening revivals of the 1730s and 1740s. The old Calvinistic belief of damnation and predestination declined and was replaced with salvation through good deeds and divine grace. Also during this period, the deceased were viewed as being in an eternal sleep (see chapter six under Postmortem Photographs); thus, it became popular to surround the final resting place with familiar, homelike objects: carved drapery, pillows, chairs, beds, and flowers. Around the 1970s our attitude toward death changed again. Today we typically commemorate the person's life, rather than the afterlife, and this is reflected in contemporary art on headstones. You'll find sandblasted images of a person's occupation, hobbies, pets, or whatever else the deceased held special in life.

## EPITAPHS AND INSCRIPTIONS

*epitaph, n. An inscription on a tomb, showing that virtues acquired by death have a retroactive effect.*
—*Ambrose Bierce,* The Devil's Dictionary

The most obvious reason for a grave marker is to tell who was buried where; the inscription and the epitaph are to memorialize the deceased. Many markers offer nothing more than the person's name and death date. Others elaborate, giving a date of birth, sometimes places of birth and/or death, age at death, parents' or spouse's names, and a verse. Some may even offer a minibiography of sorts, telling you immigration and migration data or an occupation.

**Along with the inscription of vital statistics, you might find a verse, also known as an epitaph.** The epitaph or verse carved on the marker, just like funerary art, revealed society's changing attitude toward death. Colonial verses were meant to provide instruction, not comfort. A common warning to the living about the stark reality of death was

> Stranger, stop and cast an eye,
> As you are now, so once was I,
> As I am now, so you shall be,
> Prepare for death and follow me:

This verse had many variations, such as this one:

**For More Info**

If you find a coat of arms carved on an ancestor's marker, see "Headstones, Hatchments, and Heraldry, 1650–1850," in *Gravestone Chronicles II*, by Theodore Chase and Laurel K. Gabel. This is an excellent account of New England markers, as well as a heraldic glossary and a list of heraldic painters and engravers who worked in and around Boston.

\di'fin\ *vb*

**Definitions**

Dear friends who live to mourn and weep,
Behold the grave wherein I sleep;
Prepare for death for you must die,
And be entombed as well as I.

As the attitude toward death changed, not only do we see a change in artwork from death's heads to willows and urns, we also see a change in the epitaph. It's now used to convey feelings of grief, sadness, happiness, or hope.

Many people chose verses from the monument maker's or funeral director's catalog. Verses are most often the living's choice of a memorial to the deceased, but on occasion a person specified before death what was to be carved on his or her marker. Those who specified a verse often reveal their personality. Julian C. Skaggs certainly had a sense of humor to have inscribed on his marker, "I made an ash of myself." Indeed, he was cremated in 1974, which makes the pun especially appropriate and humorous. (Quoted in J. Joseph Edgette's "The Epitaph and Personality Revelation," in Richard E. Meyer, ed., *Cemeteries and Gravemarkers: Voices of American Culture*, pages 90–91.)

Epitaphs came from popular or favorite poems, from other classic literary works such as Shakespeare, or from holy scriptures or prayers. As verses became more comforting, scripture passages became the most common form of epitaph. Next in popularity were plea-like prayers, asking for mercy on the soul. The origin of the verse may be difficult to trace, however; scripture verses may not be identified, assuming the living were familiar with the passage. Or, the verse could come from a particular religion's version of the scriptures.

Children's epitaphs are usually the most heart-wrenching and personal, revealing the parents' loss, pain, and anguish. The epitaphs of older people tend to have a philosophical quality to them, and reflect on the deceased's life.

Also common were short expressions of grief and sorrow, such as "gone but not forgotten" and "rest in peace." Some verses might have come from an eighteenth-century English literary genre known as the "graveyard school" of poetry. These poems often used the setting of the graveyard and

While some affect the sun, and some the shade.
Some flee the city, some the hermitage;
Their aims as various, as the roads they take
In journeying thro' life;—the task be mine,
To paint the gloomy horrors of the tomb;
Th' appointed place of rendezvous, where all
These travellers meet. . . .
'Midst skulls and coffins, epitaphs and worms. . . .

—Robert Blair, *The Grave*

Quotes

The boast of heraldry, the pomp of pow'r,
  And all that beauty, all that wealth e'er gave,
Awaits alike th' inevitable hour.
  The paths of glory lead but to the grave. . . .

Yet ev'n these bones from insult to protect,
  Some frail memorial still erected nigh,
With uncouth rhymes and shapeless sculpture deck'd
  Implores the passing tribute of a sigh.

Their name, their years, spelt by th' unletter'd muse,
  The place of fame and elegy supply:
And many a holy text around she strews,
  That teach the rustic moralist to die. . . .

—Thomas Gray, *An Elegy Written in a Country Churchyard*

focused on death and bereavement. Perhaps the most famous of the grave-yard poets and poems were Robert Blair's *The Grave* (1743), Edward Young's nine-volume work *The Complaint, or Night Thoughts on Life, Death, and Immortality* (1742–1745), and Thomas Gray's "An Elegy Written in a Country Churchyard" (1751).

Because colonial Tidewater Virginians were so concerned with social status and ancestry, you may find every genealogist's dream on one of these markers. Some have a person's genealogy inscribed on the headstone. John Herbert's headstone in the Old Blandford Churchyard in Petersburg, Virginia (as quoted in "The Funerary Monuments and Burial Patterns of Colonial Tidewater Virginia, 1607–1776," by Elizabeth A. Crowell and Norman Vardney Mackie III, *Markers* 7 [1990]: 103–38, at 129), reads

Here lyeth Interred the Body of
Iohn Herbert son of Iohn Herber[t]
Apothecary and Grandsonn of
Richard Herbert Citizen & Groce[r]
of London who departed this Life
the 17th day of March 1704 in the
46th year of his age

On the graves of colonial Virginia women, too, you will find their status in life. If the woman was of inherited status, then her father's name will appear on the marker along with her husband's name. If she married someone with status, but she had no inherited status herself, then she will be named as just the "wife of . . . ," but not the "daughter of . . . ."

There are many books available with gravestone epitaphs, but unfortunately, not all of them cite the source of the headstone verse or where the stone is located. Still, these books, which usually contain the most humorous and inter-

## CEMETERIES AND POETRY

It's no coincidence that the English poets of the Romantic and Victorian periods penned verses reflecting the changing attitude toward death that is also found in the cemetery. The American transformation from the graveyard to the garden cemetery clearly had British influence.

The Romantic Period (1798–1832) in both England and America was the start of an industrial revolution that shifted both societies from primarily agrarian to one of industrial dominance. Industrial areas rapidly depleted the country landscape in both countries. During this transformation, reflected both in poetry and the garden cemetery, naturalists and poets voiced their concerns. Nature and landscape were popular themes of the English poets William Blake, William Wordsworth, and Samuel Taylor Coleridge. In America, Mount Auburn Cemetery in Cambridge, Massachusetts, founded in 1831, was a Romantic poet's ideal of natural surroundings. In fact, it was designed and constructed based upon eighteenth-century English landscaped gardens.

Long before we had public parks, the cemetery was used as a "pleasure ground" for strolling and picnicking. One young Englishman, Henry Arthur Bright, while visiting his American friends Nathaniel Hawthorne and Henry Wadsworth Longfellow in the 1830s, remarked upon our cemeteries' popularity with people using them for strolling, making love, contemplating, and mourning. Cemeteries during the Romantic and Victorian periods became a place for solitary introspection for many literary figures and philosophers. Of course, poetry wasn't the only genre that reflected this change in attitude. Sermons, private correspondence, journals, and literature also revealed this trend toward nature.

esting of epitaphs, might be worth your time, especially if they deal with a specific cemetery, locality, or region that interests you. Check online bookstores, such as BarnesandNoble.com and Amazon.com, by typing in the keyword "epitaphs." Also try used and out-of-print online and brick-and-mortar bookstores. You'll even find plenty of epitaphs on the Web (type "epitaphs" into a search engine), but be cautious about using both book and Web sources. I found one Web site that supposedly gave the epitaph on Lizzie Borden's grave and that of her father. Having visited and photographed the markers in Fall River, Massachusetts, myself, I knew what was inscribed on them. The Web site reported an epitaph that wasn't on either marker and gave the wrong name of Lizzie's father. Remember, go to the original source whenever possible, even when it involves the epitaph.

**Figure 5-1** The winged death head represented the mortal remains of the deceased and was popular in the seventeenth century. Trinity Churchyard, Manhattan. *Collection of the author.*

**Figure 5-2.** Winged death head and two coffins (on either side of skull), signifying the mortal remains of the deceased. North Burial Ground, Providence, Rhode Island. *Collection of the author.*

**Figure 5-3** Skull and crossbones, symbolic of the mortal remains. Phillip Pettinger stone, Edison, New Jersey. *Collection of the author.*

**Figure 5-4** The hourglass represents the flight of time. Sarah Harris stone, 1723, North Burial Ground, Providence, Rhode Island. *Collection of the author.*

**Figure 5-5** The soul effigy gradually replaced the winged death head and skull and crossbones in the 1700s. It represented the image of the soul. Edward Thurber Lare stone, 1768, North Burial Ground, Providence, Rhode Island. *Collection of the author.*

**Figure 5-6** The urn-and-willow motif became popular in the late 1700s and early 1800s. The urn was symbolic of the death of the flesh, while the willow represented mourning and earthly sorrow. North Burial Ground, Providence, Rhode Island. *Collection of the author.*

**Figure 5-7** Roses represented motherhood and beauty. A rose in full bloom indicated a full life; whereas, a rosebud indicated a life that hadn't fully bloomed. A rose on a broken stem represented a life broken or cut short. Maude Louise Richardson stone, 1877, Evergreen Cemetery, Colorado Springs, Colorado. *Collection of the author.*

**Figure 5-8** Archways, pillars, and gates represented the passageway into the next life. Luther Clark stone, 1918, White Chapel, South Lake, Texas. *Collection of the author.*

**Figure 5-9** A forefinger pointing up meant the soul had gone to heaven. Isabella F. Campbell stone, 1885, North Burial Ground, Providence, Rhode Island.
*Collection of the author.*

**Figure 5-10** A forefinger pointing down did not mean the soul had gone to hell, but that God was reaching down for the soul. Virginia City, Nevada.
*Collection of the author.*

**Figure 5-11** Handshakes represented God's welcome into heaven. If there are sleeves on each hand, then the handshake represented holy matrimony. Note that the sleeve on the viewer's left is feminine and the one on the viewer's right is masculine. Sena Martin stone, 1876, Colorado Springs, Colorado. *Collection of the author.*

**Figure 5-12** Books represented the Holy Bible (or other form of gospel) or the book of life. When no words identify the book, then it is presumed to be the book of life. It may be opened, closed, held in a hand, or sitting on a shelf. A closed book would be symbolic of the finality of life. (See figure 4-1 on page 114 for an open book on top of a marker.) Evergreen Cemetery, Colorado Springs, Colorado. *Collection of the author.*

**Figure 5-13** Palm leaves and lilies were symbolic of the resurrection. This marker shows several symbols: the palm leaf for the resurrection, the urn representing the death of the flesh, a fig leaf (barely visible) on the urn for rejuvenation; and a partially uncarved marker to represent the transition from life to death. Tenke marker, East Hillside Cemetery, Glen Head, New York. *Collection of the author.*

**Figure 5-14** Angels were often represented with wreaths of mourning, dropping flowers on the grave, or pointing to heaven. Annie Carlson marker, 1916, Fairmount Cemetery, Denver, Colorado. *Collection of the author.*

**Figure 5-15** Angels are God's messengers and guardians; they deliver the soul to heaven. Hawley marker, 1909, Eureka Springs, Arkansas. *Collection of the author.*

**Figure 5-16** Doves represented the Holy Spirit. Doves may be depicted with wings at rest or in flight. This symbol was commonly used on children's graves, but you'll find it on adult graves, too. Gracie Shelden stone, 1888, Evergreen Cemetery, Colorado Springs, Colorado.
*Collection of the author.*

**Figure 5-17** Lambs were symbolic of purity, gentleness, and innocence. This Christian symbol also related to biblical references of Christ as the shepherd and believers as his flock. George Edward Rice III stone, 1937, Evergreen Cemetery, Colorado Springs, Colorado.
*Collection of the author.*

**Figure 5-18** Lambs were almost always represented lying down, and they were most common on children's graves. Doris Rosenberg stone, 1918, Sons of Israel Cemetery, Colorado Springs, Colorado. (Note the rock on the top of this marker. See Jewish burial practices in chapter seven.)
*Collection of the author.*

**Figure 5-19** During the Victorian period, the use of flowers and drapery became popular in funerary art. The folds of the drapery were carved with much detail, including fringes and tasseled cords. The use of flowers and drapery was to give the cemetery a homelike appearance and to make the deceased feel at home. Margaret J. Eaton marker, 1885, Evergreen Cemetery, Colorado Springs, Colorado.
*Collection of the author.*

**Figure 5-20** Crosses and crowns were common religious symbols on grave markers. The cross represented the deceased's faith in God, while the crown was symbolic of God and the eternal life. Each religion had its own representation of the cross. See Appendix A for some examples. Mrs. H.E.B. Little marker, Evergreen Cemetery, Colorado Springs, Colorado.
*Collection of the author.*

**Figure 5-21** A stone that is half carved, half unfinished represented the transition from life to death. Harlan stone, Evergreen Cemetery, Colorado Springs, Colorado.

*Collection of the author.*

**Figure 5-23** Women representing comfort were a common figure on tombstones. Like angels, women can be found in mourning, pointing to heaven, or dropping flowers on the grave. They might also be used with other symbols, such as in this stone with the urn, weeping willow, and evergreen bush. Charlotte Kruttschnett marker, 1867, Virginia City, Nevada. *Collection of the author.*

**Figure 5-22** An inverted torch represented the end of a family line, that is, there were no more male heirs to carry on the surname. Reformed Dutch Church Cemetery, Locust Valley, New York. *Collection of the author.*

**Figure 5-24** Figures of sleeping babies or small children were common during the Victorian period. These figures often appeared with no clothing or with a modest covering, symbolizing that babies and children had nothing to hide or cover up. Edward Issac Zeigler, 1891, Mt. Allen Cemetery, Hays, Kansas. *Collection of the author.*

**Figure 5-25** In coastal states in particular, shells were used to decorate graves or as part of the marker itself. Conch shells represented the female reproductive tract, assuring rebirth into the afterlife. Blanch marker, Park Cemetery, Carthage, Missouri. *Collection of the author.*

**Figure 5-26** Simple folk like simple memorials, of course, such as this marker carved to look like a log cabin. Riverside Cemetery, Denver, Colorado. *Collection of the author.*

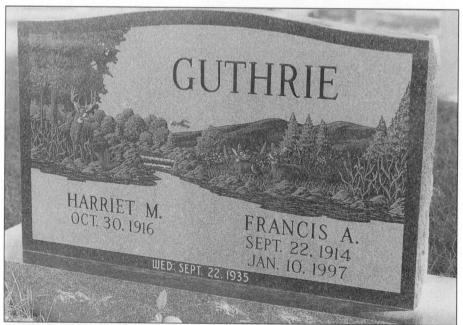

**Figure 5-27** Today's sandblasting techniques can turn a granite marker into an artist's canvas. Although this photograph appears in black and white, the color on this headstone was vivid and remarkable. Guthrie stone, Evergreen Cemetery, Colorado Springs, Colorado.
*© 2001 Susan Rust.*

**Figure 5-28** The Masons were formed in America as early as the 1730s. The compass was perhaps the most common symbol for this organization, followed by the ''all-seeing eye.'' J.B. Newman, 1880, Evergreen Cemetery, Colorado Springs, Colorado. *Collection of the author.*

**Figure 5-29** The two-headed bird was the symbol for a 32nd Degree Mason. Frank Haas, 1913, Riverside Cemetery, Denver, Colorado. *Collection of the author.*

**Figure 5-30** Another 32nd Degree Mason, but this elaborate marker also included an inverted torch behind the banner, indicating the end of a family line. Williams marker, Fairmount Cemetery, Denver, Colorado. *Collection of the author.*

**Figure 5-31** The women's auxiliary branch of the Masons is the Order of the Eastern Star. Their symbol is the inverted five-pointed star, usually with initials F.A.T.A.L.—Fairest Among Thousands, Altogether Lovely. Lillian McKerchner marker, 1896, Fairmount Cemetery, Denver, Colorado. *Collection of the author.*

**Figure 5-32** The Independent Order of Odd Fellows (I.O.O.F.) was founded in 1819. The common symbol on members' markers was the three links of chain, and sometimes the letters F.L.T.—Friendship, Love, and Truth. The women's auxiliary branch of Odd Fellows, Daughters of Rebekah, began in 1851. Their symbol contained stars inside a crescent moon, a dove, and the DofR emblem. Keyt marker, 1910, Fairmount Cemetery, Denver, Colorado. *Collection of the author.*

**Figure 5-33** Insignia of the United Daughters of the Confederacy, which was organized in 1894. Laura Darnell stone, 1923, Cripple Creek Cemetery, Colorado. *Collection of the author.*

**Figure 5-34** The Knights of Pythias was founded shortly after the Civil War. Their symbols included a knight's helmet with a bird atop, crossed weapons, a shield with skull and crossbones and the initials FCB—Friendship, Charity, and Benevolence. The women's group was the Pythian Sisters. On this symbol, the additional three chain links indicated the deceased also belonged to the Odd Fellows. Snyder marker, Fairmount Cemetery, Denver, Colorado. *Collection of the author.*

**Figure 5-35** The Improved Order of the Red Men was founded in 1834. It was a fraternal and benevolent society founded on the customs and traditions of the American Indian. Symbols for this organization included the Indian head or an eagle with a hatchet, peace pipe, arrow and quiver. The initials T.O.T.E.—Totem of the Eagle—often appeared. The women's auxiliary branch was the Degree of Pocahontas. Improved Order of the Red Men, Tuscarora Tribe No. 39, marker, Cripple Creek, Colorado. *Collection of the author.*

**Figure 5-36** The Woodmen of the World was founded in 1883. Most members lived in rural communities in the South and Midwest. Their emblem was a sawed-off tree stump, an ax, and the motto "Cu, Tacet Clamat"— Though Silent He Speaks. Tree stump markers were common, but if the person was a member of the Woodmen of the World, the insignia would appear somewhere on the marker. Woodmen of the World insignia, Simla Cemetery, Simla, Colorado. *Collection of the author.*

**Figure 5-37** According to David A. Brose in "Treestump Tombstones in an Iowa Cemetery," *The Palimpsest* 70 (Summer 1989):73–74, carvers preferred Bedford, Indiana, limestone for these markers, since it was easiest to re-create the look of tree trunks. Art Hurshane marker, 1899, Evergreen Cemetery, Colorado Springs, Colorado. *Collection of the author.*

**Figure 5-38** Egyptian motif, New Orleans, Louisiana. *Collection of the author.*

\di'fin\ *vb*

**Definitions**

---

**CRYPTIC CLUES IN TERMS ON HEADSTONES**

Two clues to watch for on a woman's headstone:

**relict of:** a widow, the husband predeceases the wife

**consort of:** woman who predeceases her husband

On colonial Virginia markers:

**gentleman:** the individual was entitled to a coat of arms

**honorable:** referenced one who held a high office (governor, treasurer, etc.)

**esquire:** members of the Governor's Council

**mister:** although not entitled to a coat of arms, a social status above yeoman

---

## FRATERNAL ORGANIZATION MARKERS

Offering life insurance and burial benefits, secret societies and fraternal benefit organizations were extremely popular during the late nineteenth and early twentieth centuries, and you'll find evidence of membership on gravestones or in the cemetery. At one time, there were as many as two thousand such groups, but some existed for only a short time. The more popular ones, such as the Masons (Freemasons, or Ancient Free and Accepted Masons), may have separate sections in the cemetery. While the symbols for these organizations may be unique to the group, they also used other common funeral icons, such as urns. Usually a combination of symbols will help identify the group.

**Tip**

Shown on pages 145–147 in figures 5-28–5-37 are representative insignia and emblems of several organizations; however, **if you find an unfamiliar emblem, local funeral directors and monument makers may be able to identify it for you.** Reproductions of the Sears, Roebuck and Montgomery Ward catalogs from the late nineteenth and early twentieth centuries may also help. Both stores sold pins with organizational insignias. Laurel K. Gabel, in her article "Ritual, Regalia and Remembrance: Fraternal Symbolism and Gravestones," *Markers* 11 (1994): 1–27, has illustrations and examples of several common emblems.

## REVIVAL MARKERS

Another Romantic and Victorian trend was a revival of classic symbols. Cemetery entrances and memorials were reminiscent of Greek, Roman, and Egyptian architecture. Some considered these symbols pagan and inappropriate, but they remained popular. (See figure 5-38 on page 147.)

## WHAT'S NEXT?

OK, we've got your ancestors buried and you found them in the cemetery. Now, let's work backward and look at how your ancestors died and came to be buried.

# SIX

# American Burial Customs and Folkways

*"Look at this," Grandma said when we got to Stiva's [Funeral Home]. "It's a packed house. We should have gotten here sooner. All the good seats up front by the casket are going to be gone. . . ."*

*Grandma was worming her way up to the casket. . . . A closed casket is a dangerous situation, since lids have been known to mysteriously spring open in Grandma's presence. Best to stay close to Grandma and keep watch that she doesn't get her nail file out to work at the latch.*

—*Janet Evanovich,* Seven Up

D eath and cemeteries are a daily part of a genealogist's life. We squeal with delight when a death certificate we've ordered for an ancestor arrives in our mailboxes. There's a spring to our step when we walk among graves in a cemetery. We get goose bumps if an ancestor had a particularly unusual demise, which might in turn have created more records like newspaper accounts and coroner's inquests. Despite our morbid fascination with our ancestors' passings and our yearning to walk on their graves, we sometimes give little thought to the few days in between death and burial. The time when practically no records were created, except perhaps for a notation in a diary or letter. A time when family gathered to prepare the corpse for burial, to make or select a coffin, to mourn the loved one during the wake and funeral, and then, finally, to bury the earthly remains.

## ATTITUDES TOWARD DEATH

As we've seen from the art and epitaphs on grave markers, society's attitude toward death has changed over the centuries, and it is sometimes based on cultural or ethnic differences. The New England Puritans, for example, viewed death in its stark reality. They had little regard for the physical remains of a person, and they hastily buried their loved ones with little ceremony. While they privately felt grief, public expressions were not considered appropriate. The Puritans prepared their children for death by reading to them—or having the child read—gruesome verses in the Bible, lecturing them about the deaths of other children, or dragging them to the edge of an open grave to make them aware of their own mortality. Death was part of their daily life and prayer, and they believed that their salvation was never certain.

Although those in the colonial Chesapeake region experienced just as much, if not more, mortality from the climate and disease than their New England counterparts, they did not dwell on the topic of death and dying. They had an attitude of stoic fatalism, accepting whatever hand fate dealt them. While the Puritans would reflect upon death in their letters and journals, the colonial Chesapeake settlers treated death as a fact of life.

These attitudes toward death prevailed into the late 1700s and slowly changed over time. During the Victorian period, 1832 to 1901, public displays of mourning and grief became acceptable and were expected.

Following are some of the customs and traditions that have surrounded the death and burial of our ancestors. **Keep in mind that these traditions can vary from one family to another and depend on the individual time period, and ethnic and religious background (see chapter seven).**

**Reminder**

## DEATH AND DYING

Death for our ancestors came in many varieties. In America, diseases, epidemics, accidents, and childbirth have been primary causes of death. Fires, floods, and other natural disasters claimed people's lives. Few people knew how to swim, especially children, so drowning was common. Mining disasters and no safety devices or regulations on farm machinery or in the workplace increased the chances of dying in a fatal accident. Wars raised the death toll dramatically; lynchings, hangings, dueling, and other violent acts took a number of lives. Doctors in their ignorance of medical science prior to the twentieth century probably claimed more lives than they healed. Bleeding a patient for a variety of ailments was common, and the average blood letting took a pint of blood. With so much against them, it's amazing any of our ancestors lived to be a ripe old age.

Yet our ancestors did not become immune to death. While some American ethnic groups and cultures had different attitudes toward death and dying, all felt the loss of a loved one as deeply as we do today. When an individual approached death's door, family and friends would gather to keep a continuous vigil by the dying person. Known as a "death watch," "death vigil," or simply "sitting up," relatives might travel for miles to keep the loved one company in the final days. If a doctor was present, the charge for his final visit to the family may be included in the estate settlement. On the other hand, if the person died when no doctor was present, a physician would not typically go to the home

**See Also**

See Appendix B: Historical Time Line of Deadly Diseases and Epidemics and Appendix C: Glossary of Historical Terms for Causes of Death

just to pronounce an individual dead. The physician did, however, have to notify the city or town of the death so the clerk could issue a burial permit.

Bell ringing announced the death of someone in the town or community and served two purposes: (1) to frighten away evil spirits, and (2) to toll the age of the deceased, spreading by word of mouth a death in the community. In some places, funeral notices were posted in public places.

## A POTPOURRI OF SUPERSTITIONS

There are hundreds of superstitions surrounding death and dying. Here are but a few:

- A bird flying into the room of a sick person was an omen of death. Folks believed that birds transport human spirits.

- Clocks should be stopped at the hour of death. This served a practical function, as well, so that everyone knew the time the person died. Starting the clock again after burial was symbolic of beginning another period in the family's life.

- Shades and drapery should be drawn at a funeral, otherwise the next person to die will be the one the sun shines on.

- Mirrors should be covered or turned to face the wall. Folks believed that the spirit of the deceased could enter the mirror and that the next person to look in the mirror would die.

- Kissing or touching the corpse was a superstition that prevented the living from dreaming about the deceased. It was also the realization that the loved one would never be felt or seen again.

- There is an unwritten rule against interrupting the movement of a funeral procession. The belief is that anyone who interferes with the deceased going to the grave will attract the wrath of evil spirits.

- It's bad luck if a bride and groom meet a funeral procession.

- Pall bearers wear gloves to handle the casket so that the spirit of the deceased does not enter their body through their hands.

- Every wonder why widows wear black? It's so the husband's spirit would not come back and pester her. Black made her less visible to the spirit world. These black garments were known as the "widow's weeds."

- The corpse should be removed from the house feet first. Two theories surround this one: (1) We come into the world head first, so should go out feet first; (2) if the head goes out first, the deceased can beckon someone to follow him to the grave.

- A clap of thunder after a burial indicates the soul has reached heaven.

## PREPARING THE CORPSE

Before undertakers took over the handling of the dead between 1850 and 1920, it was up to family or neighbors to prepare a body for burial. Even then, many families continued to handle death and funeral arrangements on their own. They took care of washing and dressing the corpse, then laying it out for visitors to pay their respects. On occasion the family would hire women known as "layers out of the dead." When infants or mothers died in childbirth, midwives often handled these tasks. Martha Ballard recorded these notations in her diary (*A Midwife's Tale: The Life of Martha Ballard, Based on Her Diary, 1785–1812*, by Laurel Thatcher Ulrich [New York: Vintage Books, 1990], 37, 39, 236):

**August 1787**

13 . . . Mrs Patin & I laid out the Child. . . .

20 . . . I heard there that Mrs Clatons Child departed this life yesterday. . . . Shee departed this Life about 1 pm. I asisted to Lay her out. Her infant Laid in her arms. . . .

**February 1801**

3 John Expired at 1 h 10 m this morning. AE 2 years, 7 months & 13 days. . . . Mrs Saunders, Oliv Fletcher and myself put on the Grave Cloaths. . . .

4 I was Calld to my sons to see the Desection of the Son of Esquire Davis which was performed very Closly. . . .

Blanch White of New York City is one of this country's earliest advertised female undertakers. In 1768 she advertised herself in *The New York Journal or General Advertiser* as an "Upholster and Undertaker" with "Funerals furnish'd with all things necessary. . . ." Lydia Darragh, however, advertised in Benjamin Franklin's *Pennsylvania Gazette* two years earlier on 4 December 1766 that she intended "to make grave-clothes, and lay out the dead." About thirty years later, in the Philadelphia City Directory for 1794, Rebecca Powell was the only woman listed as a "layer out of the dead"; by 1814, fourteen women were listed under this trade (see figure 6-1 on page 153). Ironically, even though women in early America handled preparing corpses for burial, when the undertaking businesses began, they were run exclusively by men.

To give the deceased the appearance of sleeping, the arms were folded across the chest, feet were tied together, coins were placed on the eyelids to keep them shut, and a cord or handkerchief was placed under the chin and over the head to keep the mouth from dropping open. The body needed to be arranged like this before rigor mortis set in; otherwise it would be impossible to place the body in the coffin. Burial attire ranged from a shroud to the departed's best clothes.

Before embalming, the typical time between death and burial during the summer was usually about twenty-four hours. Cold winter weather and placing the body on ice helped preserve the corpse so family members at a distance could arrive, but most burials took place within three or four days of the death.

## LAYERS OUT OF THE DEAD.

| | |
|---|---|
| Bliss Susannah, 47 Vine | January H. back 39 Arch |
| Bulfinch Mary, 26 Columbia avenue | Norton Rebecca, back of 17, Sterling alley |
| Field — 137 Spruce | Powell R. back 36 n. 3d |
| Fiss Deborah, 205 n. 8th | Robbins Eliz. 153 Vine |
| Graff Rebecca, 192 Vine | Walker Widow, 14 Sterling alley |
| Hutman — 4th ab. Coats' | |
| Heyler Catherine, 66 n. 3d | Wolbert Catherine 193 St. John |
| Jacobs — 22 Appletree alley | |

**Figure 6-1** "Layers Out of the Dead," 1814 Philadelphia City Directory. While some of those listed here appear only with a last name, the city directories from 1810 to 1820 reveal that they were all women. Habenstein and Lamers in *The History of American Funeral Directing* use this same entry as an illustration; however, they incorrectly identified it as coming from the 1810 Philadelphia City Directory. *FHL 983348.*

embalm, v.t., To cheat vegetation by locking up the gasses upon which it feeds. . . . Many a dead man who ought to be ornamenting his neighbor's lawn as a tree, or enriching his table as a bunch of radishes, is doomed to a long inutility. . . .

—Ambrose Bierce, *The Devil's Dictionary*

**Definitions**

Embalming became popular during the Civil War, when it was necessary to transport bodies from the battlefields to home grave sites. Early embalming was done in the home of the deceased. Not everyone agreed with the practice of embalming because they feared it mutilated the body, and some just couldn't afford the extra expense. But by the 1920s, almost all corpses were voluntarily embalmed, and the use of theatrical makeup and regular clothing to make the deceased look natural and lifelike became widespread. Even today embalming is not required by law, except in certain circumstances, which vary from state to state. Prior to embalming, the family or undertaker might pack the body in ice to keep it preserved, but the melting ice water needed to be drained frequently and replaced.

**Undertaker:** One who "undertakes" funeral arrangements; term used until the late nineteenth century.

**Funeral director:** Term coined in the 1880s, eventually replacing the term "undertaker."

**Mortician:** Use of this term began in the early twentieth century, but its use is not as popular.

## BURIAL CONTAINERS

*There's one thing in this world which isn't ever cheap.*
*That's a coffin.*
*There's one thing in this world which a person don't ever try to [talk] you*
*  down on.*
*That's a coffin.*
*There's one thing in this world which a person don't say, "I'll look around*
*  a little, and if I find I can't do better I'll come back and take it."*
*That's a coffin.*
—*Mark Twain's* Life on the Mississippi

Early Americans were not buried in coffins but were wrapped in shrouds or blankets for burial. About the mid eighteenth century, wood coffins came into use. These burial receptacles were made by the local cabinetmaker, carpenter, blacksmith, livery stable keeper, or upholsterer. The type of wood used revealed the economic status of the deceased: polished and stained hardwoods were for the wealthy; pine was for the poor. The sawdust and wood shavings from making the coffin were placed inside; superstition held that if these were tracked inside a house, someone in the house would die. Coffins were custom-made around a person's measurements. There was no time for dallying; an unembalmed body could swell quickly, especially in summer months, then it wouldn't fit into the coffin. If a person died in winter, there was not as much rush to construct the coffin. These early coffins were made so that the entire lid was removed for viewing the body, and there was no special lining. The deceased would be wrapped in a sheet or quilt. In some families, women made special quilts just for burials.

Metal coffins became vogue in the first half of the nineteenth century and were mass-produced. Coffin shops and warehouses opened at the same time. The family could choose a casket from the undertaker's catalog, from his display room, or by visiting a casket showroom. By 1860 there were patents for coffins made of iron, cement, marble, potter's clay, and a combination of iron, wood, and glass. By 1900, the word "casket" had replaced the term "coffin," and the construction of those with patents extended to vulcanized rubber, fabricated metals, papier-mâché, aluminum, cloth and wood, wood and glass, terra-cotta, and celluloid. Not all of these patented caskets were in wide use, mainly because of their weight or other problems. The three types most commonly used were wood, metallic, and cloth-covered metal.

The use of underground vaults as an outside receptacle to protect the coffin was not popular until the nineteenth century, and it was mostly the wealthy who could afford them.

**\di'fin\ *vb***

**Definitions**

The term "coffin" generally refers to the six-sided "mummy-shaped" burial container, wide at the shoulders and narrow at the feet. A "casket" is rectangular-shaped and was first introduced in the late 1840s, and widespread by the early 1860s. For the purposes of this book, the terms are used interchangeably.

## THE WAKE

The custom of sitting with and viewing the deceased was and is still known by various names: "the wake," "the visitation," "calling hours," and "waking the dead." Part of the practice was practical; part of it social. Before funeral parlors, this event took place in the home of the deceased. In the days before houses had screens, bugs and flying insects were a problem at wakes, especially during the summer months. Rats, dogs, and cats were other intruders. Round-the-clock vigils were necessary to protect the corpse, not only from animals and insects, but from body snatchers, too (see page 166). Attending the body also ensured that the person was dead. Premature burial was a common fear (see page 169).

The social scene of a wake varied depending on the culture and ethnic group. Perhaps the most festive wakes took place in the homes of the Irish, where there was an indulgence of food and spirits. On some occasions, the deceased would be propped up in a corner to enjoy the party, too. But the Irish were not the only group to partake in such social affairs. Even the colonial planter class of

Virginia and the Puritans in Massachusetts had lavish wakes and funerals with huge amounts of food and liquor.

## FUNERALS

*In order to know a community, one must observe the style of its funerals and know what manner of men they bury with most ceremony.*

—*Mark Twain's* Roughing It

In early America, funeral services might have been held after the burial, since there was no way to adequately preserve the body. There may not have been a clergy member present when the death occurred, especially if your ancestors lived in a rural area visited by an itinerant minister. Or, if your ancestor died in the winter when the ground was frozen, the funeral and burial might have been delayed until the spring thaw, with the body stored in an outbuilding or unheated room.

Plenty of food and drink was served at both Puritan and colonial Chesapeake area funerals. Adults and children consumed rum, wine, and brandy as the mourners gathered, as they proceeded to the grave, and after the interment. This overindulgence in food and spirits was common among many cultures and ethnic groups.

Before the early 1900s, most funerals were by invitation only. In urban areas, a man dressed in black—eventually the undertaker—hand-delivered funeral notices and invitations. It was considered rude not to attend a funeral you had been invited to. Funeral invitations were mailed to relatives and friends at a distance. These were written on black-bordered stationery and envelopes, so the recipient knew immediately that someone had died. In the 1900s, when newspaper obituaries and telephoning became the means of alerting friends and family of a death, the custom of formal, written invitations to the funeral went out of fashion.

Funeral services, like wakes, were social occasions and were typically held in the home of the deceased, then eventually in the church or the funeral parlor. The odor of the decomposing body was overwhelming during a funeral service, and this spawned the custom of having floral arrangements around the coffin—to help mask the odor. If the weather was pleasant, the funeral ceremony might be held outdoors in the yard or on a porch. Funeral wreaths were hung on the grieving family's door to not only easily identify the house to which folks visited and paid their respects, but to also forewarn unwanted visitors, such as traveling salesmen.

After the service, a funeral assistant stayed behind to restore the family's home back to normal, while loved ones followed in a procession on foot to the graveyard. The clergy led the processional, followed by the flower carriage, then the bearers, the hearse, immediate family and relatives, then finally friends. Before the use of hearses became common, underbearers carried the coffin, while pallbearers—relatives or men of dignity—held the corners of the pall (a cloth laid over the coffin) to keep it from dragging on the

**Notes**

In 1898, the average urban funeral cost about $100; today the average cost is more than $5,000.

**Quotes**

"When I was younger I hated going to weddings. It seemed that all of my aunts and the grandmotherly types used to come up to me, poking me in the ribs and cackling, telling me, 'You're next.' They stopped it after I started doing the same thing to them at funerals."

—*Author unknown, circulated via the Internet*

Quotes

## AT THE FUNERAL

Do not criticize the person in whose honor the entertainment is given . . . .

If the odor of flowers is too oppressive for your comfort, remember that they were not brought there for you, and that the person for whom they were brought suffers no inconvenience from their presence.

Listen, with as intense an expression of attention as you can command, to the official statement of the character and history of the person in whose honor the entertainment is given; and if these statistics should seem to fail to tally with the facts, in places, do not nudge your neighbor, or press your foot upon his toes, or manifest, by any other sign, your awareness that taffy is being distributed . . . .

Do not bring your dog.

—Mark Twain, from an unfinished Burlesque of Books on Etiquette,
as quoted in *Letters From the Earth*, edited by Bernard DeVoto

ground. Palls were usually black; children's coffins were draped in white, as were coffins for women who died in childbirth. If the distance from the church or home was long, then there would either be a change of underbearers, or they would stop and rest. Over time, when the pall was eliminated, only one set of bearers was necessary.

In the mid 1800s, when undertakers began taking over the management of death, they established "funeral parlors" and "funeral homes" to symbolize the parlor and homelike quality people had grown accustomed to. The funeral director handled the entire affair, from planning the funeral to contacting the preacher, to arranging for the music and selecting the flowers, to preparing the body and providing the casket. He also secured the burial permit from the town or city, and sometimes he would facilitate matters himself by getting the doctor's signature on the death certificate and taking it to the clerk.

The undertaker's carriage transported the deceased with mourners following on foot and later in carriages. Motorized hearses replaced horse-drawn carriages in the early 1900s. Starting in the late nineteenth century, the plume atop a hearse indicated the status of the deceased (see figure 6-2 on page 157).

No plume: deceased was poor
Two plumes: moderate financial circumstances
Three to four plumes: fairly well to do
Five to six plumes: deceased was well off
Seven to eight plumes: deceased was wealthy

At the cemetery, there would be a brief graveside service that focused on giving the body back to the earth. The casket was placed on planks over the

**Figure 6-2** Illustration of a horse-drawn hearse with six plumes. Dover copyright-free clip art, *Ready-to-Use Old-Fashioned Transportation Cuts,* by Carol Belanger Grafton (Mineola, N.Y.: Dover Publications, 1987).

open grave. Sometimes the coffin would be opened at the cemetery one last time for family and friends to place personal items inside with the loved one. Likewise, if any jewelry was to be removed from the body, it was done at the graveside. The casket would then be lowered by passing ropes under the coffin and removing the planks. Some religions and cultures sprinkle the coffin with dirt to symbolize the body returning to the earth. The custom of dropping flower petals on the casket in the grave has the same earthly symbology. Before outer, underground vaults were in wide use, wooden planks might be placed on top of the casket to prevent the coffin from caving in under the weight of the dirt. When the grave was filled, sometimes family members would remain, sometimes not.

## BURIAL

Puritans buried their deceased in clustered church yards, whereas those in the Chesapeake area were more likely to use private family burial plots on farms and plantations. Because of the distance between plantations and churches in Virginia, most people lived too far from the church to be buried in the church graveyard. Elite Puritans and colonial Virginians who lived near a church might be buried in the church under the floor. The closer to the altar, the more elite the person was.

At the graveyard, the sexton dug the grave and tolled the bell, informing the town of the age and sometimes the sex of the deceased. If there was no cemetery sexton, then friends and neighbors of the deceased would dig the grave. Grave digging was done by several men who worked in shifts. The old adage of being buried "six feet under" was for practical reasons. The odor of the decaying body needed to be suppressed so that animals would not dig up the remains. When caskets were routinely placed in an outer vault, the need to bury someone six feet below the surface was not necessary.

Before cemeteries were plotted so that people knew where the bodies were buried, grave diggers had to rely on someone's memory to make sure they weren't about to dig a grave where someone was already buried. You've no doubt heard of water witches—those folks who can find underground water by using a dowsing or divining rod. Before graveyards became crowded and

**See Also**

For information on types of headstones and markers, see chapter three.

157

folks needed a plot map to determine where graves were, someone used the same method to witch a grave. You can try it, too. Using two straightened, wire coat hangers with about a two- to three-inch bend at the ends for handles, hold a rod in each hand. When you walk over a grave, the wires should turn out. If there's underground water, the wires should turn in and cross. Another method to determine where graves were was to hit the ground with a hammer or stomp on it with heavy boots. A grave will have a hollow sound to it, because the ground never settles back as solidly. Or, by sticking a metal rod into the ground, a grave digger could tell if a grave was already there—because the earth has been disturbed, the rod should go through easily.

One of the biggest obstacles to grave digging, of course, was the weather. If your ancestor died in the winter months in an area that had severe snow or ice storms that froze the ground, then great-uncle Bob may have been placed in an outbuilding until the thaw.

In many cemeteries, the body was laid on an east-west axis, with feet to the east and head to the west. In nature-based cultures, this was done so that the deceased faced the rising sun. Christians believe that on Judgment Day, Christ's Second Coming will be from the east, so they positioned the body so that the soul would rise in the proper direction. East is also the direction of Jerusalem, and when the archangel Gabriel's horn trumpets, it will come from the east. By the same token, if everyone in the cemetery was buried east-west, but your ancestor was buried on a north-south axis, you may want to check court records. Those buried in the opposite direction might have done some dastardly deed in life, such as committed a murder or some other crime, that would warrant this punishment after death. If you have Catholic ancestors who were buried outside of consecrated ground, the deceased may have committed suicide or committed some other sin (see chapter seven).

Husbands and wives also have certain positioning in the grave. Just as the bride stands to the groom's left during the wedding ceremony, a wife will also be placed to her husband's left in the grave. This custom stemmed from the belief that woman was created from the left side (rib) of Adam. Today, however, many joint graves have the caskets stacked one on top of the other, with the first one to die being on the bottom. You may find that the wife's inscription is to the north (if the grave is on the east-west axis), indicating her position to the left of her husband.

Women and their infants who died in childbirth or shortly thereafter were often buried in the same grave. Here, the custom stems from the superstition that the mother will never rest if she doesn't know what happened to her infant; her spirit will forever be looking for her baby.

## OTHER TYPES OF "BURIALS"

Along with burials at sea, cremation, and open-air disposal, some cultures practice mortuary cannibalism or suspend the body through cryogenics. A few American Indian tribes have practiced the former, mostly in the form of eating body parts of an enemy to show bravery. Symbolically, Christians practice mortuary cannibal-

**Quotes**

"We've had people put stuff in the casket. . . . With one guy, his kids put a cell phone in his pocket, and it rang at the cemetery."

——funeral director John McDonough to author Katherine Ramsland in *Cemetery Stories*

ism in the sacrament of communion. Since cryogenic suspension is a relatively recent method of disposing of the dead, it will not be discussed here.

Open-air disposal of a dead body is practiced by some American Indian tribes. The body is placed in a tree or left on the ground where it decays and is consumed by birds and animals. **(For more on Native American burial customs, see chapter seven.)**

See Also

Burials at sea were common for those serving in the navy or when someone died aboard ship, and there was too much time between the death and arrival to keep the body from decomposing. Those buried at sea were wrapped in a shroud with weights attached to the body to keep it from floating to the surface. In rare cases, a body might be preserved in alcohol until the ship reached its arrival port.

Cremation dates from antiquity and is the process of reducing the corpse and burial container to ashes. While cremation has been popular in other countries and among some American Indian tribes, cremation was not a popular means of body disposal for most Americans until the late nineteenth century. The first crematorium in America was in 1884 in Lancaster, Pennsylvania. Today, cremation is more popular in some states than in others. According to Kenneth V. Iserson in *Death to Dust: What Happens to Dead Bodies?* (pages 248–249), nearly 50 percent of the deaths in Nevada are cremated, whereas in Mississippi less than 2 percent are. The same is true of certain ethnic and religious groups. Slightly more than 50 percent of Japanese Americans choose cremation, but only 5 percent each of Mexican and African Americans do. Iserson details religious attitudes toward cremation (page 274):

Require cremation: Buddhism, Hinduism

Prohibit cremation: Baptist Society, Free Presbyterian Church, Islam, Judaism (Orthodox/Conservative), Shintoism, Zoroastrianaim

Disapprove of cremation: Armenian Orthodox, Church of Jesus Christ of Latter-day Saints, Plymouth Brethren, Roman Catholic, Russian Orthodox

Allow cremation: Christian Spiritualists, Church of England, Churches of Christ, Congregational Church, Episcopal Church, Jehovah's Witnesses, Judaism (Reformed), Methodist, Moravian, Seventh-Day Adventist, Unitarian/Universalist

No position: Baptist Church, Christian Scientists, Lutheran, Friends (Quakers)

Some families prefer to scatter a loved one's remains atop a mountain or in the ocean, or keep them in an urn in their homes; others place the cremated remains in a columbarium, a building or room at the cemetery with niches for urns and places for memorial plaques.

## MEMORIAL CUSTOMS

Memorial customs and traditions varied widely, yet nearly every family expressed its grief in some fashion or another.

> ## POSTERITY HILARITY
>
> It was around Halloween one year when I was making a presentation to a class of eighth graders about cemeteries and gravestones: I was stressing how we should think of cemeteries as museums without walls and that the headstones are valuable historic artifacts. A young gentleman sitting in the back of the room appeared to pay little attention to my talk, keeping his head down. At the point where I encouraged the students to visit their departed loved ones in a cemetery to photograph or make rubbings of the headstones, the disinterested student looked up and raised his hand. He asked, "But what do you do if your grandmother has been castrated and put in an urn?"

## Household Decoration

Along with hanging a funeral wreath on the household front door, families covered the doorbell or knocker in crepe paper: black for an adult, white for the young, black with a white rosette and ribbon for a young adult. By the 1880s, families and funeral directors began using combinations of purple, lavender, and gray. For the funeral service, mirrors might have been covered, shades drawn, and clocks stopped at the hour of death.

## Wearing Black

While our colonial ancestors considered death and funerals as somber occasions, they typically did not have special mourning clothes, unless the family was wealthy. The custom of wearing black, although ancient, became more popular in America in the mid-1800s during the Victorian period. Black was believed to make the living less visible to the spirits that hovered around the corpse. Most of the etiquette for wearing black pertained to women; men might wear dark clothing with black ties or armbands. Widows were expected to wear black dresses during the first two years after their husbands died. After a year and a half, a widow could add some trim in gray, lavender, or white. Widows who were in the first two years of mourning did not attend festive occasions, such as weddings and parties. If a woman were mourning the loss of a parent or child, she wore dark clothing for a year. For the loss of a grandparent, sibling, or close friend, mourning garb was to be worn for six months; and if an aunt, uncle, niece, or nephew died, then three months was an appropriate mourning time.

## Mourning Jewelry and Tokens

From the late seventeenth century throughout most of the eighteenth century, funeral gifts, similar to party favors, were given to the living. You may find some of these among your family heirlooms. Popular were rings, brooches, scarves, and gloves. Andrew Eliot, a minister in Boston in the mid-1700s, received nearly 3,000 funeral gloves, rings, and scarves in his thirty-two years of preaching and attending funerals. Gloves were given as invitations to funerals.

**For More Info**

For more details on wearing black, right down to the type of fabrics, see "Victorian Mourning Customs From Collier's Encyclopedia published in 1901" at <www.poesattic.com/articles/colliers.html>.

Even pauper funerals gave out some token to the living. Colonial mourning rings were made of gold, enameled in black, and decorated with a winged death head, coffin, or skeleton. The name or initials of the deceased along with the date of death were engraved on the ring. Funeral spending on mourning tokens got so out of hand in Massachusetts that the colony passed laws in the 1720s and 1740s prohibiting these gifts and the consumption of spirits; however, the activities continued.

During the Victorian period, rings, lockets, and brooches were mass-produced and particularly popular among the middle class. These jewelry items might contain a miniature portrait of the deceased and/or a lock of the deceased's hair. Braided-hair watch chains, bracelets, and necklaces were also popular, and sometimes whole wreaths of the loved one's hair were braided and woven into elaborate designs and then framed. Mourning jewelry was made from black enamel, onyx, jet (a fossilized coal), vulcanite (hardened black rubber), or other materials. Mourning rings of this time period were decorated with symbols you'd find in the cemetery: weeping willows, broken columns, and urns. Like the mourning rings of colonial times, they were engraved with the name or initials of the deceased and the death date.

## Mourning Stationery

Just as there were proscribed "rules" for the wearing of black for a Victorian woman, there was also special stationery that she was to use during her period of grieving, whether to notify people of the death or for other correspondence. Widows in their first year of mourning used stationery and envelopes with quarter-inch black borders. As a widow entered her second year of mourning, the width of the black border decreased to an eighth of an inch for the first six months of that period, then during the last six months of the two-year period, the border decreased to a sixteenth of an inch. **If you have family letters in your possession, you can tell in which phase of mourning the widow was by measuring the border.**

**Hidden Treasures**

## Memorial Portraits, Prints, and Needlework

Before photographs, it was common to have a painting made of the deceased, a memorial lithograph designed, or a needlework memorial stitched. These hung on parlor and bedroom walls and were popular from the late 1600s through the mid-1800s.

Although posthumous portraits were mostly an upper-class trend, you may run across one in your ancestry in a museum, archive, or in the home of a distant cousin. These portraits typically show the deceased in bed as if asleep. Common to the middle class in the nineteenth century were posthumous mourning portraits, especially of children. The deceased was portrayed alive in these images, and the portrait was either painted from the corpse or from a daguerreotype photograph. **In these portraits, there are "disguised" death symbols, giving you a clue that the child was deceased when the painting was commissioned.** There may be clouds surrounding the child, a willow tree in the background, a timepiece, or a wilted flower in the child's hand. Mourning portraits were most

**Tip**

**Figure 6-3** Mourning embroidery worked by Nancy Torrey (1793–1869), 1809. Inscribed at lower left on the glass mat: "WROUGHT. BY. NANCY. TORREY. 1809." Epitaph printed on paper and applied to the silk-worked plinth, "AFFECTIONATELY INSCRIBED/To the/Memory/of/Mr. Caleb Torrey,/Who ob$^t$. March 16, 1808,/AGED 50." Nancy's memorial pictures her mother, Mary (Miller) Torrey, aged forty-three; Nancy, then fourteen; her sister Mary, aged thirteen; her brother Caleb, aged seven; and her sister Hannah, aged three.

*Allen Mewbourn, photographer.*
*From the collection of Betty Ring.*

common among middle-class Protestants who lived in the Northeast; however, others from all over the country commissioned them, too. Posthumous mourning paintings went out of fashion as photography became more popular at the end of the nineteenth century.

Girls attending seminaries, finishing, and boarding schools in the early 1800s through about 1830 made many of the memorial needlework art that has survived today. (See figure 6-3 above for an example of mourning embroidery.) Patterns for mourning samplers also appeared in contemporary women's magazines. These usually contained tombs, urns, weeping willows, and black-garbed people in mourning. As the attitude toward death changed to a more aesthetic quality, birds, trees, angels, and churches were added. For the most part, the custom of making handmade mourning needlework went out of popularity by the end of the Civil War. Surviving samplers may be found in museums, and you can also find pieces for sale on the Internet at antique store sites and on eBay. Type "mourning samplers" into a search engine.

In the 1840s, Nathaniel Currier mass-produced mourning lithographs with a blank space for the deceased's name and vital statistics. These resembled the needlework memorial pattern—a tall white or gray memorial stone with the inscription beginning "Sacred to the Memory of. . . ." These lithographs went out of fashion by the 1870s and were replaced by photographs and memorial cards that families could send to relatives, hang on their walls, or place in photo albums.

## Postmortem Photographs

During the wake, families of all classes might have photographs taken of the deceased, especially when babies and children died. These images were seen as

**For More Info**

For more information on photographs and postmortem photographs, see Jay Ruby's *Secure the Shadow: Death and Photography in America*; Maureen A. Taylor's *Uncovering Your Ancestry Through Family Photographs* (Cincinnati: Betterway Books, 2000); and Katherine Scott Sturdevant's *Bringing Your Family History to Life Through Social History* (Cincinnati: Betterway Books, 2000).

## TWAIN'S HUCK FINN

They had pictures hung on the walls. . . . One was a woman in a slim black dress, belted small under the armpits, with bulges like a cabbage in the middle of the sleeves, and a large black scoop-shovel bonnet with a black veil, and white slim ankles crossed about with black tape, and very wee black slippers, like a chisel, and she was leaning pensive on a tombstone on her right elbow, under a weeping willow, and her other hand hanging down her side holding a white handkerchief and a reticule, and underneath the picture it said "Shall I Never See Thee More Alas." Another one was a young lady with her hair all combed up straight to the top of her head, and knotted there in front of a comb like a chair back, and she was crying into a handkerchief and had a dead bird laying on its back in her other hand with its heels up, and underneath the picture it said "I Shall Never Hear Thy Sweet Chirrup More Alas." There was one where a young lady was at a window looking up at the moon, and tears running down her cheeks; and she had an open letter in one hand with black sealing wax showing on one edge of it, and she was mashing a locket with a chain to it against her mouth, and underneath the picture it said "And Art Thou Gone Yes Thou Art Gone Alas." These was all nice pictures, I reckon, but I didn't somehow seem to take to them. . . . Everybody was sorry [the young girl who made them] died, because she had laid out a lot more of these pictures to do, and a body could see by what she had done what they had lost. But I reckoned that with her disposition she was having a better time in the graveyard.

—from *Huckleberry Finn*, by Mark Twain

a means to help the family through the grieving process and to remember the loved one, as well as something to share with friends and family who could not be present for the funeral. (See figure 6-4.) Another reason for the popularity in postmortem photography, especially of babies and children, was the high infant and child mortality rate. Many youngsters never lived long enough for parents to have a photograph taken. Families of the nineteenth century treated postmortem photographs the same as they did pictures of the living: They hung them in their parlors and bedrooms, set them on the mantel in the living room, placed them in family photo albums, sent them to relatives, carried them in their wallets, attached them to tombstones (see chapter three), and placed them in jewelry. You can find these images in all formats: daguerreotypes, ambrotypes, tintypes, cartes de visite, cabinet cards, stereographs, postcards, snapshots, instant prints, and 35mm slides and prints.

Photographing the deceased is as old as photography itself; it dates from the 1840s. Photographers routinely advertised in newspapers and city directories that they were available to take photographs of the deceased within an hour's notice. As previously mentioned, the wake, funeral, and burial might happen within a twenty-four hour period. Photographers could not waste any time,

**Figure 6-4** Postmortem photograph of Samuel Forman from the Williston Collection (Mss 44, IV/A). *Photo courtesy of the New England Historic Genealogical Society. All rights reserved.*

especially if they needed to pose the body before rigor mortis set in. Before funeral parlors became popular, photographers took postmortem pictures in the deceased's home. The average cost of a postmortem "sitting" ranged from ten to fifteen dollars.

Even after viewings were held in funeral homes, taking photographs of the deceased remained common. James K. Crissman in *Death and Dying in Central Appalachia* (page 76) tells of one postmortem photograph:

> The body was taken to the funeral home where it was embalmed, clothed, and placed in the casket. The sisters [of the deceased] requested that the body be transferred to the home for a short period of time. . . . When the corpse was returned, the funeral director noticed that the clothing of the deceased was rumpled and unkempt. There was evidence that the body had been moved around in the casket. When questioned, the sisters confessed that they had never had their picture taken with their brother while he was alive. They had removed him from his casket, stood him between them, and had a "family" portrait taken.

Taking postmortem photographs was widespread among all middle-class families of the nineteenth century, but certain ethnic groups showed more preference for the custom than others: African Americans, Asian Americans, Italian Americans, Polish Americans, and Russian Americans, as well as the Scotch

Irish and German Lutherans. Jews, on the other hand, did not typically practice funeral or corpse photography.

Between the 1840s and 1880, the most common style of postmortem photograph was intended to deny death. According to Jay Ruby in *Secure the Shadow: Death and Photography in America* (page 63), this was known as the "last sleep," and these photographs showed mostly the upper half of the body. The idea was to make the deceased look asleep. The photographer and family placed the corpse upon a sofa or bed, or for children, in a cradle or buggy. Like posthumous mourning portraits, you might find flowers, a book or Bible, a rosary, or some other object placed in the hands. Because the illusion was to present the loved one as asleep, the deceased was never photographed in a coffin.

In the 1860s, photographic memorial cards became popular and continue even today. These memorials showed a photograph of the deceased while still alive with vital statistics and sometimes a verse. The text might have been printed on the same side as the photograph or on the back. (See also Funeral, Memorial, and Prayer Cards in chapter one.)

Starting in the 1880s through the early 1910s, it became more common to photograph the deceased's entire body, usually in the casket. This shift in attitude coincided with the changes in the funeral industry—embalming became widespread, lined caskets replaced coffins, and floral arrangements were more elaborate. Another trend in postmortem photography of this time was to take pictures of the deceased with living family members. A mother holding a deceased infant on her lap was common, as was a loved one sitting next to the deceased laid out in bed. As mentioned earlier, funerals were not just a time to grieve the loss of a loved one, but they were also social occasions, similar to family reunions. So it is not unusual to find everyone gathered around the casket or the graveside for a family portrait. Sometimes widows would have their portraits taken in their "widow's weeds" (mourning garb; in Old and Middle English, "wede" referred to a garment worn in mourning). Even taking pictures of just the funeral flowers was popular, especially to send to the distant family who ordered the flowers but could not attend the service.

Taking photographs of dead loved ones was not purely a nineteenth-century custom. It is just as popular today as it was then; however, because society considers it morbid or unhealthy, and death is not as openly discussed today as it was in our ancestors' days, many people are embarrassed to admit they have taken postmortem photographs, and most unknowingly are carrying out a social custom practiced by their ancestors. Today, there is no longer a need for a professional photographer; individuals can take photographs themselves at the funeral home or during the wake. I took photographs of my grandmother in her casket when she died in 1981. Those photographs are in my family album. In Ruby's *Secure the Shadow* (pages 167–168), he relates that even Ann Landers in her newspaper column in 1991 had to admit how widespread the custom still is. She received nearly a thousand letters from readers in support of taking pictures of the dead when she expressed her view that she thought it was "weird." Some people even wrote that they didn't take pictures because they were afraid of being thought morbid, but now they deeply regret not getting a last photograph.

**For More Info**

For a firsthand account of how photographers photographed the deceased, see "Taking Portraits After Death," by N.G. Burgess, <www.daguerre.org/res ource/texts/burgess.html>, originally published in *The Photographic and Fine-Art Journal* 8 (March 1855): 80.

## BODY SNATCHING

*Dig them up. Put them back in. Dig them up. Put them back in.*
*He didn't go to medical school to become a grave digger.*
—Sheri Holman's The Dress Lodger

**Warning**

**Quotes**

body-snatcher, *n.* A robber of grave-worms. One who supplies the young physicians with that which the old physicians have supplied the undertaker. A hyena.

——Ambrose Bierce's
*The Devil's Dictionary*

If you thought body snatching was just a colorful legend around which good horror movies are made, think again. In particular, **if your ancestors were buried in close proximity to one of the early American medical colleges, they may not be resting peacefully in their graves.** According to Kenneth V. Iserson in *Death to Dust: What Happens to Dead Bodies?* (page 337), legend has it that "few bodies remain in the several graveyards near the University of Maryland School of Medicine in Baltimore." He further states that "by the time New York passed its [anatomy] law [in 1854], grave robbers were emptying six hundred to seven hundred graves around New York City annually to supply anatomical specimens." David Burrell in "Origins of Undertaking" found one source that suggests "Ohio alone experienced over five thousand stolen bodies in the nineteenth century," probably because Cincinnati had "more medical schools than any other city in the West."

Body snatching was widespread; otherwise coffin makers wouldn't have been trying to meet the needs of those who wanted to keep their loved ones buried, and newspapers wouldn't have been reporting incidents of body snatching within their pages. Manufacturers made special coffins to discourage grave robbers and body snatchers, from heavy metal caskets with locks on the lids to "torpedo coffins" that contained explosive devises. The Clover Coffin Torpedo Manufacturing Company of Columbus, Ohio, was one such company to market these exploding caskets.

As medical schools in the early and mid nineteenth century sprung up, so did the need for cadavers to give students hands-on lessons in anatomy. Today, medical schools require anywhere from three hundred to eight hundred bodies a year, but there are state anatomy laws providing colleges with cadavers, and people freely donate their bodies to science. But this was not always the case. In order to get fresh cadavers, medical schools hired professional body snatchers—known as "resurrectionists"—or equally as common, the medical students themselves took to body snatching. On occasion, people were murdered for their bodies. While this practice was more common in the British Isles, there are reported cases in America, too, of bodies being procured through homicide.

Body snatching was not limited to the areas surrounding medical schools. Bodies were taken from rural and urban cemeteries alike, then shipped to needy colleges. Most professional body snatchers sold cadavers for five dollars, but in Ohio and some other states, thirty dollars was the going rate for a corpse. To save themselves the trouble of robbing a grave after a body had been interred, savvy resurrectionists and medical students made arrangements with unscrupulous undertakers or cemetery sextons. While the unsuspecting family buried an empty, weighted coffin, their loved one was sacked and taken to the medical school.

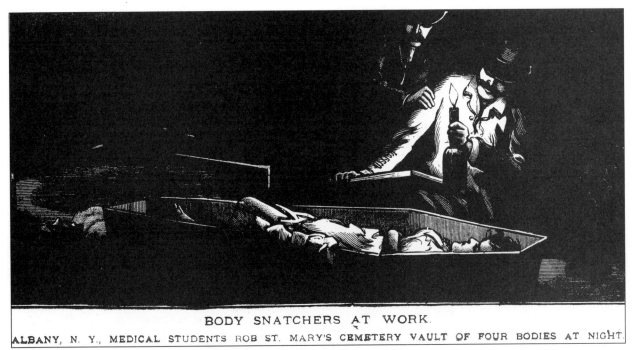

BODY SNATCHERS AT WORK.
ALBANY, N. Y., MEDICAL STUDENTS ROB ST. MARY'S CEMETERY VAULT OF FOUR BODIES AT NIGHT.

**Figure 6-5** Illustration from the *National Police Gazette*, 11 March 1893, page 12.

Ruth Sprague's headstone in Maple Grove Cemetery, Hoosick Falls, New York, is hard, irrefutable evidence:

> RUTH SPRAGUE
> dau of Gibson
> & Elizabeth Sprague.
> died Jan. 11, 1846; aged
> 9 years 1 mo's & 3 days.
>
> —
>
> She was stolen from the grave
> by Roderick R. Crow & dissect
> ed at Dr. P.M. Armstrongs' office
> in Hoosick N.Y. from which place
> her mutilated remains were
> obtained & deposited here.
>
> —
>
> Her body dissected by fiendish Men,
> Her bones anatomised,
> Her soul we trust has risen to God
> where few Physicians rise.

Could your ancestors have been victims of body snatchers? **Believe it or not, there are certain corpses that were more desirable to resurrectionists and anatomists.** Because Jews buried their loved ones within twenty-four hours of death, these bodies were especially appealing to the medical schools. Embalming was not practiced until late in the nineteenth century, so freshly buried bodies were

Notes

## BODY-SNATCHERS AT WORK

Special Dispatch to *The New York Times.*

CLEVELAND, Dec. 10.—As two gentlemen were passing through Lake View Cemetery in this city, yesterday afternoon, they discovered that a newly-made grave had been opened, and that the head and shoulders of the corpse of an old lady protruded above the ground, bent over the edge of the grave, with the face half buried in the loose dirt which had been thrown up. The body-snatchers had opened the grave at the head, and, digging down and around the coffin, had sawed away the wood from just below the shoulders, and fastening a hook in the mouth had drawn the body out of the coffin and nearly out of the grave, when it is surmised, the earth must have caved in, and so wedged the body that it could not be got out. They must have struggled hard to remove their horrible plunder even then for a terrible gash extending from the mouth across one cheek showed where the hook had slipped and torn and mangled the corpse. The men must have either been frightened or discouraged then, as they did not attempt to dig away the earth that had caved in. The Police found a shovel, and the saw which had been used in opening the coffin. The body was that of Mrs. Lear Williams, 68 years of age, and who recently had a tumor weighing 80 pounds removed from her person. She is supposed to have died from the effects of the operation. Mrs. Williams died in Massillon, Ohio, and her remains were brought on and interred here on Friday last. A plain gold ring, which was on her finger, is missing, which would go to show that the work was done by professionals. It is rumored that Mrs. Williams was suffering from another tumor at the time of her death, and that this proved an incentive for the violation of the grave. A young man who was passing through the cemetery Saturday night says he saw two men run away from the direction of this spot, and thinks they were then frightened from their work.

—*The New York Times*, 11 December 1877, Tuesday, page 1, column 4.

preferred before they began decomposing. Sometimes families would hire grave watchers to sit by the grave until the body was presumed to have decomposed sufficiently that the medical schools would not want them. Or, they might scatter flowers, pebbles, or twigs on the grave to detect any disturbance.

If your ancestor was a criminal, ended up as an unclaimed body, or died in the almshouse (poorhouse), he or she may have come to rest on the anatomy table. Was your ancestor buried in potter's field? Those were the graves most frequently raided; however, African-American cemeteries, too, were less safe than other cemeteries, especially in the South. Even family burial plots in rural areas were not immune. Body snatchers often preferred these sites since they were isolated and the threat of discovery was less. City church burial grounds were mostly unaffected by body snatchers; not because they were sacred, but because they were more likely to be in populated areas. Were your ancestors buried in a cemetery east of the Mississippi? Because medical schools were more prevalent in the East during the mid- and late-1800s, there aren't as many cases of body snatching reported out West. Additionally, most of the physicians who went West were already trained.

Although some states, such as New Hampshire, Michigan, and Connecticut, had anatomy laws as early as the 1830s and 1840s, many of these laws were repealed. Only Massachusetts and New York had enacted anatomy laws by the end of the Civil War. Body snatching began its decline in the late 1890s, by which time many states had passed anatomy acts that provided cadavers to medical schools. But as late as the 1920s body snatchers were still selling bodies to medical schools in Nashville, Tennessee, and surplus bodies were being shipped to medical schools in Iowa City.

Body snatching for the anatomist's table wasn't the only reason people disturbed graves. Of course, stealing jewelry was one reason, but another was for human teeth. Teeth, especially the front teeth, were just as valuable a commodity as a whole body was. While replacing someone's molars with synthetic teeth was common, human front teeth were coveted for their durability and color.

How do you discover if one of your ancestors fell victim to body snatchers? **Check newspaper articles for several days after your ancestor's death.** If someone discovered that the grave had been disturbed or the body snatched, the newspaper often mentioned the name of the deceased who was "missing."

**Research Tip**

---

### FUNERAL SERVICE MEMORABILIA

Visit the National Museum of Funeral History for the country's largest display of funeral service memorabilia. The museum houses rare artifacts, such as photographs, hearses, coffins, and mourning clothes. There's even a gift shop.

National Museum of Funeral History
 415 Barren Springs Dr., Houston, TX 77090
 Phone: (281) 876-3063
 Web site: www.nmfh.org

---

## PREMATURE BURIAL

*There are certain themes of which the interest is all-absorbing, but which are too entirely horrible for the purposes of legitimate fiction. . . .*
*To be buried alive is beyond question the most terrific of these extremes which has ever fallen to the lot of mere mortality.*
—*Edgar Allan Poe's "The Premature Burial"*

Edgar Allan Poe wasn't the only one who feared being buried alive. In fact, the fear was so widespread that special coffins containing life-saving devices were designed and patented and the Association for the Prevention of Premature

Burials was founded in 1896. The first life-saving coffin was patented and marketed in 1843. Christian Eisenbrandt invented a coffin whereby the occupant could release a spring lid with the slightest movement of the hand or head. The problem was it was only good before the person was buried in the ground. Later caskets contained bells and alarms that could be activated inside the coffin to alert people above ground that the deceased had "awakened." Theodore Schroeder and Hermann Wuest of Hoboken, New Jersey, patented a casket in 1871 that had a tube inserted into the coffin that extended above ground, so the buried person could open it for air and simultaneously set off an alarm. Life-saving coffins continued to be patented well into the 1880s. One of the advantages of embalming, however, was it removed fears of being buried alive.

## WHAT'S NEXT?

As mentioned, burial customs vary from one ethnic and religious group to another. Let's take a look at some of these rituals your ancestors may have practiced.

SEVEN

# Ethnic and Religious Funeral and Burial Customs

*May you be in heaven a half hour before the devil knows you're dead.*

—*Old Irish saying*

I n the previous chapter, we looked at traditional "American," that is Anglo, burial customs and traditions. The customs in this chapter are broad cultural trends of ethnic or religious groups in America; keep in mind that there can be many modifications of these burial rituals. You'll notice that not every American ethnic or religious group is covered, of course. The inclusions of some groups and not others is based solely on the availability of significant resources on the topic. Following each discussion is a list of suggested further reading. Sources without publishing information appear in the bibliography. **For links to burial practices not covered here, go to The Funeral Directory at <www.thefuneraldirectory.com/ancientrites.html>** or "Different Approaches to Death, Funerals, and Mourning" at <www.globalideasbank.org/ w2go/WTG-12.html>. Or in your Internet search engine or library catalog, type in the ethnic or religious group, then keywords such as "burial and funeral customs" or "death rituals."

**Internet Source**

## AFRICAN AMERICAN

To African Americans, death was a time for celebration, with singing, dancing, and music rather than sadness, because the deceased had been freed from the misery of earthly existence. Naturally, family and friends mourned the loss of the loved one, but this attitude stemmed from their many years in bondage.

Slaves handled all of the white and African-American families' burial needs: washing and dressing the bodies, digging the graves, and taking care of the white family's cemetery. Slaves were often buried in unmarked graves on the plantation owner's property, in a separate section of the white family's ceme-

**Figure 7-1** African-American cemetery, Vicksburg, Mississippi.
*Collection of the author.*

**Figure 7-1** African-American cemetery, Vicksburg, Mississippi.
*Collection of the author.*

tery, or segregated into a different burial ground. Slaves themselves supposedly preferred this segregation—although they really didn't have a choice in the matter—as there were fears and superstitions that burial next to the white slave owners would tie them to their slaveholders for eternity. There was little ceremony for a deceased slave, although those slaves allowed to gather would express jubilance, rather than feelings of somberness, since the deceased was now free from suffering. To slaves, dying meant "going home."

Slave owners determined if a marker would be placed, and children's graves rarely were marked by something other than field stones. Markers were generally chosen for those adult slaves whose service to the owner or family awarded them an acknowledgment as "faithful servants." Angelika Krüger-Kahloula points out that in life slaves were considered property, but by placing a marker on slaves' graves, whites gave them human identities.

After the Civil War, African-American funeral businesses began, often started by African-American women who had handled death preparation during slavery. Over time, African-American funeral directors handled all of the African-American family's needs. The wake took place in the funeral parlor, at the church, or in the deceased's home, where food and drink were served. Coins were initially placed on the eyes of the deceased to keep them closed; however, coins may also have been placed inside the casket or on the grave, supposedly as a token for admittance into the spirit world. Perhaps the most well-known African-American funerals are those that took place in New Orleans, where the procession included a lively band, singing, and dancing. Rain on the day of a funeral was considered bad luck, so every attempt was made to have the funeral on a sunny day. The sun signified that heaven was open and welcoming.

Southern African-American cemeteries established after the Civil War were often in rural, isolated areas and usually along dirt or gravel roads. Some Southern cemeteries may have had separate sections for blacks. In either case, you'll find small grave markers, a pile of rocks and stones, or no marker at all. The markers that do exist may be homemade, rather than purchased. You'll find the graves irregularly situated, although there was a preference for placing the body with feet to the east. There are usually no grave vaults in the ground to protect the casket, so sunken, uneven graves are common. (See figure 7-1 on page 172.)

### Suggested Reading

"African American Cemeteries: A World Apart," by Maryellen Harshbarger McVicker. http://mo-river.net/history/boonslick/appendix_a.htm.

"The African American Funeral Custom: Our 'Home Going' Heritage," by Erich March. www.goolsbymortuary.com/history.htm/.

"Antebellum Louisiana: Disease, Death, and Mourning." http://lsm.crt.state.la.us/cabildo/cab8a.htm.

"The History of African American Death: Superstitions, Traditions, and Procedures." www.northbysouth.org/1998/death/deathhistory.htm.

*Medicine and Slavery: The Diseases and Health Care of Blacks in Antebellum Virginia*, by Todd L. Savitt. Urbana: University of Illinois Press, 1978.

"Tributes in Stone and Lapidary Lapses: Commemorating Black People in Eighteenth- and Nineteenth-Century America," by Angelika Krüger-Kahloula. *Markers* VI (1989): 33–100.

Sources

## AMISH

Early Amish funerals were held in the home, and as one might expect, were simple affairs. Flowers and black crepe were not used, and unless embalming was required by law for public health reasons, no embalming was done. The Amish did follow the custom of wearing black. The four bearers were selected from among the deceased's friends; if the deceased was single, then single friends were chosen, and if the deceased was married, then married friends carried the casket. These bearers also helped ready the home, dig the grave, and prepare the wagon to transport the coffin to the cemetery, which was next to the church or in the country.

The funeral consisted of a sermon and prayers, but no eulogy was offered. As church bells tolled the death, the preacher led the procession to the burial ground, where the bearers lowered the coffin into the grave and then filled the grave. Then the preacher offered a few more words and a benediction.

Today, the Amish use funeral homes like other groups, although they prefer a funeral director who is familiar with Amish burial customs. The funeral director embalms the body and dresses it in white clothing in preparation for the visitation. No makeup or cosmetics are used. The wake and the funeral take place in the family's home. There is no singing, either at the funeral or at the graveside, where the preacher reads a hymn and there is more prayer. After the service, family and friends return to the deceased's home for a simple meal.

As in the past, Amish tombstones of today are plain and fairly uniform like those of the Quakers. On the stone is the name, birth and death dates, and age in years, months, and days. The plots are bare, and no foliage is planted.

Sources

## Suggested Reading

Amish Country News. "Amish Religious Traditions," Part Six: The Funeral Service, www.amishnews.com/amisharticles/religioustraditions.htm.

*Amish Society*, 4th ed., by John A. Hostetler. Baltimore: Johns Hopkins University Press, 1993.

*Death in Early America: The History and Folklore of Customs and Superstitions of Early Medicine, Funerals, Burials, and Mourning*, by Margaret M. Coffin.

## ROMAN CATHOLIC

After death, the body was laid out and a light was kept burning during the wake or visitation. A small cross would be placed in the deceased's hands, or the hands were arranged to form a cross over the chest. The body was also sprinkled with holy water.

When the casket arrived at the church for the funeral mass, it would be positioned so that the deceased's feet were turned toward the altar. If the body

**Figure 7-2** Catholic marker. Stanchfield family stone. The monogram on this stone represents the first two letters of Christos—Christ in Greek: X (chi) and P (rho). Mount Calvary Catholic Cemetery, Salt Lake City, Utah.

*Collection of the author.*

was of a priest, however, the position would be opposite, with the head to the altar. The mass began with a recital of the Vespers for the Dead. Candles that burned throughout the mass were lit around the casket. After the mass, there was an absolution or Absolute, which are special prayers said to pardon any sins of the deceased before the body is laid into the grave.

At the cemetery, the priest blessed the grave, although if the grave was dug in consecrated (that is, blessed) ground, this was not necessary. Interment in a mausoleum, however, required special blessing. Graveside services were typically brief, and after the coffin was lowered into the grave, holy water was again sprinkled onto the casket. In some parishes, the holy-water sprinkler was offered to the family of the deceased so they could continue to sprinkle holy water upon the grave. The priest and those present threw dirt onto the casket in the grave to symbolize the return of the body to the earth.

While many Catholics were buried in Catholic cemeteries, according to canon law, Catholics were free to choose wherever they would like to be buried. Only those baptized into the Catholic faith were to be buried in a Catholic cemetery; however, if this was the only cemetery in a community, then those of other faiths could be buried there. There were usually separate sections set aside for infants and young children. Like most Christian cemeteries, the graves were laid on an east-west axis, with feet to the east. While cremation is not prohibited in the Catholic faith, it is frowned upon.

Suicide victims, those killed in a duel, or notorious sinners who die without repentance may not be buried in consecrated grounds. If the suicide victim was of unsound mind when taking his or her own life, then an exception was made for a Catholic burial. Mary Clark of Greenwich, Connecticut, for example, apparently was trying to commit suicide in 1908. The local newspaper reported that she stabbed herself in the abdomen with a kitchen knife, and the death certificate added that she had also set her hair on fire. Her official cause of death on the death certificate was "burns of scalp, neck, and shoulders; laceration of the abdomen," but the newspaper also stated that she was not of sound mind. Before she attempted to take her own life, she had taken a serious fall on a trolley car, hitting the back of her head. She had not been "right" ever since, and had she recovered from the wound and burns, she would have spent the rest of her life in an institution. Thus, even though she brought about her own death, because she was not of sound mind, she could still be buried in a Catholic cemetery, which she was.

### Suggested Reading

"Christian Burial," and "Cremation," in *The Catholic Encyclopedia*, 1908. www.newadvent.org/cathen/.

Sources

## CZECH AMERICAN

In the Czech community, there were two cemeteries: one established for the Freethinkers (identified as the name in Czech and *hrbitov*, which is Czech for "cemetery") and one for the Catholics (given saints' names in English). Many

Czechs settled in the Midwest and plains states, where they found hilltops just outside of town to place their cemeteries. Like other Christian cemeteries, Czechs buried their loved ones on an east-west axis, with feet to the east. Foliage was used extensively in the Freethinker cemeteries, with a preference for tall evergreens that resembled European forests: Austrian pine, blue spruce, red cedar. Trees were also planted in the Catholic cemeteries, albeit fewer of them. Commercially produced headstones were most common, but wood, concrete, or metal markers marked earlier and less well-to-do individuals and families. For an ancestor buried in the early 1900s, you might find a flat, slab-type marker covering the entire grave. Some of the concrete slabs may be rounded.

Sources

### Suggested Reading

"Czech Cemeteries in Nebraska from 1868: Cultural Imprints on the Prairie," by Karen S. Kiest in *Ethnicity and the American Cemetery*, edited by Richard E. Meyer.

"Ethnic Influences," in *Soul in the Stone: Cemetery Art From America's Heartland*, by John Gary Brown.

## DUTCH

For the colonial Dutch, the *Aanspreker* acted as an undertaker, handling all of the funeral and burial arrangements. After he was notified of a death, he went to the family's house and took the names of those who should be notified of the death and invited to the funeral. The wake and funeral took place in the home of the deceased, known as the *sterfhuis*. Like many other cultures, beer and spirits were served. The Dutch were buried in clothes that had been prepared for the occasion before death occurred. The *Aanspreker* offered prayers at the funeral and at the grave. Once the coffin was lowered into the ground and the grave was refilled with dirt, everyone went back to the *sterfhuis* to drink and eat. Women typically did not go to the cemetery, but stayed home to prepare the refreshments.

Burials for ministers and men of prominence took place within the church; other people were buried in a town or church cemetery or on family farms. Graves in early Dutch cemeteries were placed wherever convenient, not necessarily in family plots or nearby other family members.

Sources

### Suggested Reading

*Death in Early America: The History and Folklore of Customs and Superstitions of Early Medicine, Funerals, Burials, and Mourning*, by Margaret M. Coffin.

Get NJ, Burial Customs. http://getnj.com/jchist/41.html.

## GERMAN AMERICAN

Because there are several nationalities of German Americans, burial customs were varied, although there are some similarities. Distinguishing German-

American monuments from other ethnic groups is the sense of sadness and loss as reflected in the symbols they choose for their grave markers: angels and females in mourning, urns, wreaths, drapery or shrouded figures. Also common on their early markers were hex signs believed to ward off evil spirits—rosettes, stars, and stars within circles—particularly for the Pennsylvania Germans, but also for German Americans who immigrated between 1830 and 1890. Tulips, hearts, trees of life, suns, moons, and stars were other common motifs. Eighteenth-century Pennsylvania German epitaphs might begin with *Hier ruhet* ("Here rests") or *Hier Legt* ("Here Lies"). Into the nineteenth century, before the use of English became commonplace, you'll find *Zum Andenken an* ("To the Memory of"). Early German headstones may have inscriptions in German, using German lettering. Birth dates were often inscribed, and maiden names of women may also be included. Early markers may just be crosses, in wood or wrought or cast iron, but these usually have elaborate detailing. German sections in cemeteries have an orderly, row-by-row layout.

### Suggested Reading

"Death-Customs, Superstitions, Epitaphs," excerpted from Elmer L. Smith's *Pennsylvania Dutch Folklore*. Lebanon, Pa.: Applied Arts Publishers, 1960. www.horseshoe.cc/pennadutch/culture/customs/death.htm.

"German Americans," in *Silent Cities: The Evolution of the American Cemetery*, by Kenneth T. Jackson and Camilo José Vergara.

"Pennsylvania German Gravestones: An Introduction," by Thomas E. Graves. *Markers* V (1988): 61–95.

Sources

## HISPANIC AMERICAN

Like Native Americans and German Americans, Hispanic Americans descend from several nationalities with variations of funeral rituals. All, however, have respect for the dead. This is evident in the Hispanic culture's celebration of All Souls' Day on November 2, or the Day of the Dead.

Most people know that Halloween, celebrated on October 31, was initially called All Hallows' Eve, the day before All Hallows or All Saints' Day. This day was established by the Roman Catholic Church as a memorial to those Christian saints who had died for their beliefs. The custom of dressing in costume was originally to honor the saints, not to frighten away evil spirits. The Church also encouraged its members to visit their neighbors on All Hallows' Eve, sharing "soul cakes" (breads and pastries) with the town's poor. Following All Saints' Day was All Souls' Day on November 2. This religious memorial day was to commemorate all of the dead. As the holiday spread across Europe and into the American colonies, each culture created its own customs for celebrating, but most prominent is the Mexican tradition of the Day of the Dead.

In Mexico and Mexican-American communities, the Day of the Dead, or *Día de los Muertos*, is celebrated by making special foods and offering feasts to loved ones buried in the cemetery. Typically, November 1, All Saints' Day, is in remembrance of deceased infants and children, while November 2, All

**Figure 7-3** Headstone of Marcial Fuentes, 1930, Oak Creek Cemetery, Oak Creek, Colorado.

*Collection of the author.*

Souls' Day, honors adults who have died. During the celebration, families make pastries, cookies, candies, and cakes in the form of skeletons, coffins, and skulls. Children play with toy skeletons, coffins, and skulls. Because the spirit is expected to return home on October 31 and depart November 2, families also honor the dead by creating elaborate altars in their homes decorated with candles, flowers, and photographs of the deceased. Food is also offered on the altar.

Similar to American culture's Memorial Day or Decoration Day, Mexican-American families tend the graves, clean headstones, and decorate cemetery plots with flowers, wreaths, crosses, or other religious artifacts. Families hold reunions and gather for picnics in the cemetery. Sometimes a local mariachi band is hired for the festivities. In the evening, candles and lamps are lit, and food, drink (alcoholic), and cigarettes are offered to the deceased.

You'll find your Hispanic ancestors buried in Catholic, public, and family cemeteries, sometimes in their own section, or you may find an entirely Hispanic cemetery. For those buried in separate sections or cemeteries, the grave arrangement is likely haphazard, with emphasis on individuals' graves, rather than family groupings. Landscaping is usually that of whatever foliage grows naturally, rather than the planting of evergreens or other trees; however, the Hispanic culture loves flowers, so you'll find all types of artificial flower arrangements, no doubt appealing for their vivid colors.

Most early burials, that is, before about 1820, had no markers; plain Latin crosses to mark the grave became popular after this time, and you can find them made from wood, cement (sometimes having colorful marbles, tile pieces, or trinkets pressed into them), and wrought or cast iron. As Hispanic groups became more acculturated, they began to use headstones. Hispanic Americans like to display coloring on many of their markers, painting them with bright colors: red, yellow, green, and blue. They also use religious statues of Christ, the Virgin Mary, and the Virgin of Guadalupe, and they also create miniature religious shrines. Inscriptions are often simple, giving just the name and vital information, and may be written in Spanish; rarely are origins in the home country given. (See figure 7-3 on page 178.) Shells are common decorations for graves.

### Suggested Reading

"The Agua Mansa Cemetery: An Indicator of Ethnic Identification in a Mexican-American Community," by Russell J. Barber, in *Ethnicity and the American Cemetery*, ed. by Richard E. Meyer.

"Camposantos: Sacred Places of the Southwest," by Laura Sue Sanborn. *Markers* VI (1989): 159–180.

"The Day of the Dead," by Dale Hoyt Palfrey. www.mexconnect.com/mex_/muertos.html.

"Día de los Muertos (Day of the Dead)." www.niu.edu/newsplace/nndia.html.

*Halloween: An American Holiday, An American History*, by Lesley Pratt Bannatyne. New York: Facts on File, 1990.

"Hispanic Americans," in *Silent Cities: The Evolution of the American Cemetery*, by Kenneth T. Jackson and Camilo José Vergara.

"The Mexican Graveyard in Texas," in *Texas Graveyards: A Cultural Legacy*, by Terry G. Jordan.

"What do Mexicans Celebrate on the 'Day of the Dead?' " by Ricardo J. Salvador. www.public.iastate.edu/~rjsalvad/scmfaq/muertos.html.

Sources

# IRISH AMERICAN

When most people think about funeral wakes the Irish come to mind because of their lively celebrations when a loved one dies. For those who practiced traditional Irish burial customs in the nineteenth century and before, the body was prepared either by family, friends, or the undertaker. It was then laid out for visitation and covered in white linen that had the letters IHS embroidered on the chestplate (a Roman Catholic monogram meaning "Jesus, savior of mankind"). Lighted candles surrounded the body. The wake lasted for two to three nights, and the corpse was not to be left alone. During the wake, a window was left open so the spirit of the deceased could depart. *Caoiners*, or professional mourners, offered songs and chants during the wake. Even today, games are often played during the wake, as well as lively storytelling about the deceased, bantering, debating, joke-telling, smoking, eating, and drinking.

Before the casket was taken to the cemetery, family and close friends kissed the corpse, because it was the last time family and friends would have a chance to say good-bye, then the lid was placed on the coffin, and the procession set off for the graveyard. The four nearest of kin carried the coffin. The church bell tolled for the deceased, and as the procession approached the burial ground,

**Figure 7-4** Celtic cross. Geoghegan marker. Mount Calvary Catholic Cemetery, Salt Lake City, Utah. *Collection of the author.*

**Figure 7-5** Marker showing Irish origins. Catherine Maguire, Native of Co. Monaghan, Ireland. St. Mary's Cemetery, Greenwich, Connecticut. *Collection of the author.*

black crape arm and hat bands were distributed to the mourners. Rain on the day of a funeral was considered a good omen because it rains all the time in Ireland. After the coffin was lowered and the grave was filled, the shovel and spade were laid across the top in the form of a cross. Then the priest said a graveside prayer.

Irish Catholics have obvious symbols on their tombstones. Common are the Celtic cross (see figure 7-4), the Virgin Mary, and the sacrificial lamb on the altar, as well as the monogram IHS. Rarely, however, is St. Patrick, the patron saint of Ireland, portrayed on Irish-American markers.

On headstones, you may find Irish origins—the name of the county, civil parish or even townland in Ireland—a crucial key if other records or family stories have not yet revealed your ancestor's origins. Several Irish-American headstones and cemeteries have been transcribed and published, such as Rosemary Muscarella Ardolina's *Old Calvary Cemetery: New Yorkers Carved in Stone* (Bowie, Md.: Heritage Books, Inc., 1996) and *Tombstones of the Irish Born: Cemetery of the Holy Cross, Flatbush, Brooklyn,* by Joseph M. Silinonte (Bowie, Md.: Heritage Books, Inc., 1994). Check the catalog of the Family History Library. Keep in mind, however, that the person recording the inscriptions may have failed to note the place of origin, so you always want to see the original stone for yourself.

Irish Catholics were typically buried in a Catholic cemetery because it was consecrated ground. Irish Protestants could be buried in a public cemetery, in a church graveyard, in a fraternal organization section of the cemetery, or in family plots.

**Sources**

**Suggested Reading**

"Folklore and Burial Customs," by Rory Donohue and David Gilmore, Town of Glenamaddy Web site. www.glenamaddy.net/files/history/burial_custo ms.shtml.

*A Genealogist's Guide to Discovering Your Irish Ancestors*, by Dwight A. Radford and Kyle J. Betit. Cincinnati: Betterway Books, 2001.

"Irish Americans," in *Silent Cities: The Evolution of the American Cemetery*, by Kenneth T. Jackson and Camilo José Vergara.

"The Irish Wake," www.toad.net/~sticker/wake.html.

*Of Irish Ways*, by Mary Murray Delaney. New York: Harper & Row Perennial Library, 1973, chapter twelve.

## ITALIAN AMERICAN

In Italian-American culture, the funeral mass took place after the body had been waked for at least forty-eight hours. The wake generally took place in the home where shades were closed, mirrors were covered, and clocks were stopped at the hour of death. Friends and relatives paid their respects to the deceased's family. The immediate family was expected to be in attendance and remain with the body around the clock. There would be plenty of food, wine, Italian pastries, and liqueurs, such as amaretto, anisette, or crème de cacao.

The undertaker was chosen with great care. If possible, he was someone from the same region in Italy as the deceased, or one who would cater to the traditional customs associated with death. The immediate family selected the

**Figure 7-6** Albino DeBartolo mausoleum. Photographs, flowers, and religious artifacts line the shelves. Italian Cemetery, Colma, California. *Courtesy of Rick Sturdevant.*

**Figure 7-7** Marker showing Italian origins. Frank Beni, born in Gigliana, Italy. Oak Creek Cemetery, Oak Creek, Colorado. *Collection of the author.*

**Figure 7-8** Marker showing Italian origins and who erected the monument. Rev. Michael Raimondo, born in Alba, Provincia di Dovara, Italy. Erected by Beny Raimondo, C. Rinetti, and F. Capitolo. Mount Calvary Catholic Cemetery, Salt Lake City, Utah. *Collection of the author.*

clothing in which to bury the deceased, and the family brought to the funeral home any items such as rosary beads, that would be placed in the casket. Once the undertaker prepared the body, the immediate family insisted upon seeing and approving the undertaker's work before the body was displayed for the wake.

Until about the mid-1900s, women wore black dresses, stockings, and shoes during the mourning period, which ranged from a week to a year, depending on a woman's relationship to the deceased and her age. Men wore black armbands and black ties.

Even the monument maker might have Italian origins. Italian tombstones and monuments were often elaborate sculptures of saints, the Madonna, or the deceased. If the family could afford a mausoleum, it was often decorated inside with photographs of the deceased and religious articles. Italian Americans also commonly incorporated ceramic photographs into the tombstone, with faces of the deceased set so that they somehow always seemed to look directly into the eyes of anyone who looked into theirs. Italian Americans were also likely to be buried in a Roman Catholic or Italian cemetery.

Albino DeBartolo serves as a good example of someone who had only Italian businesses handle his funeral needs. Albino died in San Francisco in the 1940s. The mortuary that handled the arrangements was Valente, Marini, and Perata Funeral Home. His memorial marker was made by L. Bocci and Sons (see figure 7-6 on page 181). Albino was buried in the Italian Cemetery in Colma, five miles outside of San Francisco. The attorney who handled his probate was an Italian: Julian Pardini. Albino had been in America for nearly forty years, yet he and his family still patronized Italian businesses.

Some of the people who handled various aspects of your ancestor's funeral may still be in business. One Italian stone carver in the San Francisco Yellow Pages boasts being the fifth generation of stone carvers. That's more than one hundred years of potential records.

### Suggested Reading

"Death, Wakes, Funerals: Italian American Style," by J. Michael Ferri, in *Dominant Symbols in Popular Culture*, edited by Ray B. Browne, et al. Bowling Green, Ohio: Bowling Green State University Popular Press, 1990, 224–230.

"The Italian-American Funeral: Persistence through Change," by Elizabeth Mathias. *Western Folklore* 33:1 (1974): 35–60.

"Italian Americans," in *Silent Cities: The Evolution of the American Cemetery*, by Kenneth T. Jackson and Camilo José Vergara.

*South Italian Folkways in Europe and America,* by Phyllis H. Williams. New Haven: Yale University Press, 1938.

"Windows in the Garden: Italian-American Memorialization and the American Cemetery," by John Matturri, in *Ethnicity and the American Cemetery*, edited by Richard E. Meyer.

Sources

# JEWISH

Rather than mourn the death of loved ones, Jews reflect upon and celebrate the deceased's life. Like other cultures and religions, before funeral homes became widely used, the preburial events took place in the home of the deceased. Today, Jews patronize funeral directors knowledgeable in Jewish customs and traditions. (For a directory of Jewish funeral directors, see chapter one under Funeral Home Records.)

The time between death and burial is known as the period of Aninut, during which the body is never left unattended. Burials take place within twenty-four hours of the death, unless interment would take place on a Sabbath, then it is delayed a day; if a person dies in the morning, the burial may take place as early as sundown that same day. A Holy Society, known as the Chevra Kadisha (Hebrew for "holy society"), prepares the body for burial, bathing the corpse

**Figure 7-9** Marker of Rebecca Freida Soifer, 1986, Sons of Israel Cemetery, Colorado Springs, Colorado.
*Collection of the author.*

**Figure 7-10** A bronze emblem is attached to the headstone of Abram Abramowitz, a Holocaust survivor. Sons of Israel Cemetery, Colorado Springs, Colorado. *Collection of the author.*

**Figure 7-11** Selma E. Picsione's signature is carved on her marker. Note the rocks atop her headstone. Sons of Israel Cemetery, Colorado Springs, Colorado. *Collection of the author.*

in a ritual bath known as the Taharah (Hebrew for "ritually pure"). The Chevra Kadisha also places ground soil from Israel into the casket to always keep the body connected to the Holy Land.

The Shiva (Hebrew for "seven") is a seven-day mourning period that begins after burial. During this time, the family stays at home waiting for relatives and friends to come and pay their respects. Mirrors in the home are covered; men are not supposed to shave, and women are not supposed to wear makeup. During Shiva, there should be no concern for personal appearance or comfort, and the immediate family sits on boxes or stools, rather than furniture. To display grief, a family member may "rend," or rip, his or her own garments. This is normally done symbolically by wearing a small piece of black cloth that has been deliberately ripped.

Every day for the next year, the family will say a prayer for the dead, known as the Kaddish. Each year on Yahrzeit (Yiddish for "anniversary"), the anniversary date of the death based on the Hebrew Calendar, the family will burn a candle in their home for twenty-four hours. They will attend service in a synagogue and recite the Kaddish again. It is also customary to visit the grave site every year on the anniversary as a tribute to a deceased parent. Alternately, this may be done around Mother's or Father's Day or before the Jewish High Holy Days of Rosh Hashanah and Yom Kippur.

Synagogues and independent mutual aid societies, such as *landsmanschaftn*, owned the Jewish cemeteries or sections. Because of the small allotment of land in many of these cemeteries, graves are crowded and may not be in family groupings. When the headstone is placed on the grave, there is usually another ceremony for family and friends called an "unveiling."

The Star of David is perhaps the most common symbol on the Jewish-American headstone after the 1800s. Another universal symbol is the menorah, the five- or seven-branched candlestick, typically used on women's markers (see figure 7-9 on page 183). Other common symbols are

- water pitcher, representing a Levite, or servant to the priests
- the blessing hands, signifying a descendant of the Cohens or priests

- a palm branch and citrus fruit, known as the Lulav and Etrog, symbolic of the harvest festival of Sukkot
- the tree of life, or Etz Chaim, representing the Torah or first five books of the Bible

If there is a Hebrew inscription on the tombstone, it will always include the religious name of the deceased, which is his or her Hebrew given name followed by the Hebrew words for "son of" or "daughter of," then by the deceased father's given Hebrew name. The Hebrew inscription may also include tributes to the person, especially if he or she was very pious or an unusually good person in life. For instructions on how to read Hebrew on tombstones, see the Web site below.

The custom of putting rocks or pebbles on top of Jewish headstones is ancient, and although the origins are obscure, it is meant as a sign of respect and as a sign that family and friends visited (see figure 7-11 on page 184).

**Sources**

### Suggested Reading

"American Jewish Cemeteries: A Mirror of History," by Roberta Halporn in *Ethnicity and the American Cemetery*, edited by Richard E. Meyer.

"Cemetery Research," in *Discovering Your Jewish Ancestors*, by Barbara Krasner-Khait. North Salt Lake, Utah: Heritage Quest, 2001.

"Jewish Americans," in *Silent Cities: The Evolution of the American Cemetery*, by Kenneth T. Jackson and Camilo José Vergara.

"The Jewish Funeral." www.biomed.lib.umn.edu/hw/jewish.html. Originally published in *The Director* 69 (October 1997): 18, 20.

"Jewish Funeral and Mourning Customs," by Sharon Ann Soudakoff. www.thefuneraldirectory.com/jewishcustoms.html.

*Only Yesterday We Drained the Cup of Sorrow: American Jewish Cemeteries and History*, by Roberta Halporn. Brooklyn, N.Y.: Center for Thanatology Research and Education, 1991.

"Reading Hebrew Tombstones." www.jewishgen.org/infofiles/tombstones.html.

*Traveler's Guide to Pioneer Jewish Cemeteries of the California Gold Rush*, by Susan Morris. Berkeley, Calif.: Judah L. Magnes Museum, 1995.

## LATTER-DAY SAINTS (MORMON)

The Church of Jesus Christ of Latter-day Saints, with headquarters in Salt Lake City, Utah, is the main denomination that bases its beliefs on the teachings of Joseph Smith who founded the faith in upstate New York in 1830. This discussion of funeral and burial practices will be limited only to those who migrated to the western United States beginning in 1846 under Brigham Young. The Church of Jesus Christ of Latter-day Saints sees itself as a new branch of Christianity (a restored Christianity), and it has neither Roman Catholic, Protestant, nor Orthodox roots, thus allowing it to develop its own culture and customs, including those surrounding funerals and burials.

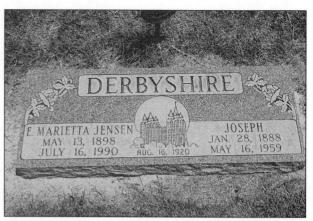

**Figure 7-12** Latter-day Saints' markers often contain detailed genealogical information, especially the woman's maiden name. This marker gives the couple's birth and death dates, names of parents (including mothers' maiden names), and major life accomplishments. Beecher stone, Salt Lake City, Utah, Cemetery. *Collection of the author.*

**Figure 7-13** Common to Latter-day Saints married couples' markers is the addition of the marriage date and an illustration of the temple where the couple was married. This stone shows the Salt Lake City Temple. Derbyshire marker, Salt Lake City, Utah, Cemetery. *Collection of the author.*

Like other groups, at the family's discretion, there may be a viewing held in the funeral home after a person dies. No food or drink is served. Those who are Temple Worthy (the highest degree of member commitment) and have received their special undergarments (a symbolic piece of underclothing received during endowment to represent their commitment) will be buried in them. Deceased Temple Worthy men and women are both dressed in special Temple Clothes that were worn during the endowment ceremony and only in the Temple: white robes with a green apron. In areas of the country that do not have a high Latter-day Saint population, Temple Worthy family members or ward (congregation) members will dress the body at the funeral home. In areas of high Latter-day Saint population, the local funeral home will know the customs for dressing the deceased. Those who are not Temple Worthy are dressed in whatever clothing the family deems appropriate, and the grave is still dedicated by the priesthood.

Funerals are held at the funeral home or sometimes at the Latter-day Saints chapel. Along with the eulogy, prayers are offered and hymns sung. After the service, everyone follows in a procession to the cemetery. The grave is then dedicated by a priesthood holder, who is always a man. Latter-day Saints believe in a literal resurrection; during the Second Coming the body will be reunited with the spirit. This is the main reason the Latter-day Saints Church frowns upon cremation; however, it is not prohibited. After the graveside service, the family goes to the church or sometimes to the family's home for a dinner prepared by ward members and relatives.

Latter-day Saint burials and cemeteries are not unlike other Christian cemeteries in that they also bury their dead on an east-west axis. For those who historically practiced polygamy, the wives were buried next to their husband in a row; this was common throughout Latter-day Saints towns in the Rocky Mountain states. The practice of plural marriage ended with the 1904 Second

**Figure 7-14** Every genealogist's dream headstone. Caleb Haight marker, Salt Lake City, Utah, Cemetery. *Collection of the author.*

**Figure 7-15** The Wives of Wilford Woodruff. Phoebe W. Carter was no doubt the first wife and held a position of authority in this polygamous household. Woodruff marker, Salt Lake City, Utah, Cemetery. *Collection of the author.*

Manifesto; a First Manifesto was given in 1890 in preparation for Utah statehood.

Latter-day Saint headstones often tell where the deceased was born and show a few common symbols and artwork. The all-seeing eye of God, also common to Masonic members' headstones, stems from the early Mormon leaders' association with the Freemasons in the nineteenth century. Other symbols are the hand of God descending from a cloud, the handshake, a beehive (symbolic of industriousness), and for more recent markers, a sandblasted image of a temple. The temple symbol is usually for a single stone where a husband and wife are buried together, and the image is usually of the temple where they were married, such as the ones in the Utah cities of Salt Lake City, Logan, or Manti. This reflects the Latter-day Saints' belief that being Temple Worthy and married in the Latter-day Saints Temple means the union will extend past the resurrection into eternity. Any of these symbols may be combined with others, such as broken rose stems, roses in full bloom or as buds, a broken chain, or the sun.

### Suggested Reading

"Acculturation and Transformation of Salt Lake Temple Symbols in Mormon Tombstone Art," by George H. Schoemaker. *Markers* 9 (1992): 197–215.

*Encyclopedia of Mormonism*, ed. by Daniel H. Ludlow. New York: Macmillan Library Reference, 1991.

Sources

## NORTH AMERICAN INDIAN

It would be impossible to cover burial rituals for every North American Indian tribe, which differ with each tribe's beliefs and religion, so this brief overview covers only a few tribes and sample customs. For more information, see the Suggested Reading list that follows.

## Aleuts

Having no fear of death, the Aleuts kept the body in the family quarters until burial. Widows mourned for forty days; when a baby died, the father fasted for ten days and the mother for twenty days.

## Arapahos

Arapahos believed in underground burial in a large grave. After lowering the body and placing personal items, clothing, and blankets into the grave, the deceased's horse was shot and buried in the same grave. Family members cut their hair and wore no paint or old clothing during the mourning period.

## Apaches

Apache men and women mourned the loss of a loved one by cutting their hair and wearing old clothing. They placed the deceased on a horse along with personal items for the procession to the grave. Apaches buried their dead and the deceased's personal possessions in rocky crevices, killed the horse, then broke any of the personal items that wouldn't fit into the grave and left them at the site. The procession of mourners took a different route back to the camp and never looked back. To discourage the ghost of the deceased from returning, the tribe burned the clothes they wore for the funeral, bathed themselves, and burned pungent plants such as juniper and sage.

## Creeks

The Creeks buried their dead in a round hole under the hut where the death occurred. The corpse was wrapped in a blanket and buried in a sitting position. Mourners expressed their grief by howling and smearing their faces with grease and wood ashes.

## Navajos

Navajos placed a blanket inside the casket with the body. The body was dressed in one set of clothing, and another set placed in the casket along with food, water, and items the deceased held dear. Because Navajos feared the dead, they had outsiders—slaves or funeral directors—handle and bury the body. At the graveside, everyone in attendance walked around the grave counterclockwise and sprinkled dirt onto the coffin. No footprints could be left on the grave, which would deter the spirit guide.

## Shawnees

Friends of the deceased prepared the corpse by painting and dressing it in new clothing. Then the body would be taken to the cemetery. Before covering the grave, Shawnees sprinkled tobacco inside the grave over the body. The possessions of the deceased were then distributed to those who helped with the funeral. The spouse in mourning did not wear any paint or jewelry for a twelve-month period and was not to change clothing.

## Sioux

The Sioux painted the deceased's body red, dressed it in its best clothing, then wrapped it in a buffalo robe. Food was placed next to the corpse's head inside the buffalo robe. Then the body would be placed in a tree or elevated platform, with the head to the north.

## Wichitas

Wichitas buried their loved ones in an elevated place, which they then covered with logs or stone slabs in a conical formation. Unlike Christian burials, the head was placed to the east. Tribal members mourned the loss for four days.

### Suggested Reading

*Everyday Life Among the American Indians*, by Candy Moulton. Cincinnati: Writer's Digest Books, 2001.

*Native Cemeteries and Forms of Burial East of the Mississippi*, by David I. Bushnell. Washington, D.C.: Government Printing Office, 1920.

*North American Indians Burial Customs*, by H.C. Yarrow. Ogden, Utah: Eagles' View Publishing, 1988.

"Releasing the Spirit: A Lesson in Native American Funeral Rituals," by Gary F. Santillanes. www.biomed.lib.umn.edu/hw/releasing.html. Originally published in *The Director* 69:10 (October 1997): 32, 34.

"The Soul of the Indian," by Dr. Charles Alexander Eastman. www.magna.com.au/%7Eprfbrown/eastman6.html.

Sources

# QUAKER

Known officially as the Religious Society of Friends, colonial Quakers viewed death as the climax of life, a time that they welcomed rather than feared. Death

**Figure 7-16** Quaker burial ground, Westbury, New York, Meeting House. Note the uniformity of graves.
*Collection of the author.*

**Figure 7-17** Grave of Elizabeth Seaman, Quaker burial ground, Westbury, New York, Meeting House. Notice the months are recorded as numbers.
*Collection of the author.*

**Figure 7-18** An immigrant ancestor's origins is what every genealogist hopes to find on a marker. Agnes Young, born in Falkirk, Scotland, 1836. Evergreen Cemetery, Colorado Springs, Colorado. *Collection of the author.*

**Figure 7-19** Example of a Chinese marker. Jean Ching Yee headstone, 1989. Salt Lake City, Utah, Cemetery. *Collection of the author.*

was the opportunity to escape the harsh realities of the world. Quakers had little interest in the remains, and special committees of Friends handled funerals and burials. Mourning was considered vain and proud, as was wearing black at burials. Unlike the New Englanders and Chesapeake settlers, Quakers did not give out mourning tokens, such as rings or gloves, because they believed in absolute simplicity.

Quakers recorded deaths in meeting registers, giving the name of the de-

**Figure 7-20** Vietnamese marker. The cross with rosary beads indicates the Cao family was Catholic. Salt Lake City, Utah, Cemetery. *Collection of the author.*

**Figure 7-21** This Greek marker gives not only the couples' origins, but a map of Greece, their photographs, and testimonials. Vamianakis stone. Mt. Olivet Cemetery, Salt Lake City, Utah. *Collection of the author.*

ceased, date of death, age, and when buried. They wrote months as numbers, so if you are researching a time period before the calendar change of 1752, the 1st month was March and the 12th month was February. You can find this method of recording dates on grave markers, too (see figure 7-17). It's important to transcribe the dates exactly as they are written and not to convert numbers to names of months, so there is no confusion for later researchers. For more on Quaker records, see the multivolume *Encyclopedia of American Quaker Genealogy*, by William Wade Hinshaw (Ann Arbor, Mich.: Edwards Brothers, 1936–1950).

Quakers usually referred to their graveyards as burial or burying grounds, and located them adjacent to the meeting house. The burial grounds were supposed to be fenced. Early Quaker burials were not marked. Between the 1820s and 1830s, Friends were allowed to use field stones to mark graves, inscribed with just the initials and the years of death. After the 1840s–1850s, low, plain carved stones, often with curved tops, were allowed, with names and vital statistics only. You won't usually find family plots in a Friends' burying ground; bodies were interred row by row as members died (see figure 7-16 on page 189). Sometimes a meeting would allow a non-Quaker in the burying ground, especially an admired person, such as a friendly Indian or a fellow abolitionist. Friends were supposed to seek burial only in Friends' burying grounds, not mixed with others where their beliefs would not hold.

Sources

### Suggested Reading

*Albion's Seed: Four British Folkways in America,* by David Hackett Fischer.

"Death Register [Rahway and Plainfield, New Jersey, Monthly Meeting of Friends]." http://members.tripod.com/~PlainfieldFriends/deathreg.htm.

"The Old Discipline," from the 1806 Book of Discipline of Philadelphia Yearly Meeting. www.voicenet.com/~kuenning/qhp/olddisc/.

"Quaker Beliefs and Grief," by Angie Lewis. www.indiana.edu/%7Ehperf 558/culture/lewis%5Fculture.html.

## WHAT'S NEXT?

Maybe you or your genealogical society would like to undertake a cemetery transcribing or indexing project. Or, perhaps the cemetery where your ancestors were buried is in need of some serious repair and maintenance. Let's look at what's involved in these projects.

# EIGHT

# Cemetery Projects and Preservation

*And genealogists come up from Boston—get paid by city people for looking up their ancestors. They want to make sure they're Daughters of the American Revolution and of the Mayflower. . . . Well, I guess that don't do any harm, either.*

—*Thornton Wilder,* Our Town

D uring the summer of 1993, I spent several hours a day at local cemeteries. I wasn't related to a single soul buried in any of them. I was doing a project for a unique class called Cemeteries and Local History, offered through The University of Alabama. My class assignment was to transcribe or "inventory" 500 tombstones and to do a "field study," that is, learn about the community and local history through my visits to the cemetery (see chapter three). Although I had class requirements to fulfill, there are many good-hearted genealogists and genealogical societies who do this same type of project without having a grade as an incentive.

Tackling a cemetery transcribing project is easy, right? You walk from grave to grave and copy what was inscribed on the stone, *exactly* as it was written. This is true, but as I discovered, there's a little bit more to it than that.

**Internet Source**

For another college-level cemetery class, "The Cemetery as a Social Document," taught by Dr. Gail S. Ludwig, go to <h ttp://ludwig.missouri .edu/101/>.

## CEMETERY TRANSCRIBING PROJECTS

*I delight in being able to transcribe data on a stone that is illegible and feel sad walking away from one that is too badly eroded to be read.*
—*Janice Helge, "Managing a Cemetery Project"*

**Before beginning a transcribing project, check to see if one has already been done for that cemetery.** Check with the cemetery or town office, local libraries and

**Tip**

**RESOURCES FOR TEACHERS**

Are you looking for projects to give your students an appreciation for cemeteries? Visit Linda Prather's Cemetery Studies at <www.angelfire.com/ky2/cemetery/> and <www.angelfire.com/ky2/cemetery/teacher.html> for cross-curriculum lessons in language arts, math, art, science, social studies, and writing, and to see how other teachers study the cemetery. Another great site with lesson plans and classroom activities is GraveNet at <www.edutel.org/gravenet_index.html>.

genealogical and historical societies, the local chapter of the National Society, Daughters of the American Revolution, as well as large repositories, such as the Family History Library. Even if one has been completed, how old is it? Will you be double-checking and supplementing with the newer graves since that transcription was done? Or, perhaps your project will be more in-depth than the previous one. The earlier transcription may give just the vital information, not the type of stone, the artwork, or the epitaphs. When I undertook my project, I knew that some of the cemeteries I wanted to transcribe had been done, but these did not include the composition of the stone or the artwork, so I was adding new information.

Also before beginning, think about your final product, how it will look, and what you want to include. As I noted in chapter two, practically every published book of cemetery transcriptions you pick up is different. Wouldn't it be nice if you could expect the same kind of information in all cemetery transcribing projects? The final product model I'm recommending is an adaptation of the one my instructors suggested for the class I took.

## Introduction

In the introduction, give a brief history of the project, who was involved, and the dates of the project. Also explain the arrangement of the transcriptions in the book, and give an explanation of any supplemental research you did in records such as newspapers, censuses, and county histories. This is also the appropriate place to acknowledge anyone outside of the project who contributed knowledge, help, or funding.

## Overview of the Cemetery

Begin with the name of the cemetery and directions to it, along with who currently owns and maintains the cemetery. Give the location based on the legal land description if you can, as well as directions from the roads and highways you took to get there, or include a map. You might also want to give directions based on a Global Positioning Device as discussed in chapter four, or use the USGS Web site maps as described in the sidebar on page 50. Follow this with an overview of the characteristics of the cemetery (see chapters three and four). If you have found when the land was initially purchased and the cemetery was established, include this information here, too. Use the Cemetery Survey Form in Appendix E, or use a stack of four-inch by six-inch or five-inch by eight-inch note cards on a clipboard. Since many cemeteries are located on hilltops, it can get quite breezy, and if you're working with a cemetery on the plains of Colorado or Kansas, you might be dealing with gale force winds. **Note cards might prove easier to work with than wind-blown paper.**

Tip

I also included in the overview for my class project information about the typical composition of the majority of markers (granite, marble, wood, metal); the direction the stones faced (east-west axis); the prominent artwork carved on the stones (doves, lambs, flowers, horses, cattle brands, tractors—remember, the eastern plains of Colorado are ranching communities); typical trees, plants, or flowers growing on or around each grave (evergreens are popular here); common decorations on graves (those awful, plastic artificial flowers are really popular); generally, where the wife was buried in relation to the husband (overwhelmingly to his left); and whether graves were mounded and scraped clean of grass and weeds (some were, some weren't). (See chapter three for more details on all of these aspects.) Looking at the overall cemetery, I also noted the type of cemetery (rural country), what other foliage grew there (indigenous trees), whether the cemetery was located on a hilltop (yep), and whether it had a fence and a lich-gate (the symbolic passageway into the cemetery—this cemetery had both).

Additional items you may want to include in your study are
- the condition of the stone
- if any repairs have been done to the stone
- presence of graffiti or biological growth, such as lichen and moss
- erosion from weathering
- whether the stone is tilted, sunken, or has fallen over
- whether the stone no longer marks the grave (caretakers might move fallen stones and prop them up against a fence or elsewhere)
- the name of the carver, if identified on the stone (check bases, backs, and tops of markers)

From this in-depth field study, I was able to conclude that this area was economically depressed at the turn of the century since many graves were only marked with the metal marker supplied by the funeral home. This was a bonus, however, because it revealed the mortuary that handled the arrangements, thus leading to more records. Those with inscriptions contained mainly the deceased's name and birth and death years, indicating that families could not afford to have much more inscribed or any artwork carved.

## Map of the Cemetery

If there is already a map, ask the cemetery office for permission to reproduce it in your book and to use it for your project. Even if the caretaker offers, do not keep or use the original map any longer than to make a photocopy. You would not want to be responsible for it if something happened. If there is no map, then you will need to make map sketches yourself. These need not be

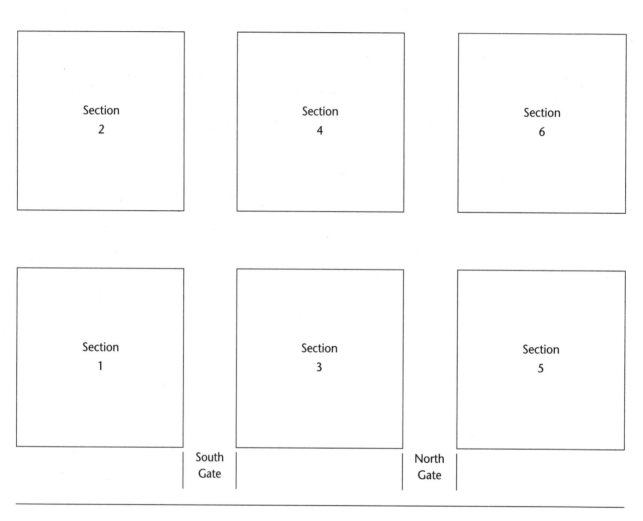

**Figure 8-1** Map of Ramah Cemetery from *Communities at Rest: An Inventory and Field Study of Five Eastern Colorado Cemeteries*, by Sharon DeBartolo Carmack.

especially detailed; the idea is to know the layout of the cemetery and for your readers to be able to use the map to find their ancestors' graves. **You will need the map before you begin your project, so you can note where you started and where you left off each day.** The town cemetery in Ramah, Colorado, did not have a map, so I made my own and numbered the sections according to how I transcribed them (see figure 8-1).

## Transcriptions

This is the heart of your study, of course. Note from the main gate where you start reading stones, then go stone by stone. Along with carrying a pen and a set of Cemetery Transcription Forms (see Appendix E) on a sturdy clipboard, I wore a carpenter's apron so I could easily carry the following supplies with me and not have to run back to the car to get anything.

- extra pens
- white chalk for hard-to-read inscriptions
- camera to photograph interesting stones to use as illustrations in the final product (see chapter four for tips on photographing markers)

Using the form, copy each inscription as written, then write a description of the stone. You can use figure 8-2 on page 198 as a guide. Do not make any abbreviations unless they are part of the inscription. Remember, you're creating a source document. When you are unsure about a letter or word, use brackets to note your guesses and question marks, such as R[o?]ger or [Roger?]. If you are adding any information, such as a surname that's implied from markers neighboring it, include that in brackets, too. If you come to a spot that has no headstone, but it appears to be a grave because the ground is sunken or has curbing or fencing around it, note that as well.

When you get home—and it's best to do this after each trip, rather than waiting until the project is complete—type the information onto the same computerized form (or similar format) to use for the camera-ready copy. The Association for Gravestone Studies sells a reasonably priced IBM-based database specifically for recording gravestones and cemeteries. You can order it through their Web site at <www.gravestonestudies.org/Store/software.htm>.

Another database program for your desk or laptop is Aspen 2000 for Windows by Design Software <www.designsw.net/aspen.htm>. This software program offers an easy method of organizing, indexing, and publishing cemetery, funeral home, and obituary records. The reports can be exported into many popular file formats, including Web pages. The utilities include a Soundex code generator, a birth date calculator, and a dictionary of standard genealogical abbreviations. You can download a demo at the Web site.

Of course, with today's technology, you don't have to do your transcriptions with pen and paper like I had to several years ago. With a PalmPilot or similar handheld computer, you can use a database program to create the fields you need to input the information once. Two such databases for Palms are Jfile 4.1 by Land-J Technologies <www.land-j.com/jfile.html> and HanDBase 2.1 by DDH Software <www.handbase.com>. If you want one specific to recording cemetery data, check out Cemetery V1.0 <www.palmgear.com/software/shows oftware.cfm?prodID=9184>. For more information on how to use a Palm for cemetery projects, see Steve Paul Johnson's article "A Tombstone in Your Palm," at <http://interment.net/column/records/palmpilot/index.htm>.

## Proofreading

Before you take your camera-ready copy to the printer, proofread your transcriptions. This is best done as a two-person project. Take your final copy with

**Headstone Transcription Form**

**Name of Cemetery:** Ramah Public Cemetery
**Location of Cemetery:** US Highway 24, south of Ramah, on a hill, abt ¼ mi S on E. Ramah Rd.
**Starting point:** South Gate
(In first column, give row/grave number)

| | Headstone Inscription | Marker Description |
|---|---|---|
| sec 6 Row 1 stoN grave 1 | Called Higher Margaret wife of C.H. Cox 1888 - 1912 [Cox [on base] | Headstone composition: Marble<br>Footstone: N/A<br>Artwork: drapery; Kingdom of Heaven<br>Grave Decorations: none<br>Other:<br>Condition of Stone: excellent<br>Condition of Inscription: good<br>Direction of Grave: east - west<br>Direction Inscription Faces: West<br>Photograph taken? (Yes) No |
| 2 | Single grave<br>no identification on marker | Headstone composition: field stone<br>Footstone:<br>Artwork:<br>Grave Decorations:<br>Other:<br>Condition of Stone:<br>Condition of Inscription:<br>Direction of Grave: E-W<br>Direction Inscription Faces:<br>Photograph taken? Yes (No) |
| 3 | Robt. L. Stone<br>July 28, 1868<br>Sept. 23, 1918 | Headstone composition: Marble slab on ground<br>Footstone: N/A<br>Artwork: none<br>Grave Decorations: none<br>Other:<br>Condition of Stone: good<br>Condition of Inscription: good<br>Direction of Grave: east - west<br>Direction Inscription Faces: West<br>Photograph taken? Yes (No) |

**Figure 8-2** Completed transcribing form. A blank one is in Appendix E.

you to the cemetery. Have someone read to you the inscription on the stone, spelling any unusual names, while you double-check what you have written. If you hand copied the stones' inscriptions originally and then typed them, there are two chances for you to inadvertently make a mistake. **This final proofing is essential to ensure that your copy is as accurate as it can be.**

Important

## Comparing Against Cemetery Records

If cemetery records still exist, go a final step and compare your transcriptions with the cemetery records. No doubt you will find discrepancies, and once you have verified that you copied everything accurately from the inscriptions, note these discrepancies in your final version. Remember to indicate which material is which, either using brackets, italics, or a different font to make it clear which information came from the tombstones and which came from the cemetery records.

## Bibliography

Assuming you used newspapers, county histories, censuses, and other records to supplement your project, cite these sources in your bibliography. Clearly indicate what supplemental information comes from which source.

## Index

**An index is not optional, of course, and the more detailed the better.** If you have three James Greenwoods in your study, identify them in the index by their death dates. And please don't arrange the tombstone inscriptions in alphabetical order to avoid making an index! Remember, you'll destroy the possible family connections with other surnames by doing so.

Important

## CEMETERY SURVEY PROJECTS

**In a cemetery survey project, you or your society are not copying headstone inscriptions, but rather making a master index of all known cemeteries, burial sites, and single graves in a state or area.** These statewide projects are a large undertaking, of course, and may take years to compile. This type of project should also be viewed as ongoing; once you've published the directory, people will discover new burial grounds for inclusion in the next edition. Only a few states have published cemetery directories so far (see chapter two), and other states are working on compiling them.

\di'fin\ *vb*

Definitions

Some of these projects are genealogical society-driven; others may involve a host of organizations. According to Jeannie Regan-Dinius in "Preserving the Past for the Future: Indiana's Statewide Cemetery Registry," *The Hoosier Genealogist* 41 (June 2001): 78–83, Indiana's Department of Natural Resources, Division of Historic Preservation and Archaeology (DHPA) oversees the state's cemetery project. As cemetery registry coordinator, Jeannie has recruited preservationists and members from historical societies and museums, and genealogical societies to help identify burial grounds throughout the state. For each cemetery or burial site, the DHPA created a survey form to complete that will contain

**Technique**

## TRANSCRIBING HEADSTONES IN A LARGE CEMETERY

In November 2000, Pikes Peak Genealogical Society published its ninth cemetery volume, finishing a five-year effort to index the cemeteries of El Paso County, Colorado. The only cemeteries not covered were a private mausoleum that ignored the society's requests for permission to index its interments and Evergreen Cemetery, which had previously been indexed through 1972. Evergreen burials since then are not included in the society's publications, but are easily accessible from the cemetery office.

In January 2001, the society released a CD-ROM with information from all nine PPGS volumes, the Evergreen volume, and a book published by Sharon Carmack that covers three El Paso County cemeteries she indexed. PPGS-indexed cemeteries yielded nearly 27,000 names in 54 cemeteries; the Evergreen database added about 50,000 names, and the Carmack-recorded cemeteries contributed about 550 names. Many PPGS-recorded cemeteries were only a single grave, but two exceeded 5,000. The project began in 1996 and involved approximately forty volunteers over five years, although the working group rarely numbered more than twenty. People would come and go for various reasons: moving, health issues, waning interest, personality conflicts.

The volunteers met once a month to discuss procedures, organize field work, report on progress, and turn in completed work. The cemetery project chair planned and led the meetings and directed the effort's focus. At the beginning, the group spent much time establishing procedures, figuring out how to configure the database, and deciding how the results would be published.

The project chair encouraged volunteers to team up with a friend to serve as team leaders for a particular cemetery. Thus several cemeteries were being worked at a time, and many people got experience in leadership positions. To begin, the project chair secured permission from the person responsible for the cemetery to index and publish the tombstone and sexton records. If sexton records existed, permission to copy them was requested. From that point, the team leaders copied the records and plat maps and recruited volunteers to key them into a database. (We used a DOS-based shareware program, PC File 7.0, because it could be inexpensively loaded on everyone's computer.)

The database was divided into logical sections of one hundred to two hundred graves each, and volunteers were given a packet or two that included walking papers and maps of the sections they were to record. The sexton records were printed in lot/block/plot order (whatever names the cemetery used to identify burial locations) so volunteers could easily go down the rows and record the information from the markers. Each printed page had four names with the name as it appeared in the sexton record, birth and death dates if available, lines for inscriptions and other comments, and notation of presence or absence of marker. Volunteers were asked to check off information that was the same as it was on the marker, note variations, and add additional information. If a person didn't have a marker, the volunteers noted that. If a marker appeared for someone not recorded (or not recorded properly) in the sexton records, the volunteer noted the location, name, dates, and inscription in space available at the bottom of the page or on the back of the sheet.

The volunteers usually worked in pairs—with either a friend or a spouse—which made the time more enjoyable and the transcriptions more accurate, as two sets of eyes were reading the inscriptions. Not working by themselves, they were probably also safer in some of the remote cemeteries. Sometimes we scheduled project work days and carpooled together to complete a cemetery in one day.

Team leaders kept track of who had what packets, when they were assigned, and when they were returned. They also usually checked everyone's work by rewalking the sections with the original papers. Volunteers generally entered their own marker information into the section of database they were given and turned in the papers and the disk. Those who didn't have computers handed the work off to someone else.

When the cemetery was completely walked and the database reassembled, proofing papers were printed and the information was proofed against the sexton records and the volunteers' walking papers. When questions arose that couldn't be answered, the team leaders went back out to the cemetery and checked the marker in question. When discrepancies existed between the sexton records and the markers, they were noted in the database and printed in the final book.

After that, the project editor edited the database for style and consistency, the project chair created an index of maiden names and people whose names appear in the sexton records or on markers but aren't buried there (spouses who weren't deceased yet, parents or children's names, etc.). This special index was added into the index of burials. The publisher worked with the team leaders to compile a history of the cemetery, take photographs, take GPS readings, draw maps, and put together a list of volunteers and others who were to be thanked for their help. The chair, editor, and publisher worked together to compile the manuscript that went to the printer.

### Advice Before Starting a Cemetery Transcribing Project

- Look at other cemetery indexes in your local or regional genealogy library to see what you like and don't like.

- Use a cemetery-indexing manual as a basis for your own procedure and style manual.

- Recruit volunteers and ask if any of them have been involved in such efforts before.

continued

- Identify people with special skills: volunteer leadership, training, computer/ software expertise, proofing/editing/layout, mapmaking, etc.

- Use a database program that can export its data to other programs; this will facilitate contributing files to USGenWeb Tombstone Project managers and other publishing projects.

**What Would We Have Done Differently?**

- **Form a steering committee.** Most people who volunteer for cemetery projects merely want to walk the cemetery and record the inscriptions. That's the fun part. We spent a lot of time with the whole group hashing out details of how to do the recording and entering in the database. With so many people, this wasn't efficient and wasted much time. It would have been better to have three or four key people decide the details, then tell the volunteers what was wanted of them.

- **Use a few typists rather than expecting all the volunteers to key in their own data.** Most volunteers don't want to learn to use a database program and some struggle to do so. It would be better for database consistency and accuracy to train a few people with aptitude and interest to use the database and style you choose and ask them to do the data entry.

- **Prepare a simple training manual for field volunteers.** Despite what you tell them, most people remember better if you *show* them what you want. Take pictures of markers (digital cameras work great here) and print them with the sexton records and handwritten annotations to show volunteers how you want them to record what they see in the cemetery. Give examples of the many kinds of problems, discrepancies, and other situations they may encounter and show them how to record them.

—Linda Vixie

general information about the cemetery, a description of the site's physical condition, needed preservation efforts, religion and/or ethnicity of those interred, condition of markers, an inventory of any buildings on the site, and bibliographic resources used for each cemetery. The DHPA plans to place the information on the Internet and link it with a geographic information system (GIS) so researchers can create maps showing the location of the cemetery. You can find out more about this project by contacting Jeannie Regan-Dinius, Cemetery Registry Coordinator, Department of Natural Resources, Division of Historic Preservation and Archaeology, 402 W. Washington Street RM W274, Indianapolis, IN 46204, or e-mail her at <jrdinius@dnr.state.in.us>.

A statewide cemetery project is definitely not one that a small group of volunteers can tackle alone. The managing committee needs to enlist the aid of other groups, county commissioners, and town and county clerks, as well as the public by sending out letters or brochures and placing advertisements in newspapers that such a project is underway.

## COMPILING A STATEWIDE CEMETERY DIRECTORY: AN ONGOING PROJECT

"Ohio cemeteries are being rapidly destroyed and many from which I have obtained inscriptions over the past years are already destroyed." Esther Weygandt Powell, the dean of Ohio genealogists, wrote this statement in 1960 on the first page of her *Ohio Records & Pioneer Families*.

As early as 1955, a fledgling state genealogical organization—Ohio Genealogical Society (OGS)—formed a committee to collect locations of cemeteries and other inscriptions. This committee set its goal to create a statewide directory of cemeteries and their locations in Ohio's eighty-eight counties. "Wood County was easy," said Mary Jane Henning. "I called a cousin who happened to be a county commissioner, and he replied, 'I have just the man for you.' " In that county, the commissioners identified the perfect researcher, one who was both a geographer and a local historian. From there, the committee approached elected officials throughout the state. In most counties, one or two respected local historians compiled lists for their county. A few county recorders undertook the task. Ohio Genealogical Society published *Ohio Cemeteries* as a statewide directory in 1978.

By this time, local genealogical societies were organizing in almost every county. Their volunteers were eager to visit all local cemeteries and began copying and publishing books of tombstone inscriptions. As interest grew within a single county, volunteers discovered more family graveyards in remote rural areas. Researchers found clues to cemeteries' existence in published late-nineteenth-century county histories and in church and family histories. The time was coming when *Ohio Cemeteries* needed to be updated. Some chapters of OGS participated in making additions that became the nucleus of *Ohio Cemeteries Addendum*, published by OGS in 1990, which brought the number of identified cemeteries and their locations to 13,100.

Since 1955, many changes outside the genealogical world were taking place. While local genealogical societies identified or renamed an additional one thousand cemetery sites, many of those previously listed had been destroyed or relocated, and road names were changed to numbers within many counties throughout the United States, following U.S. Postal Service guidelines.

An Ohio consumer-protection law of 1993 brought into existence the Annual Registration of Active Cemeteries and support for the governor-appointed, nine-member Cemetery Dispute Resolution Commission, under the administration of the Ohio Division of Real Estate and Professional Licensing. All registered cemeteries are now issued a six-digit permanent identification number—a tremendous help in distinguishing among the multiple Mt. Calvary cemeteries, Hopewell cemeteries, and Memorial Gardens.

continued

Beginning in 1998, the OGS Cemetery Committee initiated another statewide-quest: "Searching Ohio for Lost and Forgotten Cemeteries." The committee ran numerous stories with photos in metropolitan and county newspapers. The committee also widely distributed throughout the state brochures containing forms for replying in an effort to reach "hunters, naturalists, soil conservation staff, game wardens, utility linemen, surveyors, farmers, and old-timers" who might know where cemeteries existed. More than one hundred burial sites were added as a result.

Approaching the Ohio's Bicentennial Anniversary in 2003 gave the Society impetus to update the soon-to-be twenty-five-year-old book. In Ohio, in a cooperative effort, the OGS Cemetery Committee and the Ohio Township Association are calling on trustees of the 1,200 townships to participate in the "Trustee-Cemetery Edit Project." They will be the first to see the rough draft of *Ohio Directory of Cemeteries: 1803–2003* for their township and are being asked to offer corrections in road names, alternate cemetery names, type of ownership, and current condition of sites.

Compiling a statewide directory of cemeteries and their locations is a multifaceted, ongoing project with tremendous benefits to researchers today and far into the future.

—Lolita Guthrie

## CEMETERY AND GRAVESTONE PRESERVATION

In many areas, more and more cemetery associations are being formed with the purpose of preserving and restoring old cemeteries. As I've mentioned several times in this book, cemeteries are merely outdoor museums, and the gravestones are historical artifacts, some centuries old. It would be a shame to let further vandalism, weathering, and pollution ruin what remains. Just the act of transcribing a cemetery's headstones is one method of ensuring the information will be around for future descendants and researchers. But a more rewarding project is to restore and preserve the markers. If there is no cemetery association or similar group in your area, you might want to consider starting one. The best places to get advice beyond the scope of this book is through Saving Graves <www.savinggraves.com> or the Association for Gravestone Studies <www.gravestonestudies.org>.

**For More Info**

**Lynette Strangstad's *A Graveyard Preservation Primer* is considered the authoritative guide on this topic.** There is certainly no need to duplicate her efforts here, but let me share with you a few items to consider should you decide to tackle a restoration project. After getting permission from the appropriate authorities to undertake a restoration project, Strangstad suggests making an inventory of the cemetery, that is, not only copying the headstone inscriptions, but also noting the condition of the markers and what repairs are likely needed. Include in the inventory photographs of the stones needing attention. If the cemetery has not been mapped, she suggests creating one. If there is a map and you are working with a photocopy, freely mark on it; but under no circumstances should you mark on an original map. If you find stone fragments, do not move them, but mark their locations on the map.

Once you've made this inventory and documented what work needs to be done, then it's time to call a gravestone conservation specialist. Fortunately, Strangstad gives plenty of advice on how to find someone with this unique calling. While she also advises how to clean, reset, and repair stones, I would caution you to only undertake something like this with the advice and guidance of a specialist. Using the wrong chemicals for cleaning can permanently damage a stone; resetting and repairing stones can cause further damage if you are unsure how to do it properly. There are plenty of examples of these projects going awry; you don't want yours to be included in those horror stories.

**There are also ethical considerations and decisions to make:** Should you attempt to reset fragile, fallen, or moved stones, assuming you can determine where the graves originally were, or should you place them against a fence or somewhere else in the cemetery? Would wayward stones be better off in a museum, out of harm's way of vandals, pollution, and weathering? Who will make these decisions? And what are the legal ramifications of transporting headstones to a museum? Is the stone so fragile that a replica should be made to replace the original stone? If so, what do you do with the original?

As you can see, a restoration or conservation project should not be undertaken lightly. By no means am I trying to discourage you. But you need to enter such a project with eyes wide open. Study Strangstad's book, and talk with others who have tackled this type of activity. There is no doubt that it is an incredible amount of work, but one for which generations to come (and perhaps our ancestors) will thank you.

Notes

## WHAT'S NEXT?

Have you taken your family to the cemetery? My husband and daughter aren't particularly interested in genealogy, but they do usually enjoy going to the cemetery with me. So pack a lunch, grab the kids and your spouse (please, leave Fido at home for this family excursion), and make a day of it!

# NINE

# Making Cemeteries a Family Affair

*"If tomorrow isn't sunny," Linda said, "maybe we could take a little day trip out past Salisbury. I want the twins to get some sense of their heritage."*

*"Oh, Linda, not that damn cemetery again," Eliza said.*

—*Anne Tyler,* Ladder of Years

## FINDING THE LIVING IN THE CEMETERY

So you thought you would find only your dead ancestors in the cemetery, huh? Not true. Visiting the cemetery around Memorial Day or a town's Decoration Day, you might find living relatives of your ancestors. **If you can't visit the cemetery on one of those days, leave a note or ask someone in the area to do it for you.** Professional genealogist Marcia K. Wyett wrote a note saying she was interested in contacting relatives of the person who was buried there, and left her name and phone number. On the envelope, she addressed it to "The Relatives of. . . ." She put the note in a small self-sealing bag, bought an inexpensive plant to leave at the grave, and attached the note to the plant. (She thought this might look better than duct-taping a note directly to the tombstone.) The note attached to the plant worked like a charm. The Monday after Memorial Day, she got a call from a relative.

## MEMORIAL OR DECORATION DAYS

Most communities celebrate either Memorial Day (the last Monday in May) or a Decoration Day. In the South, Decoration Day was celebrated on the local level at the end of the Civil War to decorate the graves of the Confederate dead. Loved ones of Union dead were doing the same in the North, and eventually a national holiday was created. The Grand Army of the Republic, the veterans organization for Union men, campaigned for the national holiday, and Decoration Day was first celebrated nationally on 30 May 1868. But it was not until

**Idea Generator**

**Quotes**

The earliest tombstones in the cemetery up there on the mountain say 1670–1680—they're Grovers and Cartwrights and Gibbses and Herseys— same names as are around here now.

———Thornton Wilder
*Our Town*

1968 that the last Monday in May became the official day to celebrate Memorial Day. Several southern states recognize a Confederate Memorial Day (also known as Confederate Decoration Day or Confederate Heroes Day):

April 26: Alabama, Florida, Georgia, Mississippi
May 10: North Carolina, South Carolina
May 30: Virginia
June 3: Kentucky, Louisiana, Tennessee

Memorial and decoration days are the time of year when people tend to family and individual markers, cleaning away dead foliage and leaves, planting new flowers or trees, and placing flags by veterans' graves. **Try to plan your visits to ancestral cemeteries during these times.** Even if you're not related to those who come to care for the graves, don't be shy. Start a conversation. They may know of relatives still in the area. Or, if you're still trying to hunt down that family burial ground, one of these people may know where it is.

Tip

## PICNICKING IN THE CEMETERY

Apparently genealogists can find more to do in a cemetery than most people. Most people visit cemeteries on only three occasions: funerals, to pay their respects to loved ones, and when they are being buried. And that seems to be enough—for most people. We genealogists have that cemetery gene, remember? We like to picnic in cemeteries. When my daughter, Laurie, was a toddler, we went on several outings like this.

During the first one, we were lunching in our van. I was there to take pictures of a headstone for a client, but we were hungry, so we ate first. As we ate, I noticed a car pull up several yards ahead of me. Pretty soon, another car pulled up, and the woman from the first car then got in with the man in the second car. "Oh, please," I thought, "don't let the headstone I need to photograph be next to the couple having their lunch-hour rendezvous." Laurie and I finished our lunch and began our row-by-row search, me with 35mm camera in hand. We kept getting closer and closer to the occupied car, now with windows somewhat steamed, and sure enough, that headstone was almost directly in line with the car.

On another occasion, Laurie and I decided to eat our lunch outside, having found a bench memorial to sit upon with a nice shade tree nearby. (Some of the dead are so considerate.) We had just gotten our sandwiches out when Laurie pointed to a group of people gathering not far from us.

"Oh look, Mommy. They're having a picnic, too."

I peered in that direction. "No, Laurie. They're having a funeral."

We certainly didn't want to interfere with someone's last big shebang, so we moved our picnic basket to someplace unobtrusive.

Picnicking in cemeteries is not morbid nor something new. Cemeteries are actually the precursor to public parks. Remember, the elite garden cemetery was a place for the dead designed to be appealing for the living. People took Sunday strolls and had picnics, so you are actually carrying on a nineteenth-

> ## A VETERAN'S TWENTY-ONE GUN SALUTE
>
> I made a visit to a cemetery with my six-year-old daughter. We happened to be in this cemetery when they were burying someone, so I took this as an opportunity to show her where people go when they die. We walked around the hole that was dug up. Then people started coming out of the chapel, and we moved away to give them privacy.
>
> The newly deceased happened to be a veteran and was then given his salute by the guns. I ignored the funeral; it had nothing to do with me. But my daughter was terrified and running and ducking behind the larger headstones as I absentmindedly passed through the cemetery. This upset my baby. She was terrified and angry with me because I wasn't hiding like her. She yelled at me, "Mom, get out of the way, they're shooting guns!"
>
> —Melissa Roman

**Warning**

century tradition. (**Some cemeteries do prohibit picnicking, however, so look for "No Picnicking Allowed" signs.**)

## HOLDING A CEMETERY REUNION

A few years ago, I spoke to a fifth-grade class about tombstones and doing rubbings. The following week, we took a field trip to the local cemetery where the kids could put into practice what I had taught them. As I watched the twenty or so little monsters run amok in the graveyard—the teacher and I screaming, "Get *off* the tombstones!" and wondering if this was such a good idea after all—it occurred to me that a cemetery would also be a great place to hold a family reunion field trip.

Oftentimes, family reunions are held in an ancestral town. When I attended my husband's Carmack family reunion one summer, I suggested we caravan and take a tour of the cemeteries where family members were buried. Some gave me strange looks—others loved the idea. We went cemetery hopping the next afternoon, and I learned more about the family than I could ever find in genealogical records. With video camera in tow, not only did my husband and I get pictures of the tombstones, but we preserved on videotape stories about the deceased relatives, including wonderful clips of the older family members narrating.

"Do you know how my grandfather, David McMasters, died?" chuckled Granny in her hillbilly, Missouri Ozarks twang as we stopped by his headstone. We shook our heads no. "He was on top of his roof adjusting the lightning rod—during a thunderstorm!"

We were all shocked. Then we noticed there was a tree not far from his grave that had also been hit by lightning. We moved to another part of the cemetery.

This type of field trip isn't just for the adults who attend the reunion. It's an

## GRANDPA WAS MORE THAN A GRAVEDIGGER

When I was a little girl, one of my most favorite things to do was to go "help" my grandfather, Uri Robert McDonald, at his work. He worked for the Medina County, Ohio, garage in the township of Lafayette, and one of his jobs was to dig the graves in our local cemetery.

Back then, in the late 1950s and early 1960s, you never took a backhoe into a cemetery; you had to dig it by hand. You never started digging in the daytime, as it was considered sacrilegious. So my grandpa had to wait until dusk, and off he would go to prepare the final "home" for the dearly departed.

He would come pick me up, and we would go while there was some daylight left, so he could unload his pick ax and shovels, lanterns and tarps. While he would do that, he would mention that this was the last place that a person had to show for his life. If it wasn't for the tombstones, we wouldn't remember that person had lived and loved, had joys and sorrows. In time, we would forget about them. He would ask me to look around and see if a person's stone needed cleaning off or weeds pulled, so that if a loved one came along they would see someone else cared about them.

I would pick flowers and even brought little decorations for stones that I knew were there. If it was a child's stone, I would bring some small toy to place on it. I had my family give me little vases and things I could use and was always ready when Grandpa would come tell me a citizen had need of "our services."

When it was time, my grandfather would start the digging, which could last way into the night. I would hand him the pick or the shovel and move the lantern so he could see. By the time he would get half way (which was about three feet deep), we would take a lunch break and sit on the edge of the hole and talk about the person who would be buried there—or current events in our town or world. Then back to work until it was six feet deep and perfect for the coffin to fit in.

After we were done, we would cover the dirt with a green tarp so that during the funeral, the family wouldn't have to look at a mound of earth that would be placed back over after they left the service.

Sometimes he would take me back to help fill in the site. He would take such care to make it look very neat and "rounded." We would arrange the flowers left by the mourners and remove any rocks so that it would look nice.

I had friends who thought cemeteries were spooky and hated to go in them. They thought I was crazy to go and stay till after midnight. My grandpa taught me that they are a place to be comforted and remembered in. He used to tell me that the cemetery was the safest place to be—no one there could hurt you. He used to say, "The dead are at peace; it's the live ones who you need to be worried about."

continued

> To this day, I will still pull weeds or replace flowers or wreaths that have been blown over for those who are near my own loved ones. Long after I'm gone, I hope some other "little girl" will have a grandfather who takes the time to teach her to respect and care for my final resting place. Maybe she will sit by my stone and wonder if I was a mother, a wife, and whether I had a happy or sad life. Maybe she will put a flower on my stone to show someone cares.
>
> —Beverly Teibel

**Idea Generator**

adventure kids of all ages can enjoy. By planning ahead, you can have materials to take along for everyone to make tombstone rubbings. Kids love doing tombstone rubbings—especially of a family member who was in the Civil War or who did something remarkable. They can take the rubbings to school for show-and-tell when the teacher asks what they did on their summer vacations. They can even decorate their bedroom walls with winged death heads and skulls and crossbones. Kids like that sort of thing. I do, too.

**Cemeteries are also a wonderful place to teach children about respect for the dead and the sacredness of the final resting place.** This can help avoid future vandalism by explaining that the cemetery is a museum without walls. Many of the tombstones are hundreds of years old, like antiques. The monuments are not to be climbed upon, colored on, or knocked down.

Some families use the time of a reunion to hold a decoration/memorial day in the cemetery. This is a good time to weed, clean, and decorate country graves that are not in a perpetual-care cemetery. At the turn of the century, families made a day of it, taking a picnic lunch. Those marble or granite benches you find in older cemeteries served an actual purpose.

## Bringing the Cemetery to the Reunion

Well, this is all well and good, you say, if your reunion is being held near the family plots, but what if it isn't? What if your reunion is being held aboard a cruise ship (oh, I do pity you), or, like one branch of my family does, at a wooded resort in Ohio where my ancestors never even stepped foot? Instead, why not bring the cemetery to the reunion?

**Idea Generator**

Designate a cemetery committee ahead of time consisting of those family members who live near the ancestors' final resting places. **Have them take slides and rubbings of tombstones to present a visual tour of the cemeteries during the reunion.** Or, have those with digital cameras and PowerPoint capabilities put together a computer slide show.

During the presentation, encourage family members to reminisce about the departed family members, telling funny stories or other memories of the person. Make sure, however, that a committee member is tape-recording or taking notes of the stories. At the next reunion, these tales may be preserved into a memorial booklet, appended with photographs of the tombstones and the deceased, and distributed to reunion attendees.

## FINAL THOUGHTS

Although I have visited a number of cemeteries during my years as a genealogist, I haven't made any major breakthroughs on my visits. I found no new places of origin in Europe, no previously unknown maiden names, no dates of birth or death that I hadn't already discovered. In fact, I learned on more than one cemetery visit that an ancestor never had a gravestone marker at all. So what have I learned from all these cemetery visits? Upon reflection, I realize that I have gathered many clues to help me reconstruct what my ancestors' lives were like.

In some of the cemeteries, I have learned how much my ancestors valued their ethnic ties. For instance, my great-grandfather, Joseph Betlock, who was born in the United States in 1881 and used an Americanized form of his surname Betlach, chose to be buried in the Bohemian National Cemetery in his home-town of Owatonna, Minnesota. And I've copied down many German inscriptions from ancestral tombstones in the German-American communities of Cross Plains, Wisconsin, and Pierz and Lastrup, Minnesota. Many of those ancestors were generations removed from a European homeland but the German words tell me that they retained its language and undoubtedly some of its culture too.

I've also learned that where people are buried says something about where they defined home. After thirty years in Alberta, Canada, my husband's great-great-grandfather, Edwin Kendall, was buried in Waterloo, Iowa, where he had spent his prosperous middle years. After years of working in various Minnesota towns for the Chicago, Milwaukee, and St. Paul Railway, my great-grandfather came back to be buried in the hometown he'd left when he was in his early twenties. My grandfather Willard Betlock, after many years of retirement in Missouri, was buried in his home state of Minnesota.

Cemeteries, of course, can tell a lot about religious ties. I saw my most striking example of this in Madison, Wisconsin, where my third great-grandfather Philip Schmidt is buried in Forest Hill Cemetery. His tombstone lists his birth date and death date and on the top of the tombstone is the word "Father." Except "Mother"—his wife, Susanna Fuermann Schmidt—is not buried next to him. Instead she was buried in Holy Cross Cemetery, the Catholic Cemetery. This illustrated for me more graphically than anything else could have how much religious differences matter in life—and in death.

Even the contrast between cemeteries can tell a story. My husband's third great-grandmother Maria Little Kendall made the journey from Morristown, Vermont, to LaMoille, Illinois, as a young bride in 1836. Obviously Maria's whole world changed. Although none of Maria's houses was standing in either town, we did get a sense of the differences as we stood in the two cemeteries. In Vermont, the cemetery was situated upon a hill, looking out into the Green Mountains.

continued

The gravestones, including those of Maria's siblings and parents, were not in rows but rather haphazardly placed throughout the cemetery. The stones themselves reflected the gravestone traditions of New England. We visited in the summer and the weather was sunny but cool and the fields were lush and green. On the other hand, the small cemetery in LaMoille, Illinois, was a fenced-in square situated on the flat prairieland. The plain markers were laid out in neat sections. We were also in Illinois in the summer, but there the scorching heat had turned the fields yellow and lifeless. And although I am a proud Midwesterner myself, I felt a rush of sympathy for Maria, who must have longed for the cool green hills of Vermont many times during the rest of her lifetime in Illinois.

As for those ancestors who did not have tombstones, I've found that the lack of a tombstone tells a story too. One of my ancestors, Joseph Moeglein, died at the age of 41 in a freak accident in Madison, Wisconsin, in 1867. He left a widow and four children under the age of fifteen. Under those circumstances, it is perhaps not so odd that no headstone marks his grave in the Forest Hill Cemetery. More puzzling to me is why there was no headstone in Crystal Lake Cemetery for his widow, Sophia Borchers Moeglein, when she died in Minneapolis more than thirty years later, in 1899. By this time, her children were prosperous citizens, so it doesn't seem like the reason could be a lack of funds. I know there is a story here, and I hope that someday I will be fortunate enough to learn it.

So these cemetery visits have given me some insight into my ancestors' lives, insight that I wouldn't have gotten anywhere else. And so I'll be happy to go on collecting this type of information on my cemetery visits—although I wouldn't mind a bit if a stray maiden name or a European place of origin came my way either!

—Lynn Betlock

Including either cemetery field trips or a tombstone slide show as a part of your family reunion activities is fun for everyone. A reunion is a time of family gathering, of all generations, young and old. By visiting ancestors' graves (or seeing the stones on the screen) and sharing memories of those who have preceded you, you can also link and reunite those generations long departed.

## CRAFT-RELATED CEMETERY PROJECTS
### Making a Cemetery Scrapbook

Scrapbooking is a popular hobby among all ages. Why not create a scrapbook dedicated to your ancestors' final resting places? Along with a photograph of each ancestor's headstone, include photographs of the overall cemetery. Add a biographical sketch of each of the deceased based on your research. Give some background history of the cemetery or of burial customs. If you have postmortem photographs in your family, include copies of these. Put only copies of original, historic photographs in your scrapbook. Store the originals in archival quality products. See Maureen A. Taylor's *Preserving Your Family Photographs* (Cincinnati: Betterway Books, 2001).

Decorate your scrapbook pages with black and purple crepe paper, dried flowers, and cemetery clip art. You'll find all sorts of cemetery and funeral clip art at <www.alsirat.com/cemart/index.html>, and the site is continually adding to its collection.

## Making a Cemetery Quilt

Oh, the mind reels with ideas for this one. Have photographs of your ancestors' headstones transferred onto fabric squares, then sew them together with black patterned squares. Or, make fabric coffins—the eight-sided mummy kind—to add to a quilt. Have the artist in your family draw some winged death heads, skulls and crossbones, willows, and urns, then have those transferred onto fabric. Have tombstone rubbings reduced and put onto fabric squares, then quilt together. Make one for each of your kids and grandkids. Any child would treasure and love to sleep under their very own cemetery quilt. Also check the Internet for replica patterns. Try entering "mourning quilts" into a search engine.

## Patterns for Mourning Samplers

While I found few actual replica patterns to make your own mourning sampler, you can find a few examples on the Internet to create your own modern-day memorial needlework. In your Internet search engine, type in the keywords "mourning sampler" and "mourning sampler patterns." The closest I came to finding a replica pattern from a nineteenth-century sampler was at <www.scarlet-letter.com/RepSamDesp/19thEng/Mourning.htm>. If you're set on making a nineteenth-century replica, you may have to scout out old needlework magazines with patterns, and have someone copy the pattern for you. For a good history of mourning samplers, go to <www.cameoroze.com/articles/art_mrng.htm>.

## WHAT'S NEXT?

You may find yourself spending more and more time in cemeteries, even where your ancestors aren't buried. There's no treatment, I'm afraid, for the cemetery gene that you surely must carry, otherwise you wouldn't have bought and read this book. I hope that you have found a new sense of discovery in your ancestor's final resting place and that you'll never look at another cemetery in quite the same way.

**And maybe now's the time to start thinking about what you want inscribed on your headstone.** No sense in leaving it to chance. Jot down your name and vitals (you'll have to leave the death date blank for now), find some artwork that has special meaning to you, and compose or "borrow" an epitaph from another headstone you like. On page 214 is an illustration, drawn by Johnny Titmus, of how I'd like my grave marker to look. The artwork is a replica of the Susanna

**Idea Generator**

Jayne stone of 1776, Marblehead, Massachusetts. The epitaph comes from Margaret Atwood's *Alias Grace*. Reflecting my personality, my tombstone combines early American thoughts and art with my love of genealogy and the trends of today.

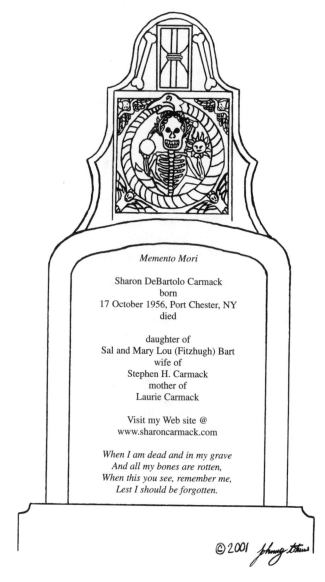

Happy cemetery hopping!

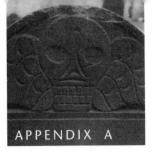

# Gravestone Art, Symbols, Emblems, and Attributes

*Note: Many of these interpretations are what gravestone scholars believe these symbols mean; however, there can be more than one interpretation for a symbol. Today, we can only speculate what our ancestors were trying to tell the living through their gravestone iconography.*

## Architectural

| | |
|---|---|
| archways, doors, and gates | passageway into the next life |
| benches | places of contemplation for mourners |
| half carved, half uncarved stone | transition from life to death |
| obelisk | eternal life; regeneration |
| pillar or column, broken | life cut short or sudden death |
| pillar or column, completed | a complete and full life; steadfastness; support of heaven |
| pillar or column, two | passageway into the next life |
| pyramid | endurance, stability, immortality |
| sphinx | power; spiritual triumph |

## Animals

| | |
|---|---|
| bat | death; misfortune |
| beehive | industriousness |
| bird | the soul, the spirit |
| dove | Holy Spirit; gentleness; peace |
| dove with olive branch | eternal peace |
| lamb | meekness, gentleness, innocence; God's flock; most popular on children's graves |
| lamb, lying down | suffering of Christ |
| lamb, standing | the triumphant, risen Christ |
| lion | bravery |
| peacock | immortality; vanity; pride |
| phoenix | resurrection |
| rooster | resurrection; awakening the spirit |

## Books

| | |
|---|---|
| book | wisdom, knowledge |
| book, open | the Bible or scriptures; perfect knowledge |
| book, closed | secrecy; chastity; final acts written |
| book, cross laying over it | faith personified |

## Clothing

| | |
|---|---|
| shoes, empty, one overturned | loss of a child |

## Figures

| | |
|---|---|
| angels, dropping flowers on grave | grief, mourning |
| angels, pointing to heaven | rejoice |
| baby or child, sleeping | the deceased child |
| baby or child, naked | new life, innocence, purity |
| woman, drooping or shrouded | mourning |
| woman, weeping | grief, mourning |

## Fruit, Nuts, and the Harvest

| | |
|---|---|
| acorn | strength, independence |
| corn | fertility; health; germination and growth |
| cornucopia | abundance; the bounty of God; thanksgiving |
| fruit | eternal plenty |
| grape clusters | body and blood of Jesus; sacrifice; the Eucharist |
| grape vine | Christ |
| pear | Christ's love for mankind |
| pineapple | welcome; perfection |
| wheat | harvest; prosperity; deceased of full years |

## Furniture

| | |
|---|---|
| bed, empty | loss of loved one, usually a child; anguish |
| chair, empty | loss of loved one; absence of authority |
| cradle, empty | loss of an infant; rebirth; protection |

## Geometric Symbols

| | |
|---|---|
| circle | eternity, completeness |
| chain links, one broken | family unity is broken |
| triangle | the Trinity |

## Hands and Fingers

| | |
|---|---|
| forefinger pointing up | soul has gone to heaven |
| forefinger pointing down | God reaching down for the soul |
| hand with ax | sudden death, life cut short |
| hands, middle and ring fingers separated | Jewish blessing hands; indicates a Jewish priest |
| handshake | God's welcome into heaven and farewell to earthly existence |
| handshake with masculine/ feminine sleeves | holy matrimony |

## Heraldry, cadency marks

| | |
|---|---|
| label (horizontal bar with three bars extending down) | first son |
| crescent (half-moon) | second son |
| mullet (five-pointed star) | third son |
| martlet (bird) | fourth son |

| annulet (ring) | fifth son |
| fleur-de-lis | sixth son |
| rose | seventh son |
| cross | eighth son |
| double quatrefoil | ninth son |

**Initials**

| AAONMS | Ancient Arabic Order of Nobles of the Mystic Shrine (Masonic) |
| AASR | Ancient and Accepted Scottish Rite (Masonic) |
| AF&AM | Ancient Free and Accepted Masons |
| AMORC | Ancient and Mystical Order of Rosae Crucis (Rosicrucians) |
| AMOS | Ancient Mystic Order of Samaritans (see IOOF) |
| AOH | Ancient Order of Hibernians |
| BPOE | Benevolent and Protective Order of Elks |
| BRT | Brotherhood of Railway Trainmen |
| DAN | Daughters of the Nile (Masonic) |
| DAR | National Society, Daughters of the American Revolution |
| DofR | Daughters of Rebekah |
| DOKK | Dramatic Order Knights of Khorassan (Knights of Pythias) |
| CSA | Confederate States of America |
| FATAL | Fairest Among Thousands, Altogether Lovely (see OES) |
| F&AM | Free and Accepted Masons |
| FCB | Friendship, Charity, and Benevolence (see K of P) |
| FFA | Future Farmers of America |
| FLT | Friendship, Love, and Truth (see IOOF) |
| FOE | Fraternal Order of Eagles |
| FOP | Fraternal Order of Police |
| GAR | Grand Army of the Republic |
| IHC, IHS | the first three letters of Jesus' name in Greek |
| INRI | Latin initials for Jesus of Nazareth, King of the Jews |
| IOF | Independent Order of Foresters |
| IOOF | Independent Order of Odd Fellows |
| IOJD | International Order of Job's Daughters |
| K of C | Knights of Columbus |
| K of P | Knights of Pythias |
| KT | Knights Templar |

| LOM | Loyal Order of Moose |
| MWW | Modern Woodmen of the World |
| OES | Order of the Eastern Star |
| SAR | Sons of the American Revolution |
| TOTE | Totem of the Eagle (Improved Order of Redmen) |
| UAW | United Auto Workers |
| UDC | United Daughters of the Confederacy |
| UMWA | United Mine Workers of America |
| USA | United States Army |
| USAF | United States Air Force |
| USMC | United States Marine Corps |
| USN | United States Navy |
| VFW | Veterans of Foreign Wars |
| WOW | Woodmen of the World or Women of Woodcraft |

## Military

| anchor, singular or crossed | maritime occupation |
| swords, crossed | battle; military strategy |

## Mortality

| arrows | darts of death; spiritual weapon |
| bone | death |
| candle | life |
| candle snuffed out | end of life |
| candles, two | dual nature of Christ |
| candles, three | the Trinity |
| candles, five | five wounds of Christ |
| candles, seven | Jesus |
| clock | the march of time; usually stopped at hour of death |
| coffin | death of the flesh |
| Father Time | mortality |
| hourglass | flight of time |
| imps | evil demons victorious over death; not popular, rarely seen after early 1700s |
| scythe | life cut off; death; harvest |
| shovel and spade | death |
| skeleton | death |
| skull | mortality; death |
| skull and crossbones | brevity of life |
| snake biting its own tail | eternity |
| urn | death of the flesh |
| urn, flames atop | soul arising out of the ashes |
| winged death head | mortal remains of the deceased |

## Musical Instruments

| | |
|---|---|
| harp | joy, praise, bridge between heaven and earth |
| lyre | harmonious union; relationship between heaven and earth |
| lute | marital bliss; friendship |
| trumpets | welcome to heaven; call of the spirit |
| trumpeters | heralds of the resurrection |

## Occupation and Crafts

| | |
|---|---|
| caduceus | medical |
| church with steeple | minister |
| fireman's helmet | fireman |
| horses, two heads | International Brotherhood of Teamsters; Chauffeurs, Stablemen & Helpers |
| lyre | musician |
| scales of justice | lawyer |
| star with initials LCHPF, half-moon with initials GIA to BLE | Ladies Auxiliary to the Brotherhood of Railroad Trainmen |
| treble clef | musician |

## Organizations

| | |
|---|---|
| anchor and sword crossed, hatchet and arrow in center, K of C | Knights of Columbus |
| chain links, three | International Order of Odd Fellows |
| circle with K in center | Kiwanis International |
| clover with H inside each petal | 4-H |
| compass with G in center | Masons |
| eagle with F.O.E. | Fraternal Order of Eagles |
| eagle, double-headed with 32 on breast | 32nd Degree Mason |
| eagle with shielded breast inside fleur-de-lis | Boy Scouts of America |
| elk | Benevolent and Protective Order of Elks |
| eye, handshake, chain with FLT | International Order of Odd Fellows |
| hatchet with T.O.T.E. | Improved Order of Redmen |
| R with dove and half-moon | Rebekah Lodge |
| R with three chain links | Rebekah Lodge |
| skull and crossbones within heraldic shield | Knights of Pythias |
| star, five-pointed inverted | Eastern Star |
| spinning wheel with thirteen stars | National Society, Daughters of the American Revolution |
| star, five-pointed rounded tips | Grand Army of the Republic |
| star, sabre, half-moon | Mystic Shrine |

## Ornamental

| | |
|---|---|
| banner | triumph, victory; often used as background for an inscription or motto |
| basket | maternal body; fertility |
| drapery and tassles | homelike; make the deceased feel comfortable; popular during Victorian era |
| fleur-de-lis | purity; the Trinity |
| gourd | fertility; resurrection |
| scroll | wisdom; life; often used as background for an inscription |
| scroll on Jewish grave | divine presence |
| shield | protection; faith; defense of the spirit |
| sword | liberty; the Crusades |

## Religious

| | |
|---|---|
| alpha and omega | Christ; the beginning and the end |
| altar shaped as a table | the Last Supper |
| altar shaped as a tomb | the death of Christ |
| angel | God's messenger and guardian |
| angel with sword | justice |
| Bible | the Word of God |
| chalice | the Eucharist |
| cherub | messenger of Divine wisdom |
| clover | the Trinity |
| crescent | emblem of the Virgin Mary |
| cross | faith in God |
| cross, variations (see Types of Veterans' Markers on page 223 for illustrations) | Armenian; Botonee; Celtic; Christian; Crucifix; Eastern, Greek, or Russian Orthodox; Episcopal; Fourchee; Gothic; Greek; Latin; Lutheran; Maltese; Presbyterian |
| crown | sovereignty, victory, eternal life |
| heart | soul in bliss (colonial) romantic love (Victorian–present) |
| heart with cross and anchor | love, faith, and hope |
| lamp or flame | immortality of the soul, hope of resurrection |
| lighthouse | safety; watchfulness, final port |
| mansion in sky | Biblical, "In my Father's house there are many mansions." |
| menorah | emblem of Judaism |
| star(s) | guidance and protection |
| star, four-pointed | emblem of Shamash; a cross |
| star, five-pointed | Epiphany; the Virgin Mary |

| | |
|---|---|
| star, five-pointed inverted | witchcraft |
| star, six-pointed | the human soul; good and evil; Star of David, emblem of Israel, the Jewish faith |
| star, seven-pointed | the Holy Spirit |
| star, eight-pointed | regeneration; the rising sun |
| star, nine-pointed | the Holy Spirit |
| star, ten-pointed | the ten Apostles who neither denied nor betrayed Christ |
| tablets, two | the Ten Commandments |
| torch | guidance, enlightenment |
| torch, inverted | end of family line |

**Resurrection**

| | |
|---|---|
| anchor | hope, being safely anchored in God's harbor |
| clouds | transition to afterlife |
| cloud, hand emerging | God |
| soul effigy | image of the soul; sometimes portrayed as cameo portrait |
| sun | dawn of life |
| sunset | end of earthly life, beginning of heavenly life |
| sun, moon, stars | glory of Christ and the saints; soul arising to heaven |
| wings | soul soaring to heaven |

**Shells**

| | |
|---|---|
| conch shell | wealth; female reproductive tract; rebirth |
| scallop shell | resurrection |

**Trees, Plants, and Flowers**

| | |
|---|---|
| bouquet | a tribute; sweet thoughts |
| daisies | youth, innocence |
| fig leaves | abundance; fruitfulness; rejuvenation |
| flowers, buds | mortal life unblossomed; renewal in the afterlife |
| flowers, broken stems | life cut short |
| iris | hope; purity |
| ivy | clinging memory of the deceased; longevity; despondency; dependence |
| laurel | spiritual victory |
| leaf | happiness |
| lilies | resurrection |
| oak leaves | strength of faith |
| olive tree or branch | reconciliation between God and man; peace |

| | |
|---|---|
| palm leaves | resurrection, victory |
| pine cone | spiritual fertility |
| poppy | eternal sleep |
| rose | motherhood; beauty |
| thistle | of Scottish heritage |
| tree | tree of life |
| trees, two | two side by side, possibly marriage trees |
| trees, fallen or cut branch, trunk | life cut short |
| tree stump | life cut short, often members of Woodmen of the World |
| vine | Christ |
| weeping willow | mourning and earthly sorrow |
| wreath | mourning |

**Veterans' Markers**

Christian Cross
Buddhist Wheel of Righteousness
Hebrew Star of David
Presbyterian Cross
Russian Orthodox Cross
Lutheran Cross
Episcopal Cross
Unitarian Church Flaming Chalice
United Methodist Church
Aaronic Order Church
Mormon Angel Moroni
Native American Church of North America
Serbian Orthodox
Greek Cross
Bahai Nine-Pointed Star
Atheist
Muslim Crescent and Star
Hindu
Konko-Kyo Faith
Reorganized Church of Latter-Day Saints
Sufism Reoriented
Tenrikyo Church
Seicho-No-Ie
Church of World Messianity Izunome
United Church of Religious Science
Christian Reformed Church
United Moravian Church
Eckankar
Christian Church
United Church of Christ
Christian Scientist Cross and Crown
Muslim Islamic Five-Pointed Star

**Figure App. A-1** Symbols available for veterans' markers.

# Historical Time Line of Deadly Diseases, Epidemics, and Disasters in America 1516–1981

*Note: This time line, prepared by Sharon DeBartolo Carmack and Katherine Scott Sturdevant, does not cover military engagements, massacres, or slave revolts. Remember that military troops often carried infectious diseases to other troops as well as to civilians. Disease and infection usually killed more soldiers during wars than wounds incurred in battles. Although we checked the accuracy of these dates in multiple sources, sometimes our sources disagreed on the exact dates or years of an event. This time line is meant as a reference guide and springboard for further research.*

| | |
|---|---|
| 1516 | First major smallpox epidemic spread among native tribes in Hispaniola brought by European colonists |
| 1531 | Measles epidemic in the Southwest |
| 1545 | Bubonic plague in the Southwest |
| 1592 | Smallpox found throughout North America east of the Mississippi and in the Southwest |
| 1602 | Smallpox epidemic in the Southwest |
| 1607–1624 | Chesapeake settlement "seasoned" by malaria, dysentery, influenza, typhoid, etc. and malnutrition and salt poisoning |
| 1615–1660 | Outbreaks of smallpox hit East Coast and Great Lakes tribes |
| 1616–1618 | Chicken pox or other infection decimated New England native populations—brought by fishermen |
| 1618 | Smallpox epidemic hit New England and spread to Virginia; hit tribes from the Penobscot River in Maine to Narragansett Bay in Rhode Island |
| 1630s | Smallpox, New England, further reduced natives |
| 1637 | Scarlet fever outbreak in Native American communities |
| 1638 | Smallpox and spotted fever, New England |
| 1648–1649 | Smallpox, Massachusetts Bay Colony |
| 1657–1658 | Measles, Boston |
| 1659 | Throat distemper, Massachusetts Bay Colony |
| 1677–1678 | Smallpox, Boston and Charlestown |
| 1679–1680 | Smallpox, Virginia |
| 1687 | Measles, Boston |
| 1689–1690 | Smallpox, New England |
| 1690 | Yellow fever, New York |
| 1693 | Yellow fever, Boston |
| 1696 | Smallpox, Jamestown, Virginia |
| 1699 | Yellow fever, Philadelphia and Charleston<br>Smallpox, South Carolina |
| 1702 | Yellow fever, New York |
| 1702–1703 | Smallpox, Boston |

| | |
|---|---|
| 1706 | Yellow fever, Charleston |
| 1711–1712 | Smallpox, South Carolina |
| 1713 | Measles, Boston |
| 1715–1725 | Widespread smallpox |
| 1720–1722 | Smallpox, Boston (inspired discovery of inoculation in 1721) |
| 1723–1730 | Smallpox, Boston, New York, and Philadelphia |
| 1729 | Measles, Boston |
| 1730s–1760s | Diphtheria annually, New England and New York |
| 1732 | Yellow fever, New York and Charleston |
| 1732–1733 | Worldwide influenza epidemic |
| 1734 | Yellow fever, Virginia |
| 1735 | Diphtheria outbreak in Kingston, New Hampshire |
| 1735–1740 | Smallpox, scarlet fever, diphtheria, New England and Middle Colonies |
| 1738 | Smallpox, South Carolina |
| ca. 1738 | Smallpox spread to Cherokees in Georgia by white slave traders |
| 1739–1740 | Measles, Boston |
| 1740s | Yellow fever among Pennsylvania troops returning from West Indies |
| 1741 | Yellow fever, Virginia |
| 1747 | Measles, New York, Connecticut, Pennsylvania, and South Carolina |
| 1752 | Smallpox, Boston |
| 1755 | Severe earthquake hit Boston, November 18 |
| 1760–1761 | Smallpox, Connecticut, Massachusetts, Rhode Island, and Charleston |
| 1762 | Yellow Fever, Philadelphia |
| 1763 | Smallpox used as biological weapon in French and Indian War |
| 1763 | Throat distemper, Philadelphia |
| 1764 | Smallpox, Boston |
| 1769 | Throat distemper, New York |
| 1772–1774 | Smallpox, New England |
| 1775–1780s | Disease spread by troop movements during Revolutionary War |
| 1775–1776 | Influenza, smallpox, and dysentery, Boston and Massachusetts, during British occupation |
| 1776 | Hurricane hit eastern seaboard from North Carolina to Nova Scotia, September 2–9 |
| 1777 | Yellow fever, Louisiana |
| 1778 | Smallpox, Boston |
| 1780 | Smallpox epidemic hit Arikara tribe, wiping out nearly 75 percent |
| 1781–1782 | Worldwide influenza epidemic |
| 1782–1783 | Smallpox introduced to Northwest tribes |
| 1784 | Deadly hailstorm hit Winnsborough, South Carolina, May 8 |
| 1786–1787 | Yellow fever, Louisiana |
| 1788 | Measles, Philadelphia and New York |

| | |
|---|---|
| 1788 | Fire in New Orleans, March 21 |
| 1789 | Influenza epidemic throughout the thirteen states of the U.S. |
| 1792 | Smallpox, Boston |
| 1792–1793 | Smallpox, Virginia |
| 1793 | Yellow fever, Philadelphia (the most famous of these epidemics) |
| | Influenza, Vermont and Virginia |
| 1794 | Yellow fever, Philadelphia |
| 1796 | Yellow fever, New Orleans, Philadelphia |
| 1796–1798 | Yellow fever, Philadelphia, northeastern cities, New Orleans, Baltimore, and Mobile |
| 1798 | Blizzard, New England, November 17–21 |
| 1800 | Smallpox vaccination caught on in South |
| 1800–1801 | Smallpox hit Omaha tribe |
| 1800s | Smallpox reduced population of Hawaii |
| 1801 | Smallpox, Columbia River Basin |
| 1801–1802 | Smallpox along Upper Missouri, hit Arikara tribe |
| 1803 | Yellow fever, New York |
| 1811 | Tornado hit Charleston, South Carolina, September 10 |
| | Earthquake hit the Mississippi Valley, December 16, destroying the village of New Madrid, Missouri |
| 1814 | Burning of Washington, DC, by the British during the War of 1812 |
| 1816 | Smallpox, Comanches |
| 1819 | Yellow fever, Natchez, Mississippi |
| 1820s | Yellow fever, Philadelphia and other eastern cities |
| 1821 | Yellow fever, Virginia by way of Norfolk |
| 1830 | Influenza epidemic among tribes in California and Oregon |
| 1832–1845 | Asiatic Cholera, New York City and other eastern cities |
| | Cholera, New Orleans and other southern cities |
| | Cholera, 1832 first time in Virginia |
| 1835 | Fire in New York City, December 16 |
| 1836 | Smallpox epidemic among the Tlingits |
| 1837 | Smallpox, Great Plains, reduced native population; Mandans reduced to fewer than 200 from about 9,000 in 1750; also impacted the Hidatsas and Arikaras |
| | Typhus, Philadelphia |
| | Mississippi steamboats *Monmouth* and *Tremont* collided near Profit Island, October 31 |
| 1837–1870 | Four major smallpox epidemics hit western Indian nations |
| 1840 | Tornado hit Natchez, Mississippi, May 6 |
| 1841 | *Erie* steamboat fire, en route from Buffalo, New York, to Chicago, August 9 |
| | Hurricane wiped out Saint Jo, Florida (near Apalachicola), September |
| 1842 | Tornado hit Natchez, Mississippi, again, June 16 |
| 1845 | Fire in New York City, started on New Street, July 14 |
| 1847 | Yellow Fever, New Orleans |

| | |
|---|---|
| 1847–1848 | Typhus, Pittsburgh; influenza worldwide |
| 1848–1849 | Cholera, New York City |
| 1849 | St. Louis, Missouri, fire in downtown district, May 17 |
| 1849–1854 | Cholera, northeastern cities |
| 1850s | Cholera, Great Plains and Overland Trails, spread through wagon trains and to native population, also in San Francisco, Cleveland, St. Louis, St. Paul; hit tribes in the Great Basin and Southern Plains |
| 1850–1854 | Cholera, annual outbreaks, Virginia |
| 1851 | Fire in San Francisco, started in Portsmouth Square, May 3 |
| 1852 | Typhus, New York City |
| 1852-1853 | Yellow fever, New Orleans |
| 1853 | Railroad accident, Norwalk, Connecticut, River Bridge, May 6 |
| 1855 | Yellow fever, Virginia and New Orleans |
| 1855–1858 | Smallpox, Virginia |
| 1856 | Trains collided, two northern Pennsylvania trains, Camp Hill, Pennsylvania, July 17 |
| | Hurricane hit Last Island, Louisiana, August 11 |
| 1857–1859 | Worldwide influenza |
| 1858 | Smallpox, Pennsylvania |
| 1860 | Factory accident, Pemberton Mill, Lawrence, Massachusetts, January 10 |
| | Lake Michigan steamer *Lady Elgin* sank, September 7 |
| 1861–1865 | Diseases spread through troops and civilians by Civil War: measles, malaria, typhoid, dysentery, smallpox, scurvy, pneumonia, syphilis, gangrene, tetanus |
| 1863 | New York City draft riots, July 13 |
| 1863–1864 | Diphtheria, northeastern cities |
| 1864 | Yellow fever, Galveston, Texas |
| 1865–1873 | Smallpox, Philadelphia, New York, Boston, and New Orleans Cholera, Baltimore, Memphis, and Washington, DC |
| 1865 | Typhoid, typhus, scarlet fever, yellow fever, Philadelphia and northeastern cities |
| | *General Lyon* steamship burned at sea off Cape Hatteras, North Carolina, March 25 |
| | *Sultana* steamboat suffered fiery explosion during trip up the Mississippi from Vicksburg to Cairo, Illinois, about eight miles north of Memphis, April 27 |
| 1866 | Cholera, Philadelphia, New York, national, especially northeastern cities |
| | *Monarch of the Seas* immigrant passenger ship, en route from Liverpool, England, to the United States, disappeared without a trace after departing on March 19 |
| 1866–1867 | Yellow fever, Galveston, Texas |
| 1867 | Cholera, New Orleans; cholera outbreak among the Comanches; yellow fever, Louisiana |

| | |
|---|---|
| 1869–1870 | Scarlet fever, Philadelphia |
| 1870 | Smallpox, Philadelphia |
| | Yellow fever, Kentucky, St. Louis |
| 1871 | Staten Island ferry *Westfield* exploded, July 30 |
| | Great Chicago Fire, October 8–9 |
| | Fire destroyed Peshtigo, Wisconsin, October 8 |
| 1871–1872 | Smallpox, Kentucky |
| 1872 | Typhoid, northeastern cities |
| | Boston fire, November 9 |
| 1872–1873 | Smallpox, measles, northeastern cities |
| 1873 | *Atlantic* steamship en route to New York from Halifax, Nova Scotia, sank, April 1 |
| | Yellow fever, smallpox, cholera, Memphis, Nashville, and Louisiana |
| 1874–1878 | Yellow fever, Florida |
| 1874–1882 | Diphtheria, northeastern cities |
| 1876 | Brooklyn, New York, theater fire, December 5 |
| | Ohio train wreck, Ashtabula, Ohio, December 29 |
| 1878 | Yellow fever, New Orleans |
| 1878–1879 | Yellow fever, Mississippi Valley, Memphis, Vicksburg |
| 1880 | Series of twenty-four tornadoes hit Marshfield, Missouri, April 18 |
| 1880s | Germ theory of disease started to spread in U.S. medical circles |
| 1881 | Hurricane hit coasts of Florida and the Carolinas, August 27 |
| 1882 | Bacillus causing tuberculosis discovered |
| 1883 | Starvation among northern Montana Territory tribes after the buffalo were exterminated by whites |
| | Coal mine floods, Wilmington Coal Field, Braidwood, Illinois, February 16 |
| 1884 | *City of Columbus* passenger ship bound for Savannah from Boston sank off Martha's Vineyard, January 18 |
| | Tornadoes hit Mississippi, Alabama, the Carolinas, Tennessee, Kentucky, and Indiana, February 19 |
| 1885 | Typhoid, Plymouth, Pennsylvania |
| 1886 | Yellow fever, Jacksonville, Florida |
| | Earthquake hit Charleston, South Carolina, August 31 |
| 1887 | Chatsworth railway disaster, near Chatsworth, Illinois, August 10 |
| 1888 | Blizzard hit East Coast, March 10–14 |
| 1889 | Diphtheria, northeastern cities |
| | Johnstown, Pennsylvania, flood, May 31 |
| 1889–1890 | Worldwide influenza epidemic |
| 1890 | Tornado hit Louisville, Kentucky, March 27 |
| 1890–1892 | Smallpox, Houston |
| 1892 | Oil City, Pennsylvania, fire, June 4 |
| 1893 | Hurricane hit Georgia and South Carolina, August 28; also coasts of Louisiana, Mississippi, and Alabama, October 1 |
| | Insect-borne diseases recognized |

| | |
|---|---|
| 1893–1894 | Worldwide cholera epidemic |
| 1894 | Forest fire in Hinckley, Minnesota, September 2 |
| | Poliomyelitis epidemic struck the United States |
| 1896 | Fire and explosion destroyed Cripple Creek, Colorado, April 25 |
| | Tornado hit St. Louis, Missouri, May 27 |
| 1898 | Cholera, Kentucky |
| | *City of Portland* sank near Cape Cod, November 26 |
| | Blizzard hit coastal northeastern United States, November 26–27 |
| 1898–1902 | Spanish-American War and Philippine Insurrection afflicted men with tropical diseases known as "diarrhea scandal" |
| 1899 | Cholera, Arkansas |
| | New York's Windsor Hotel caught fire, March 17 |
| | Tornado hit New Richmond, Wisconsin, June 12 |
| 1900 | Diphtheria, North Dakota |
| | Bubonic plague hit Honolulu, April 30 |
| | Coal mine exploded, Scofield, Utah, May 1 |
| | Fire on piers of North German Lloyd Steamship line, Hoboken, New Jersey, June 30 |
| | Hurricane hit Galveston, Texas, September 8 |
| 1902 | Typhus wiped out Eskimo population of Southhampton Island in the Hudson Bay |
| | Tornado hit Goliad, Texas, May 18 |
| 1902–1906 | Drs. Reed and Gorgas discovered cause and eliminated yellow fever from Panama Canal Zone after it killed many workers |
| 1903 | Tornado hit Gainesville, Georgia, June 1 |
| | Iroquois Theater fire in Chicago, December 30 |
| 1904 | Baltimore, Maryland, fire, February 7 |
| | *General Slocum* steamer caught fire in the East River, New York City, June 15 |
| | Train derailment, Eden, Colorado, August 7 |
| 1905 | Yellow fever epidemic, New Orleans |
| | Tornado hit Snyder, Oklahoma, May 10 |
| 1906 | Typhoid Mary (Mary Mallon) caught, New York |
| | Great San Francisco Earthquake and Fire, April 18 |
| 1907 | Steamers *Larchmont* and *Harry Knowlton* collided off Block Island, February 11 |
| | West Virginia mine disaster, Monongha, December 6 |
| | Mine explosion, Jacob's Creek, Pennsylvania, December 19 |
| 1908 | Fire at Lake View School, Collingwood, Ohio, March 4 |
| | Tornadoes hit Amite, Louisiana, Purvis, Mississippi, and Natchez, Mississippi, April 24 |
| 1909 | Hurricane hit Louisiana and Mississippi, September 10–21 |
| | Fire and mine explosion, Cherry, Illinois, November 13 |
| 1910 | Train wreck, Wellington, Washington, March 1 |
| | Forest fires in Montana and Idaho, August |
| 1911 | Triangle Shirtwaist Company fire, New York City, March 25 |

| 1912 | *Titanic* sank in the Atlantic, April 15 |
| 1913 | Tornado hit Omaha, Nebraska, March 23 |
| | Ohio River flooded, Dayton, Ohio, and Indiana hit hardest, March 26 |
| | Mine explosion, Dawson, New Mexico, October 22 |
| 1914 | Pasteurization of milk began in major cities |
| | *Empress of Ireland* sank in the St. Lawrence River, May 29 |
| 1915 | *Lusitania* sunk off Irish coast by German submarine, May 17 |
| | *Eastland* steamer overturned in Chicago River, July 24 |
| | Hurricane hit east Texas and Louisiana, August 5-23 |
| 1916 | Polio outbreak (infantile paralysis) |
| 1917–1919 | Spanish Influenza, worldwide (World War I) |
| 1917 | Munitions plant explosion, Eddystone, Pennsylvania, April 10 |
| | Tornadoes hit Illinois, Indiana, Kansas, Kentucky, Missouri, Tennessee, Alabama, and Arkansas, May 26 |
| 1918 | Brooklyn train wreck, November 1 |
| | Explosion, Aetna Chemical Company plant, Oakdale, Pennsylvania, May 18 |
| | Two trains collided near Nashville, Tennessee, July 9 |
| | Forest fires in and around Duluth, Minnesota, and northern Wisconsin, October 12 |
| | *Princess Sophia* luxury liner sank, Lynn Canal, Alaska, October 27 |
| | Subway derailment, New York City, November 1 |
| 1919 | Hurricane hit Florida, Louisiana, and Texas, September 2–15 |
| 1920 | Tornado hit Starkville, Mississippi, and Waco, Alabama, April 20 |
| 1922 | Snow storms hit eastern seaboard, January 27–29 |
| 1924 | Babb's Switch, Oklahoma, School Fire, December 24 |
| | Tornado hit Lorain and Sandusky, Ohio, June 28 |
| 1925 | Tornadoes hit Missouri, Illinois, and Indiana, March 18 |
| 1926 | Hurricane hit southern Florida and Alabama, September 11–22 |
| 1927 | Mississippi Valley Floods, late April |
| | Tornado hit Poplar Bluff, Missouri, May 9 |
| | Tornado hit St. Louis, Missouri, September 29 |
| | Gas explosion, Pittsburgh, Pennsylvania, November 14 |
| 1928 | Dam broke, Santa Paula, California, March 12 |
| | Mine explosion, Mather, Pennsylvania, May 19 |
| | Hurricane hit southern Florida, September 6–20 |
| 1929 | Cleveland, Ohio, hospital fire, May 15 |
| 1930 | Fire at Ohio State Penitentiary, Columbus, April 21 |
| 1931 | Diphtheria epidemic |
| 1932 | Tornadoes hit Alabama, Mississippi, Georgia, and Tennessee, March 21 |
| 1933 | Earthquake hit Long Beach, California, March 10 |
| 1934 | *Morro Castle* caught fire off Asbury Park, New Jersey, September 8 |

| | |
|---|---|
| 1935 | Hurricane hit Florida Keys, August 29–September 10 |
| 1936 | Tornadoes hit Tupelo, Mississippi, April 5; Gainesville, Georgia, April 6 |
| 1937 | Flooding of Ohio River Basin, January |
| | Explosion at a school in New London, Texas, March 18 |
| 1938 | Hurricane hit Long Island, Connecticut, Massachusetts, and Rhode Island, September 10–22 |
| 1940 | Fire at Rhythm Night Club, Natchez, Mississippi, April 23 |
| 1941 | Blizzard hit Midwest, March 15–16 |
| 1942 | Fire at Coconut Grove nightclub, Boston, November 28 |
| 1943 | Train derailment and collision, near Rennert, North Carolina, December 16 |
| 1944 | Tornadoes hit Shinnston, West Virginia, June 23 |
| | Fire at Ringling Brothers and Barnum & Bailey Circus, Hartford, Connecticut, July 6 |
| | Ammunition ships exploded, Port Chicago, California, July 17 |
| | Hurricane hit North Carolina to New England, September 9–16 |
| | Explosion and fire at East Ohio Gas Company, Cleveland, October 20 |
| 1944–1946 | Polio, national outbreaks |
| 1946 | Fire at La Salle Hotel, Chicago, June 5 |
| | United airliner crash, LaGuardia Airport, New York, May 30 |
| | Fire at Winecoff Hotel, Atlanta, Georgia, December 7 |
| 1947 | Tornado hit Woodward, Oklahoma, April 9 |
| | Fire and explosion, Texas City, Texas, April 16–18 |
| | Hurricane hit Florida and mid–Gulf Coast, September 4–21 |
| 1949–1952 | Polio, national outbreaks |
| 1950 | Long Island Railroad commuter train crashed into another, Richmond Hill, New York, November 22 |
| 1951 | Pennsylvania Railroad commuter crashed, Woodbridge, New Jersey, February 6 |
| 1952 | Polio outbreaks nationwide |
| | Blizzard in Sierra Nevadas, January 14 |
| | Tornadoes hit Arkansas, Tennessee, Missouri, Mississippi, Alabama, and Kentucky, March 21–22 |
| 1953 | Tornado hit Waco, Texas, May 11 |
| | Tornado hit Flint, Michigan, June 8 |
| | Tornado hit Worcester, Massachusetts, June 9 |
| 1954 | Hurricane Carol hit North Carolina to New England, August 25–31 |
| | Hurricane Hazel hit South Carolina to New York, October 5–18 |
| | Polio vaccine developed |
| 1955 | Tornado hit Udall, Kansas, May 25 |
| | Hurricane Diane hit North Carolina to New England, August 7–21 |

| | |
|---|---|
| 1956 | Mid-air crash over Grand Canyon, involving United and TWA airliners, June 30 |
| | *Andrea Doria* collided with the *Stockholm*, July 25 |
| 1957 | Fire at Katie Jane Memorial Nursing Home, Warrenton, Missouri, February 17 |
| | Hurricane Audrey hit Texas to Alabama, June 25–28 |
| 1957–1958 | Worldwide Asian flu epidemic |
| 1958 | Fire at Our Lady of the Angels Parochial School, Chicago, December 1 |
| 1960 | Hurricane Donna hit Florida to New England, August 29–September 13 |
| | United and TWA airliners collided over Staten Island, December 16 |
| 1961 | Hurricane Carla hit Texas Gulf Coast, September 3–15 |
| 1963 | Ice show explosion in Indianapolis, Indiana, October 31 |
| 1964 | Earthquake hit eighty miles east of Anchorage, Alaska, March 28 |
| 1965 | Tornadoes hit Iowa, Wisconsin, Michigan, Illinois, Ohio, and Indiana, April 11 |
| | Los Angeles race riots, August 11–16 |
| | Hurricane Betsy hit Southern Florida and Louisiana, August 27–September 12 |
| 1967 | Silver Bridge spanning Kanauga, Ohio, to Point Pleasant, West Virginia, collapsed, December 15 |
| 1969 | Floods and mudslides in Southern California, January 18–26 |
| | Hurricane Camille hit Mississippi, Louisiana, Alabama, Virginia, and West Virginia, August 14–22 |
| 1972 | Flood in Logan County, West Virginia, February 26 |
| | Flash flood, Rapid City, South Dakota, June 9–10 |
| | Hurricane Agnes hit eastern seaboard from Florida to New York, June 14–23 |
| | Two Illinois Central commuter trains collided, October 30 |
| 1973 | Staten Island gas storage tank exploded, February 10 |
| | Mississippi River flooded from northern Illinois to Louisiana delta, April |
| 1974 | 148 tornadoes hit the East, South, and Midwest, April 3–4 |
| 1976 | Legionnaires' disease outbreak in Philadelphia, Pennsylvania, July |
| | Big Thompson River flood, Loveland, Colorado, July 31 |
| 1977 | Fire at Beverly Hills Supper Club in Southgate, Kentucky, May 28 |
| | Pacific Southwest plane collided midair with a Cessna, September 25 |
| 1978 | Jonestown mass suicides, November 18 |
| 1979 | American Airlines flight crashed after takeoff from O'Hare International Airport in Chicago, May 25 |
| | Hurricane David hit Caribbean Islands to New England, August 25–September 7 |

Hurricane Frederick hit Mobile, Alabama, and Mississippi coast, September 12

1980    Hurricane Allen hit Caribbean Islands to Texas Gulf, August 3–10

MGM Grand Hotel fire in Las Vegas, Nevada, November 21

1981    AIDS epidemic invaded the United States

## Selected Sources

*And the Band Played On: Politics, People, and the AIDS Epidemic,* by Randy Shilts. New York: St. Martin's Press, 1987.

*Bargaining for Life: A Social History of Tuberculosis, 1876–1938,* by Barbara Bates. Philadelphia: University of Pennsylvania Press, 1992.

*Bring Out Your Dead: The Great Plague of Yellow Fever in Philadelphia in 1793,* by J.H. Powell. New York: Time Life Books, 1949.

*The Cholera Years: The United States in 1832, 1849, and 1866,* by Charles Rosenberg. Chicago: University of Chicago Press, 1962.

*Chronicle of America.* Mount Kisco, N.Y.: Chronicle Publications, 1989.

*Dirt and Disease: Polio in America Before FDR,* by Naomi Rogers. New Brunswick, N.J.: Rutgers University Press, 1992.

*Epidemics in Colonial America,* by John Duffy. Baton Rouge: Louisiana State University Press, 1953.

*Everyday Life Among the American Indians,* by Candy Moulton. Cincinnati: Writer's Digest Books, 2001.

*Images of Healing: A Portfolio of American Medical and Pharmaceutical Practice in the 18th, 19th, and Early 20th Centuries,* ed. by Ann Novotny and Carter Smith. New York: Macmillan, 1980.

"Major U.S. Epidemics" and "Worst United States Disasters." www.infoplease.com/ipa/a0001459.html.

*The New York Public Library American History Desk Reference.* New York: Macmillan, 1997.

*The Pessimist's Guide to History,* by Stuart Flexner and Doris Flexner. New York: Quill, 2000.

*Silent Travelers: Germs, Genes, and the "Immigrant Menace,"* by Alan M. Kraut. New York: BasicBooks, 1994.

"Some Major Epidemics in American History," unpublished chronology by Katherine Scott Sturdevant, 1992–2001. (Note: This original compilation was for internal use and did not include source citations. It contains information from years of research and hundreds of sources, books, and periodicals, sometimes one fact coming from one source.)

"Tragedies on U.S. Soil." *The Wall Street Journal,* 13 Sept. 2001, B11.

*Typhoid Mary: Captive to the Public's Health,* by Judith Walzer Leavitt. Boston: Beacon Press, 1996.

*Yellow Fever and the South,* by Margaret Humphreys. New Brunswick, N.J.: Rutgers University Press, 1992.

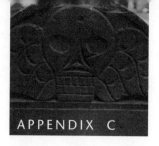

# Historical Medical Glossary for Causes of Death

*Note: This glossary was compiled by James Byars Carter, M.D., deceased, and reprinted with permission of Dr. Carter's widow. It was originally published as part of "Disease and Death in the Nineteenth Century: A Genealogical Perspective,"* National Genealogical Society Quarterly 76 *(December 1988): 289–301. Supplemental data by Sharon DeBartolo Carmack is bracketed.*

*Remember, while this glossary gives definitions of common causes of death from the nineteenth century, the diagnosis on a death certificate or any source that records the cause of death, such as the mortality schedules, might not be accurate based on what we know about medical science today (see chapter one, Death Certificates).*

**Abscess.** A localized collection of pus buried in tissues, organs, or confined spaces of the body, often accompanied by swelling and inflammation and frequently caused by bacteria. The brain, lung, or kidney (for instance) could be involved. See *boil.*

**Addison's disease.** A disease characterized by severe weakness, low blood pressure, and a bronzed coloration of the skin, due to decreased secretion of cortisol from the adrenal gland. Dr. Thomas Addison (1793–1860), born near Newcastle, England, described the disease in 1855. Synonyms: Morbus addisonii, bronzed skin disease.

**Ague.** Malarial or intermittent fever characterized by paroxysms (stages of chills, fever, and sweating at regularly recurring times) and followed by an interval or intermission whose length determines the epithets: *quotidian, tertian, quartan,* and *quintan ague* (when the interval between paroxysms of fever was twenty-four hours, it was called *quotidian ague*; when the interval was forty-eight hours, it was called *tertian ague*; and when seventy-two hours, it was called *quartan ague*). Popularly, the disease was known as "fever and ague," "chill fever," "the shakes," and by names expressive of the locality in which it was prevalent—such as, "swamp fever" (in Louisiana), "Panama fever," and "Chagres fever."

**Ague-cake.** A form of enlargement of the spleen, resulting from the action of malaria on the system.

**Anasarca.** Generalized massive dropsy. See *dropsy.*

**Aphthae.** See *thrush.*

**Aphthous stomatitis.** See *canker.*

[**Apoplexy.** Sudden loss of consciousness followed by paralysis due to a hemorrhage in the brain. Synonyms: shock, stroke.]

**Ascites.** See *dropsy.*

**Asthenia.** See *debility.*

[**Atelectasis.** Condition where the lungs of a newborn remain unexpanded; a collapse of the lung. May be caused by obstruction of a foreign body or mucous plugs or in premature birth.]

**Bilous fever.** A term loosely applied to certain enteric (intestinal) and malarial fevers. See *typhus*.

**Biliousness.** A complex of symptoms comprising nausea, abdominal discomfort, headache, and constipation—formerly attributed to excessive secretion of bile from the liver.

[**Black tongue.** See *typhoid fever*.]

[**Blood poisoning.** See *septicemia*.]

[**Bloody flux.** See *dysentery*.]

**Boil.** An abscess of skin or painful, circumscribed inflammation of the skin or a hair follicle, having a dead, pus-forming inner core, usually caused by a staphylococcal infection. Synonym: furuncle.

**Brain fever.** See *meningitis, typhus*.

[**Bright's Disease.** Named for Dr. Richard Bright (1789–1858). Acute and chronic disease of the kidneys, which could be a result of diabetic kidney failure. Usually associated with *dropsy*.]

**Bronchial asthma.** A paroxysmal, often allergic disorder of breathing, characterized by spasm of the bronchial tubes of the lungs, wheezing, and difficulty in breathing air outward—often accompanied by coughing and a feeling of tightness in the chest. In the nineteenth century, the direct causes were thought to be dust, vegetable irritants, chemical vapors, animal emanations, climatic influences, and bronchial inflammation—all of which were reasonable guesses. The indirect causes were thought to be transmissions by the nervous system or by the blood from gout, syphilis, skin disease, renal disease, or heredity. Only the latter cause was a reasonable assumption.

**Camp fever.** See *typhus*.

**Cancer.** A malignant and invasive growth or tumor (especially tissue that covers a surface or lines a cavity), tending to recur after excision and to spread to other sites. In the nineteenth century, physicians noted that cancerous tumors tended to ulcerate, grew constantly, and progressed to fatal end and that there was scarcely a tissue they would not invade. Synonyms: malignant growth, carcinoma.

**Cancrum oris.** A severe, destructive, eroding ulcer of the cheek and lip, rapidly proceeding to sloughing. In the last century, it was seen in delicate, ill-fed, ill-tended children between the ages of two and five. The disease was the result of poor hygiene acting upon a debilitated system. It commonly followed one of the eruptive fevers and was often fatal. The destructive disease could, in a few days, lead to gangrene of the lips, cheeks, tonsils, palate, tongue, and even half the face; teeth would fall from their sockets, and a horribly fetid saliva flowed from the parts. Synonyms: *canker*, water canker, noma, gangrenous stomatitis, gangrenous ulceration of the mouth.

**Canker.** An ulcerous sore of the mouth and lips, not considered fatal today. Synonyms: aphthous stomatitis. See *cancrum oris*.

[**Canine fever.** See *hydrophobia*.]

**Carcinoma.** See *cancer*.

**Catarrh.** Inflammation of a mucous membrane, especially of the air passages of the head and throat, with a free discharge. It is characterized by cough, thirst, lassitude, fever, watery eyes, and increased secretions of mucus from the air passages. Bronchial catarrh was bronchitis; suffocative catarrh was croup; urethral catarrh was gleet; vaginal catarrh was leukorrhea; epidemic catarrh was the same as influenza. Synonyms: cold, coryza.

[**Childbed fever.** See *puerperal fever*.]

**Childbirth.** A cause given for many female deaths of the century. Almost all babies were born in homes and usually were delivered by family members or a midwife; thus infection and lack of medical skill were often the actual causes of death. [See *puerperal fever*.]

**Cholera.** An acute, infectious disease, endemic in India and China and now occasionally epidemic elsewhere—characterized by profuse diarrhea, vomiting, and cramps. It is caused by a potent toxin discharged by the bacterium *Vibrio cholerae*, which acts on the small intestine to cause secretion of large amounts of fluid. The painless, watery diarrhea and the passing of rice-water stool are characteristic. Great body-salt depletion occurs. Cholera is spread by feces-contaminated water and food. Major epidemics struck the United States in the years 1832, 1849, and 1866. In the 1830s, the causes were generally thought to be intemperance in the use of ardent spirits or drinking bad water; uncleanliness, poor living or crowded and ill-ventilated dwellings; and too much fatigue. By 1850 cholera was thought to be caused by putrid animal poison and miasma or pestilential vapor rising from swamps and marshes—or that it entered the body through the lungs or was transmitted through the medium of clothing. It was still believed that it attacked the poor, the dissolute, the diseased, and the fearful—while the healthy, well-clad, well-fed, and fearless man escaped the ravages of cholera.

**Cholera infantum.** A common, noncontagious diarrhea of young children, occurring in summer or autumn. In the nineteenth century, it was considered indigenous to the United States; was prevalent during the hot weather in most of the towns of the middle and southern states, as well as many western areas; and was characterized by gastric pain, vomiting, purgation, fever, and prostration. It was common among the poor and in hand-fed babies. Death frequently occurred in three to five days. Synonyms: *summer complaint*, weaning brash, water gripes, choleric fever of children, cholera morbus.

**Chorea.** Any of several diseases of the nervous system, characterized by jerky movements that appear to be well coordinated but are performed involuntarily, chiefly of the face and extremities. Synonym: Saint Vitus' dance.

**Chronic.** Persisting over a long period of time as opposed to acute or sudden. This word was often the only one entered under "cause of death" in the mortality schedules. The actual disease meant by the term is open to speculation.

**Colic.** Paroxysmal pain in the abdomen or bowels. Infantile colic is benign paroxysmal abdominal pain during the first three months of life. Colic rarely caused death; but in the [nineteenth] century a study reported that in cases of death, *intussusception* (the prolapse of one part of the intestine into the lumen of an immediately adjoining part) occasionally occurred. Renal colic can occur from disease in the kidney, gallstone colic from a stone in the bile duct.

**Congestion.** An excessive or abnormal accumulation of the blood or other fluid in a body part or blood vessel. In congestive fever (a febrile disease characterized from its onset by "strongly-marked symptoms of deep internal congestion, and a great oppression of the powers of life"), the internal organs become gorged with blood.

**Consumption.** A wasting away of the body; formerly applied especially to pulmonary tuberculosis. The disorder is now known to be an infectious disease caused by the bacterial species *Mycobacterium tuberculosis.* Synonym: *marasmus* (in the mid nineteenth century), *phthisis.*

**Convulsions.** Severe contortion of the body caused by violent, involuntary muscular contractions of the extremities, trunk, and head. See *epilepsy.*

**Coryza.** See *catarrh.*

**Croup.** Any obstructive condition of the larynx (voice box) or trachea (windpipe), characterized by a hoarse, barking cough and difficult breathing—occurring chiefly in infants and children. The obstruction could be caused by allergy, a foreign body, infection, or new growth (tumor). In the early nineteenth century, it was called *cynanche trachealis.* The crouping noise was similar to the sound emitted by a chicken affected with the pip, which in some parts of Scotland was called *roup*; hence, probably, the term croup. Synonyms: roup, *hives,* choak, stuffing, rising of the lights.

**Debility.** Abnormal bodily weakness or feebleness; decay of strength. This was a term descriptive of a patient's condition and of no help in making a diagnosis. Synonym: asthenia.

**Diphtheria.** An acute infectious disease caused by toxigenic strains of the bacillus *Corynebacterium diphtheriae,* acquired by contact with an infected person or carrier of the disease. It was usually confined to the upper respiratory tract (throat) and characterized by the formation of a tough membrane (false membrane) attached firmly to the underlying tissue that would bleed if forcibly removed. In the nineteenth century, the disease was occasionally confused with scarlet fever and *croup.* [Synonym: throat distemper.]

**Dropsy.** A contraction for *hydropsy.* Edema, the presence of abnormally large amounts of fluid in intercellular tissue spaces or body cavities. Abdominal dropsy is *ascites*; brain dropsy is *hydrocephalus*; and chest dropsy is *hydrothorax.* Cardiac dropsy is a symptom of disease of the heart and arises from obstruction to the current of blood through the heart, lungs, or liver. *Anasarca* is general fluid accumulation throughout the body.

**Dysentery.** A term given to a number of disorders marked by inflammation of the intestines (especially of the colon) and attended by pain in the abdomen, by tenesmus (straining to defecate without the ability to do so), and by frequent stools containing blood and mucus. The causeative agent may be chemical irritants, bacteria, protozoa, or parasitic worms. There are two specific varieties: (1) amebic dysentery caused by the protozoan *Entamoeba histolytica*; (2) bacillary dysentery caused by bacteria of the genus *Shigella.* Dysentery was one of the most severe scourges of armies in the nineteenth century. The several forms of dysentery and diarrhea accounted for more than one-fourth of all the cases of disease reported during the first two years of the Civil War. Synonyms: *flux, bloody flux*, contagious pyrexia (fever), frequent griping stools.

**Eclampsia.** A form of toxemia (toxins—or poisons—in the blood) accompanying pregnancy, characterized by albuminuria (protein in the urine), by hypertension (high blood pressure), and by convulsions. In the [nineteenth] century, the term was used for any form of convulsion.

**Edema.** See *dropsy.*

**Effluvia.** Exhalations or emanations, applied especially to those of noxious character. In the mid nineteenth century, they were called "vapours" and distinguished into the *contagious effluvia*, such as rubeolar (measles); *marsh effluvia*, such as miasmata; and those arising from animals or vegetables, such as odors.

**Emphysema, pulmonary.** A chronic, irreversible disease of the lungs, characterized by abnormal enlargement of air spaces in the lungs and accompanied by destruction of the tissue lining the walls of air sacs. By 1900 the condition was recognized as a chronic disease of the lungs associated with marked dyspnea (shortness of breath), hacking cough, defective aeration (oxygenation) of the blood, cyanosis (blue color of facial skin), and a full and rounded or "barrel-shaped" chest. This disease is now most commonly associated with tobacco smoking.

**Enteric fever.** See *typhoid fever.*

**Epilepsy.** A disorder of the nervous system, characterized either by mild, episodic loss of attention of sleepiness (*petit mal*) or by severe convulsions with loss of consciousness (*grand mal*). Synonyms: falling sickness, fits.

**Erysipelas.** An acute, febrile, infectious disease, caused by a specific *group A streptococcus bacterium* and characterized by a diffusely spreading, deep-red inflammation of the skin or mucous membranes causing a rash with a well-defined margin. Synonyms: Rose, Saint Anthony's Fire (from its burning heat or, perhaps, because Saint Anthony was supposed to cure it miraculously).

**Flux.** See *dysentery.*

**[French pox.** A venereal disease, usually syphilis.]

**Furuncle.** See *boil.*

**Gangrene.** Death and decay of tissue in a part of the body—usually a limb—due to injury, disease, or failure of blood supply. Synonym: *mortification.*

**Gleet.** See *catarrh.*

**Gravel.** A disease characterized by multiple small calculi (stones or concretions of mineral salts) which are formed in the kidneys, passed along the ureters to the bladder, and expelled with the urine. Synonym: kidney stone.

**Hectic fever.** A daily recurring fever with profound sweating, chills, and flushed appearance—often associated with pulmonary tuberculosis or *septic* poisoning.

**Hives.** A skin eruption of wheals (smooth, slightly elevated areas on the skin) which is redder or paler than the surrounding skin. Often attended by severe itching, it usually changes its size or shape or disappears within a few hours. It is the dermal evidence of allergy. See the discussion under *croup;* also called *cynanche trachealis.* In the mid nineteenth century, hives was a commonly given cause of death of children three years and under. Because true hives does not kill, croup was probably the actual cause of death in those children.

[**Hooping cough.** See *whooping cough*.]

**Hospital fever.** See *typhus*.

**Hydrocephalus.** See *dropsy*.

[**Hydrophobia.** Morbid fear of water caused by the bite of a rabid animal. See *rabies*.]

**Hydrothorax.** See *dropsy*.

**Icterus.** See *jaundice*.

**Inanition.** Exhaustion from lack of nourishment; starvation. A condition characterized by marked weakness, extreme weight loss, and a decrease in metabolism resulting from severe and prolonged (usually weeks to months) insufficiency of food.

**Infection.** The affection or contamination of a person, organ, or wound with invading multiplying, disease-producing germs—such as bacteria, rickettsiae, viruses, molds, yeasts, and protozoa. In the early part of the last century, infections were thought to be the propagation of disease by effluvia (see page 238) from patients crowded together. "Miasms" were believed to be substances which could not be seen in any form—emanations not apparent to the sense. Such miasms were understood to act by infection.

**Inflammation.** Redness, swelling, pain, tenderness, heat, and disturbed function of an area of the body, especially as a reaction of tissue to injurious agents. This mechanism serves as a localized and protective response to injury. The word ending -*itis* denotes inflammation on the part indicated by the word stem to which it is attached—that is, appendicitis, pleuritis, etc. Microscopically, it involves a complex series of events, including enlargement of the sizes of blood vessels; discharge of fluids, including plasma proteins; and migration of leukocytes (white blood cells) into the inflammatory focus. In the [nineteenth] century, cause of death often was listed as inflammation of a body organ—such as brain or lung—but this was purely a descriptive term and is not helpful in identifying the actual underlying disease.

[**Intemperance.** Alcoholism.]

**Intussusception.** The slipping of one part within another, as the prolapse of one part of the intestine into the lumen of an immediately adjoining part. This leads to obstruction and often must be relieved by surgery. Synonym: introsusception.

**Jail fever.** See *typhus*.

**Jaundice.** Yellow discoloration of the skin, whites of the eyes, and mucous membranes, due to an increase of bile pigments in the blood—often symptomatic of certain diseases, such as hepatitis, obstruction of the bile duct, or cancer of the liver. Synonym: icterus.

**Kidney stone.** See *gravel*.

**King's evil.** A popular name for *scrofula*. The name originated in the time of Edward the Confessor, with the belief that the disease could be cured by the touch of the king of England.

**Lockjaw.** Tetanus, a disease in which the jaws become firmly locked together. Synonyms: *trismus, tetanus*.

**Malignant fever.** See *typhus*.

**Marasmus.** Malnutrition occurring in infants and young children, caused by an insufficient intake of calories or protein and characterized by thinness, dry skin, poor muscle development, and irritability. In the mid nineteenth century, specific causes were associated with specific ages: In infants under twelve months old, the causes were believed to be unsuitable food, chronic vomiting, chronic diarrhea, and inherited syphilis. Between one and three years [of age], marasmus was associated with rickets or cancer. After the age of three years, caseous (cheeselike) enlargement of the mesenteric glands (located in the peritoneal fold attaching the small intestine to the body wall) became a given cause of wasting. (See *tabes mesenterica*.) After the sixth year, chronic pulmonary tuberculosis appeared to be the major cause. Marasmus is now considered to be related to *kwashiorkor*, a severe protein deficiency.

[**Measles.** A highly communicable virus characterized by catarrhal symptoms and by a typical eruption on the skin and mucous membranes of the mouth. It occurs usually in young children before adolescence. Incubation is about ten days; onset is gradual. Symptoms are loss of appetite, runny nose, drowsiness, gradual elevation of temperature, and cough. Eruption first begins on the face, extending to the body and the extremities. Synonyms: Rubeola, rubella.]

**Meningitis.** Inflammation of the meninges (the three membranes covering the brain and spinal cord), especially of the pia mater and arachnoid—caused by a bacterial or viral infection and characterized by high fever, severe headache, and stiff neck or back muscles. Synonym: brain fever.

[**Milk sickness.** A disease in cows transmitted to infants, especially those who were fed cow's milk. Symptoms were chills, vomiting, trembling, and gastrointestinal disorders.]

**Morbus.** Latin word for disease. In the last century, when applied to a particular disease, morbus was associated with some qualifying adjective or noun, indicating the nature or seat of such disease. Examples: *morbus cordis*, heart disease; *morbus caducus*, epilepsy or falling sickness.

[**Mortification.** See *gangrene*.]

**Neuralgia.** Sharp and paroxysmal pain along the course of a sensory nerve. There are many causes: anemia, diabetes, gout, malaria, syphilis. Many varieties of neuralgia are distinguished according to the part affected—such as face, arm, leg.

**Paristhmitis.** See *quinsy*.

[**Pellegra.** A deficiency disease of the body's failure to absorb niacin (nicotinic acid) or its amide (niacinamide, nicotinamide). May occur secondarily to gastrointestinal diseases and alcoholism. Symptoms in advanced cases are diarrhea, dermatitis, and mental symptoms.]

[**Pertussis.** See *whooping cough*.]

**Petechial fever.** See *typhus*.

[**Puerperal fever.** Septicemia following childbirth. Synonym: *childbed fever*. See *septicemia*.]

**Phthisis.** See *consumption*.

**Pleurisy.** Inflammation of the pleura, the membranous sac lining the chest cavity, with or without fluid collected in the pleural cavity. Symptoms are chills, fever, dry cough, and pain in the affected side (a stitch).

[**Poliomyelitis.** Inflammation of the gray matter of the spinal cord. Epidemics are seasonal, occurring in summer and fall. Children are more susceptible than adults. Infection is spread by direct contact, the virus probably entering the body via the mouth. Death is likely to occur in respiratory and bulbar types. Synonym: polio.]

**Pneumonia.** Inflammation of the lungs with congestion or consolidation—caused by viruses, bacteria, or physical and chemical agents.

**Pus.** A yellow-white, more or less viscid substance found in abscesses and sores, consisting of a liquid plasma in which white blood cells are formed and suspended by the process of inflammation.

**Putrid fever.** See *typhus*.

**Putrid sore throat.** Ulceration of an acute form, attacking the tonsils and rapidly running into sloughing of the fauces (the cavity at the back of the mouth, leading to the pharynx).

**Pyrexia.** See *dysentery*.

[**Rabies.** An acute infectious disease of mammals, including domestic animals such as dogs, cats, and cattle. Characterized by involvement of the central nervous system, resulting in paralysis and finally death. Symptoms include malaise, depression or intense excitement and aggressiveness, respiratory problems, vomiting, unusual salivation. Synonyms: *canine fever, hydrophobia*.]

[**Rickets.** A vitamin D deficiency that affects the absorption of calcium and phosphorus. A form of osteomalacia (softening of the bones) in children.]

**Quinsy.** A fever, or a febrile condition. An acute inflammation of the tonsils, often leading to an abscess; peritonsillar abscess. Synonyms: suppurative tonsillitis, cynanche tonsillaris, partisthmitis, sore throat.

[**Saint Anthony's Fire.** See *erysipelas*.]

[**Saint Vitus' Dance.** See *chorea*.]

**Scarlantina.** Scarlet fever. A contagious febrile disease, caused by infection with the bacteria *group A beta-hemolytic streptococci* (which elaborate a toxin with an affinity for red blood cells) and characterized by a scarlet eruption, tonsillitis, and pharyngitis.

**Scrofula.** Primary tuberculosis of the lymphatic glands, especially those in the neck. A disease of children and young adults, it represents a direct extension of tuberculosis into the skin from underlying lymph nodes. It evolves into cold abscesses, multiple skin ulcers, and draining sinus tracts. Synonym: *kings' evil*.

[**Scurvy.** A deficiency disease of vitamin C, usually resulting from a lack of fresh fruits and vegetables in the diet.]

**Septic.** Infected, a condition of local or generalized invasion of the body by disease-causing microorganisms (germs) or their toxins.

[**Septicemia.** Condition of absorbing septic products into the blood and tissues. Synonym: *blood poisoning*.]

**Ship fever.** See *typhus*.

[**Smallpox.** An acute, viral, contagious, febrile disease, the main symptom of which is the appearance of an eruption on the skin. Abrupt onset with chills, headache, intense back pain, elevated temperature, nausea, and vomiting. Synonym: variola.]

**Spotted fever.** See *typhus*.

**Suffocation.** The stoppage of respiration. In the nineteenth century, suffocation was reported as being accidental or homicidal. The accidents could be by the impaction of pieces of food or other obstacles in the pharynx or by the entry of foreign bodies into the larynx (as a seed, coin, or food). Suffocation of newborn children by smothering under bedclothes may have happened from carelessness as well as from intent. However, the deaths also could have been due to SIDS (sudden infant death syndrome), wherein the sudden and unexpected death of an apparently healthy infant, while asleep, typically occurs between the ages of three weeks and five months and is not explained by careful postmortem studies. Synonyms of SIDS: crib death and cot death. It was felt that victims of homicidal suffocation were chiefly infants or feeble and infirm persons.

**Summer complaint.** See *cholera infantum*.

**Suppuration.** The production of *pus*.

**Tabes mesenterica.** Tuberculosis of the mesenteric glands in children, resulting in digestive derangement and wasting of the body.

**Teething.** The entire process which results in the eruption of the teeth. Nineteenth-century medical reports stated that infants were more prone to disease at the time of teething. Symptoms were restlessness, fretfulness, convulsions, diarrhea, and painful and swollen gums. The latter could be relieved by lancing over the protruding tooth. Often teething was reported as a cause of death in infants. Perhaps they became susceptible to infections, especially if lancing was performed without antisepsis. Another explanation of teething as a cause of death is that infants were often weaned at the time of teething; perhaps they then died from drinking contaminated milk, leading to an infection, or from malnutrition if watered-down milk was given. [*Note*: Pasteurization of milk did not begin until 1914.]

**Tetanus.** An infectious, often-fatal disease caused by a specific bacterium, *Clostridium tetani*, that enters the body through wounds; characterized by respiratory paralysis and tonic spasms and rigidity of the voluntary muscles, especially those of the neck and lower jaw. Synonyms: *trismus, lockjaw*.

[**Throat distemper.** See *diphtheria*.]

**Thrush.** A disease characterized by whitish spots and ulcers on the membrane of the mouth, tongue, and fauces caused by a parasitic fungus, *Candida albicans*. Thrush usually affects sick, weak infants and elderly individuals in poor health. Now it is a common complication from excessive use of broad-spectrum antibiotics or cortisone treatments. Synonyms: aphthae, sore mouth, aphthous stomatitis.

**Trismus nascentium or neonatorum.** A form of tetanus seen only in infants, almost invariably in the first five days of life, probably due to infection of the umbilical stump.

**Typhoid fever.** An infectious, often-fatal, febrile disease, usually occurring in the summer months—characterized by intestinal inflammation and ulceration caused by the bacterium *Salmonella typhi*, which is usually introduced by food and drink. Symptoms include prolonged hectic fever, malaise, transient characteristic skin rash (rose spots), abdominal pain, enlarged spleen, slowness of heart rate, delirium, and low white-blood cell count. The name came from the disease's similarity to typhus (see below). Synonym: enteric fever.

**Typhus.** An acute, infectious disease caused by several microorganism species of *Rickettsia* (transmitted by lice and fleas) and characterized by acute prostration, high fever, depression, delirium, headache, and a peculiar eruption of reddish spots on the body. The epidemic or classic form is louse borne; the endemic or murine is flea borne. Synonyms: typhus fever, malignant fever (in the 1850s), jail fever, hospital fever, ship fever, putrid fever, brain fever, *bilious fever*, spotted fever, petechial fever, camp fever.

**Virus.** An ultramicroscopic, metabolically inert infectious agent that replicates only within the cells of living hosts, mainly bacteria, plants, and animals. In the early 1800s, *virus* meant poison, venom, or contagion.

[**Whooping cough.** Also *hooping cough*. An acute, infectious disease with recurring spasms of coughing ending in a whooping inspiration. Synonym: pertussis.]

**Yellow fever.** An acute, often-fatal, infectious febrile disease of warm climates—caused by a virus transmitted by mosquitoes, especially *Aëdes aegypti*, and characterized by liver damage and jaundice, fever, and protein in the urine. In 1900 Walter Reed and others in Panama found that mosquitoes transmit the disease. Clinicians in the late nineteenth century recognized "specific yellow fever" as being different from "malarious yellow fever." The later supposedly was a form of malaria with liver involvement but without urine involvement.

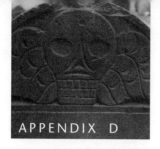

# A Case Study Using Obituaries as Family Histories

*Adapted by Katherine Scott Sturdevant from her forthcoming book* Organizing and Preserving Your Heirloom Documents *(Cincinnati: Betterway Books, 2002).*

O bituaries, particularly the Victorian, literary ones with the romantic prose about character and religion, can tell family history stories themselves. What follows is a group of seven obituaries from a single family. I transcribed them from clippings in a scrapbook that I acquired along with photographs and other memorabilia of this family in an antique store. The two granddaughters of the family had selected these things to consign for sale, on the grounds that these were irrelevant to their immediate families, being the possessions of remote relatives. I was pleased to acquire a family collection like this to use in the college classroom. By studying just these obituaries, I was able (and so were my students) to determine the basic family line of the women selling the heirlooms, all the way back to the immigrant ancestor. Read along, perhaps even jotting a few notes, as an exercise in the research value of obituaries.

Note: I slightly changed some surnames and some other identifying information in the recent years to protect the anonymity of the earlier owners.

## CASE STUDY

### Obituary

Edward Parker was born in Ireland in August, 1800, and died at the home of his son, Matthew Parker, May 28th, 1893. He was married to Sarah Davidson in 1825. To them were born nine children. Two of them died in infancy, all the rest live to mourn their father's death.

In 1832 Mr. Parker and family came to live in America, landing at Montreal, Canada, where they lived about one year. He then moved to Niagara County, N. Y. and settled on a farm where he lived for 40 years. His children having grown up and settled in the west, he and his wife concluded to spend their declining years near them. So in 1873 they came west and settled in Leland [Illinois]. His wife died in 1885. Since that time he has made his home among his children.

Mr. Parker, being persuaded of the truths of Christianity . . . died with a well grounded hope of heaven. His funeral sermon was preached at the home of Matthew Parker. . . .

❖ ❖ ❖

**Card of Thanks**
We and our families wish to express our sincere thanks to all our friends
who so kindly lent us their aid and sympathy during our late bereavement.

Matthew Parker.             Geo. Parker.
Ed. Parker.                 Richard Parker.

◊ ◊ ◊

**Death Calls Another Old Resident**
Matthew Parker, who came to Victor Township
in 1856, Passes Away Tuesday Morning

Matthew Parker was born in County Armagh, Ireland, Feb. 25, 1827,
and died April 16, 1912, at the age of 85 years, 1 month, and 21 days. In
1832 when five years of age he came with his parents, Edward and Sarah
(Davidson) Parker, to Montreal, Canada, reaching that city at a time when
the cholera was raging. After a residence of one year in the Dominion [of
Canada], they moved to Niagara county, New York.

In the fall of 1856 the deceased came to Illinois settling in Victor township, DeKalb county, where he purchased a farm and spent the greater part
of his life. May 13, 1860 he was united in marriage to Eliza Parker and had
he lived a few weeks longer would have celebrated their 52nd wedding
anniversary.

Of the four children born to Mr. and Mrs. Parker three survive, [M]ettie
and Lizzie of Sandwich and Mrs. Charles Bonney of Remington, Ind., and
one grandchild, who with the wife are left to mourn the loss of a kind father
and a loving husband.

Of a family consisting of six brothers and one sister, two brothers and
the sister survive, John, of Ransomville, New York, George, of Sandwich,
and Mrs. C. T. Archer, of Spencer, Iowa.

Mr. Parker, along with his family, united with the Congregational
Church, of Sandwich in 1901, and he was a regular attendant as long as his
health would permit.

He became a member of Leland [Masonic] lodge, A. F. & A. M., Aug.
19, 1868, and after moving transferred his membership to Meteor
Lodge. . . .

◊ ◊ ◊

**A Good Woman Called**
Eliza Parker was born in County Armagh, Ireland, September 3, 1826, and
died July 26, 1915, aged 88 years, 10 months, and 23 days.

She came to America with her parents in 1846 and settled in Niagara
county, New York.

She was married to Matthew Parker on May 13, 1860, and came to
Illinois the same year, settling on the farm north of Leland, where they lived
for forty years, moving to Sandwich in 1901. She was the mother of four
daughters, one of whom preceded her to the better world in infancy.

Her husband preceded her in death April 16, 1912.

She leaves to mourn their loss three daughters, Metta and Lizzie of Sandwich and Mrs. C. A. Bonney of Remington, Ind., and one granddaughter, all of whom were with her during her last sickness. She also leaves one brother and one sister and a host of other relatives and friends.

While of a retiring disposition, her thoughts and influence were always for the right, and it can truly be said she was a thoughtful loving mother and a good Christian woman. She joined the M[ethodist] E[piscopal] church when she was a girl and remained a member of that church until moving to Sandwich when she with her family united with the Congregational church. . . .

❖ ❖ ❖

### Funeral Rites Held for Miss Metta Parker
She Had Made Her Home Here For Thirty-Nine Years

Metta Parker, second daughter of the late Matthew and Eliza Parker, was born in Victor township, September 23, 1864, and passed away at the Woodward memorial hospital on July 10, 1940.

Her early life was spent at the farm in Victor and in Leland, receiving her education in the rural school and in the Leland public school. She received piano instruction from local teachers and later studied in Aurora and at Northwestern university in Evanston. As a result of this training she took her place in the musical activities of the community both as a teacher and as a performer.

In 1901, with her parents, she moved to Sandwich where she has since lived. She took an active part in Lotus chapter Eastern Star, for many years serving as treasurer. With her family she transferred her membership to the local Congregational church.

Though of a retiring disposition, she was loved and respected by all who knew her. She leaves to mourn her loss, two sisters, Lizzie with whom she lived, Mrs. Charles Bonney of Remington, Indiana; one niece Mrs. Harold Bunyan of Colorado Springs, Colorado, and many cousins and friends.

The funeral. . . .

❖ ❖ ❖

### Charles Bonney Dies Following Brief Illness
Funeral Services Were Held on Wednesday With Burial at Leland
[handwritten on clipping:] Mar. 8-1942

Charles Bonney, 74, a resident of this community for the past year and a half died at 9:30 o'clock Sunday evening at the home of his sister-in-law, Miss Lizzie Parker.

He was born near Cass, Illinois, on September 4, 1867, and when a lad accompanied his parents to Remington, Indiana, where he had made his home until coming to Sandwich. In October, 1908, he was united in marriage to Miss Emma Parker. One daughter, Elizabeth, was born to them.

He engaged in the grain business at Remington and was active in the affairs of the community, serving as township commissioner and as member of the school board. He was a member of the Masonic lodge.

Mr. Bonney was taken ill two weeks ago with a heart attack following a stroke of paralysis.

He is survived by his widow, one daughter, Mrs. Gerald Bunyan of Colorado Springs, Colorado, and one sister, Caroline Bonner of Remington, Indiana.

Funeral services. . . .

⬧·⬧·⬧

THURSDAY, APRIL 19, 1950 [handwritten correction to the 18th]
**Community Shocked By Sudden Death of Miss Lizzie Parker**
Suffered Stroke on Friday Evening; Dies During the Night
CHARTER MEMBER LELAND O.E.S.

The community was shocked Saturday morning to learn of the passing of Lizzie Parker. Her death came suddenly as the result of a stroke suffered the night before.

Lizzie Parker, daughter of Mr. and Mrs. Matthew Parker, was born on a farm in Victor township, March 25, 1867, and died at the hospital, April 8, 1950, having been preceded in death by her parents and two sisters.

Lizzie received her early education in the Parker school, graduating from Leland high school in 1889. The next ten years were spent teaching in rural schools and the Leland and Rollo public schools. In 1900 the family moved to Sandwich.

Miss Parker was a charter member of the Leland Chapter of Eastern Star. Last October Lotus Chapter honored her at their golden anniversary celebration as a Past Matron and with a fifty year membership certificate. She enjoyed an active part in the work and fellowship of the Congregational church.

A life of service and devotion is a testimonial to her understanding of the Christian principles of faith, love, purity, justice and truth. Because of a personality which endeared her to all, she will be greatly missed by friends and neighbors and especially her sister, Mrs. Charles Bonney with whom she made her home and her niece's family, Mr. and Mrs. Gerald Bunyan, [and their daughters] Elizabeth and Ellen.

⬧·⬧·⬧

[From the Colorado Springs, Colorado, *Gazette-Telegraph*, 1994, clipped by one of my students and mailed to me, after a class project studying the scrapbook obituaries.]

ELIZABETH BONNEY BUNYAN, 84, a Colorado Springs homemaker, died . . . at a local nursing home.

A memorial service will be held. . . .

Mrs. Bunyan was born . . . 1909 in Remington, Ind., to Charles and Emma (Parker) Bonney. She was married . . . 1938, in Colorado Springs to Gerald Bunyan who is deceased.

She is survived by two daughters, Elizabeth and Ellen, [both married], and four grandchildren.

Mrs. Bunyan received a master's degree in music from Northwestern University. She was [an active volunteer in community organizations dedicated to women's education, hospitals, and her church.] She had lived in Colorado Springs since 1938. . . .

Even though the descendants sold the scrapbook in the antique store, thinking it was part of "remote" family memorabilia, my students and I could have drawn some genealogical charts for them from just these obituaries. The scrapbook contents trace the Parkers back to their Irish immigrant ancestors, thus even achieving the dream of many genealogists, crossing the ocean with their research. Certainly all newspaper information needs genealogical verification in other sources, but the basic line is clear.

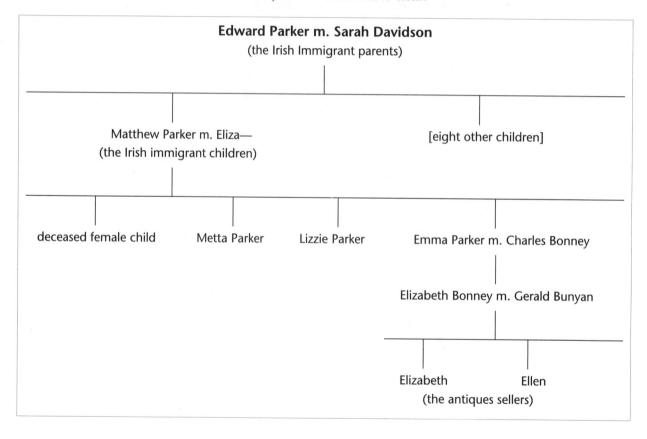

**Edward Parker m. Sarah Davidson**
(the Irish Immigrant parents)

Matthew Parker m. Eliza—
(the Irish immigrant children)

[eight other children]

deceased female child          Metta Parker          Lizzie Parker          Emma Parker m. Charles Bonney

Elizabeth Bonney m. Gerald Bunyan

Elizabeth          Ellen
(the antiques sellers)

What social history lessons or clues did you learn from these obituaries that might lead to more research? Here are some, combined with knowledge of my own that I have italicized to distinguish it from what was available in the obituaries.

- Multiple families of Irish immigrants came through Canada in the 1830s and settled in western New York. *This was common because Canada offered easier immigration and naturalization to the Irish, during the pre-famine era, to attract labor. Many families moved into New England from there.*

- The same families moved west to Illinois to continue farming. *This was also a very common migration pattern from western New York.*
- Their patterns were to form small rural towns that grew into larger towns. *This was typical of the New England Yankee migration, even with Irish followers.*
- They educated their children first in rural schools, perhaps on their own land (the Parker school) and then in town public schools and high schools. *The country school was common, and the other family documents attest to the children's school activities being very important in a small town.*
- They were active in the Masonic Lodge and the Eastern Star. *Again, this was the social life of their time and place, but would not have been so likely had they been Irish Catholic. There was also a strong background connection between being an Orangeman in County Armagh, circa 1790s–1820s, and being a Mason.*
- Child mortality was a sad fact of their lives. They remembered their lost children. *The Victorians were very sentimental on this score.*
- Although Irish immigrants might most often have been Roman Catholics, these joined Methodist Episcopal and Congregational churches. *They were northern Irish, plus they arrived in western New York during the Second Great Awakening. The Congregational Church was the old home-grown heir to Puritanism, central to Yankee towns, and the M.E. Church became popular during the Awakening.*
- Some daughters remained spinsters, although women's education was important. Even if they had "retiring dispositions," these women were teachers with music degrees from Northwestern University. They performed programs for the community. *Women's history teaches us that this role for spinsters was common.*
- The style of obituaries certainly changed. *Modern ones are disappointing.*
- Individuals in the 1800s lived through illness and death at home. By the mid-1900s we see the first hospitals and, by 1994, a nursing home. *Note how the family members went to each other's aid in early years, living together. One reason the modern heirs were disposing of property was because their mother went into a nursing home.*

Finally, this case study shows how rich with genealogical and historical information old obituaries are. Clearly, if you have them in your family papers, do not discard them. If you do not have obituaries in your collection, consider researching old newspapers for them. Do not just look for death dates, but for all the clues to family history and family life that they hold.

# Appendix E: Cemetery Transcription Forms

## CEMETERY SURVEY FORM

Name of Cemetery: _____

Town, City, Community, Township: _____

Specific Location: _____

Cemetery Office Address: _____

Sexton or Caretaker's Name: _____

Cemetery Owner: _____

Date Cemetery Established: _____

First Burial: _____

*Type of Cemetery*

☐ church ☐ family ☐ country ☐ garden ☐ urban ☐ veterans ☐ memorial park ☐ potter's field ☐ pet

*Special Sections in this Cemetery*

☐ ethnic ☐ fraternal organizations ☐ veterans ☐ religious ☐ other

*Status and Condition of Cemetery*

☐ abandoned ☐ maintained, but no longer in use ☐ currently in use ☐ well maintained

☐ overgrown, but graves easily identifiable ☐ overgrown, graves difficult to find and read

☐ graves not identifiable, but burial site known to exist through tradition or research:

Explain: _____

*Size* (approx. number of graves or acreage): _____

*Cemetery enclosure* (type of fencing, if any): _____

*Cemetery gate* (describe and if more than one entrance): _____

*Markers* (check types found in this cemetery):

☐ upright headstones ☐ footstones ☐ grave houses ☐ false crypts ☐ mausoleums ☐ family markers

☐ flat markers set flushed with the ground

*Marker Composition* (check types found in this cemetery)

☐ slate ☐ marble ☐ granite ☐ sandstone ☐ limestone ☐ metal ☐ other

*Prominent Artwork on Markers in this Cemetery*

☐ skull variations ☐ soul effigy ☐ urn and/or willow ☐ lamb ☐ dove ☐ hands ☐ flowers

☐ archways, pillars, gates ☐ broken stems or branches ☐ fraternal symbols

*Historical or other remarks about the cemetery:* _____

_____

_____

_____

_____

Transcriber's Name: _____

Date: _____

Organization: _____

# HEADSTONE TRANSCRIPTION FORM

**Name of Cemetery:**
**Location of Cemetery:**
**Starting Point:** _____

| Row#/ Grave # | Headstone Inscription | Marker Description |
|---|---|---|
| | | Headstone Composition: _____<br><br>Foot Stone: _____<br><br>Artwork: _____<br><br>Grave Decorations: _____<br>Other: _____<br><br>Condition of Stone: _____<br>Condition of Inscription: _____<br>Direction of Grave: _____<br>Direction Inscription Faces: _____<br>Photograph Taken? ☐ Yes ☐ No |
| | | Headstone Composition: _____<br><br>Foot Stone: _____<br><br>Artwork: _____<br><br>Grave Decorations: _____<br><br>Other: _____<br><br>Condition of Stone: _____<br>Condition of Inscription: _____<br>Direction of Grave: _____<br>Direction Inscription Faces: _____<br>Photograph Taken? ☐ Yes ☐ No |
| | | Headstone Composition: _____<br><br>Foot Stone: _____<br><br>Artwork: _____<br><br>Grave Decorations: _____<br><br>Other: _____<br><br>Condition of Stone: _____<br>Condition of Inscription: _____<br>Direction of Grave: _____<br>Direction Inscription Faces: _____<br>Photograph Taken? ☐ Yes ☐ No |

# Bibliography

Adams, Randy. *Eternal Prairie: Exploring Rural Cemeteries of the West.* Calgary: Fifth House Publishers, 1999.

*American Blue Book of Funeral Directors.* New York: The American Funeral Director, published every even-numbered year.

Ardolina, Rosemary M. "Cemetery Strategies: Some Lessons Learned at Calvary Cemetery in New York City." *The Irish at Home and Abroad* 3 (1995/1996): 104–107.

Baker, F. Joanne, Daniel Farber, and Anne G. Giesecke. "Recording Cemetery Data." *Markers* I (the journal of the Association for Gravestone Studies) (1980): 99–117.

Benes, Peter. *The Masks of Orthodoxy: Folk Gravestone Carving in Plymouth County, Massachusetts, 1689–1805.* Amherst: University of Massachusetts Press, 1977.

Bergman, Edward F. *Woodlawn Remembers: Cemetery of American History.* Utica, N.Y.: North Country Books, Inc., 1988.

Bliss, Harry A. *Memorial Art, Ancient and Modern.* Buffalo, N.Y.: the author, 1912.

Bouchard, Betty J. *Our Silent Neighbors: A Study of Gravestones in the Olde Salem Area.* Salem, Mass.: T.B.S. Enterprises, 1991.

Brigham, Clarence. *A History and Bibliography of American Newspapers, 1690–1820.* 2 vols. Worcester, Mass.: American Antiquarian Society, 1947.

Brose, David A. "Treestump Tombstones in an Iowa Cemetery." *The Palimpsest* 70 (Summer 1989): 73–74.

Brown, John Gary. *Soul in the Stone: Cemetery Art From America's Heartland.* Lawrence: University of Kansas Press, 1994.

Brown, Randy, and Reg Duffin. *Graves and Sites on the Oregon and California Trails.* Independence, Mo.: Oregon-California Trails Assocation, 1998.

Burek, Deborah M., ed. *Cemeteries of the U.S.: A Guide to Contact Information for U.S. Cemeteries and Their Records.* Detroit, Mich.: Gale Research Inc., 1994.

Burns, Stanley B. *Sleeping Beauty: Memorial Photography in America.* Altadena, Calif.: Twelvetrees Press, 1990.

Burrell, David. "Origins of Undertaking: How Antebellum Merchants Made Death Their Business." 9 June 1998. http://dave.burrell.net/OofUnder.html.

Carmack, Sharon DeBartolo. "Carved in Stone: Composition and Durability of Stone Gravemarkers." *NGS Newsletter* 17 (May–June 1991): 69–70.

———. *Communities at Rest: An Inventory and Field Study of Five Eastern Colorado Cemeteries.* Simla, Colo.: privately published, 1993.

———. "Digging in Cemeteries." *Reunions* 1 (Spring 1991): 22–24.

———. "Grave Concerns." *Family Tree Magazine* 1 (October 2000): 34–39.

———. "There's More Here than Meets the Eye: A Closer Look at Cemetery

Research and Transcribing Projects," *Federation of Genealogical Societies' Forum* 7 (Fall 1995): 1, 16–17.

Carter, James Byars. "Disease and Death in the Nineteenth Century: A Genealogical Perspective." *National Genealogical Society Quarterly* 76 (December 1988): 289–301.

Chase, Theodore, and Laurel K. Gabel. *Gravestone Chronicles I and II*. Boston: New England Historic Genealogical Society, 1977.

Cicotello, Louis. "Cemetery Sculpture." Lecture presented at the University of Colorado, Colorado Springs, Fall 1987.

Coffin, Margaret M. *Death in Early America: The History and Folklore of Customs and Superstitions of Early Medicine, Funerals, Burials, and Mourning*. Nashville: Thomas Nelson, Inc., 1976.

Colman, Penny. *Corpses, Coffins, and Crypts: A History of Burial*. New York: Henry Holt and Co., 1997.

Crissman, James K. *Death and Dying in Central Appalachia: Changing Attitudes and Practices*. Urbana: University of Illinois Press, 1994.

Crosby, Alfred W. *America's Forgotten Pandemic: The Influenza of 1918*. Cambridge: Cambridge University Press, 1989.

Crowell, Elizabeth A., and Norman Vardney Mackie III. "The Funerary Monuments and Burial Patterns of Colonial Tidewater Virginia, 1607–1776." *Markers* VII (1990): 103–138.

Curl, James Stevens. *The Victorian Celebration of Death*. Gloucestershire, Eng.: Sutton Publishing, 2001.

Davies, Douglas James. *Death, Ritual, and Belief: The Rhetoric of Funerary Rites*. Washington, D.C.: Cassell, 1997.

Duval, Francis, and Ivan B. Rigby. *Early American Gravestone Art in Photographs*. New York: Dover Publishing, 1979.

"Earth Almanac: On Tombs, Pollution's Toll is Graven in Stone," *National Geographic* 179 (April 1991): 140.

Edgette, J. Joseph. "The Epitaph and Personality Revelation," in *Cemeteries and Gravemarkers: Voices of American Culture,* Richard E. Meyer, ed. Ann Arbor, Mich.: UMI Research Press, 1989.

Edwards, Linden F. *Body Snatching in Ohio During the Nineteenth Century*. Ft. Wayne, Ind.: Allen County Public Library, 1955.

Farrell, James J. *Inventing the American Way of Death, 1830–1920*. Philadelphia: Temple University Press, 1980.

Felt, Joseph B. *The Customs of New England*. Boston: Press of T.R. Marvin, 1853.

Fischer, David Hackett. *Albion's Seed: Four British Folkways in America*. New York: Oxford University Press, 1989.

Flexner, Stuart, and Doris Flexner. *The Pessimist's Guide to History*. New York: Quill, 2000.

Florence, Robert. *New Orleans Cemeteries: An Exploration of the Cities of the Dead*. New Orleans: Batture Press, 1997.

Forbes, Harriette Merrifield. *Gravestones of Early New England and the Men Who Made Them, 1653–1800*. Princeton: Pyne Press, 1955.

Foster, Gary S., and Richard L. Hummel, "Applications of Developing Technologies to Cemetery Studies." *Markers* XVII (2000): 111–123.

Frenza, Paula J. "Communities of the Dead: Tombstones as a Reflection of Social Organization." *Markers* VI (1989): 137–157.

Frommer, Arthur. "Where the Bodies Aren't Buried." Arthur Frommer's Budget Travel Online. www.frommers.com/destinations/neworleans/0020031939.cfm.

Gabel, Laurel K. "Ritual, Regalia, and Remembrance: Fraternal Symbolism and Gravestones." *Markers* XI (1994): 1–27.

*Gale Directory of Publications and Broadcast Media* (formerly *Ayer Directory of Publications,* Fort Washington, PA). Detroit, Mich.: Gale Research Co., annual.

Genealogical Institute, The. *How to Search a Cemetery.* Salt Lake City: The Genealogical Institute, 1974.

George, Diana Hume, and Malcolm A. Nelson. *Epitaph and Icon: A Field Guide to the Old Burying Grounds of Cape Cod, Martha's Vineyard, and Nantucket.* Orleans, Mass.: Parnassus Imprints, 1983.

———. "Resurrecting the Epitaph." *Markers* I (1979/1980): 85–95.

Gillon, Edmund Vincent Jr. *Early New England Gravestone Rubbings.* New York: Dover Publishing, 1966.

"Gravestones Record Air Pollution," *Association for Gravestone Studies Newsletter* 13 (Spring 1989): 6.

Green, Harvey. *The Light of the Home: An Intimate View of the Lives of Women in Victorian America.* New York: Pantheon Books, 1983.

Gregory, Winifred, ed. *American Newspapers, 1821–1936.* New York: H.W. Wilson Co., 1937.

Guttmacher, Alan F. *Bootlegging Bodies: A History of Body Snatching.* Ft. Wayne, Ind.: Allen County Public Library, 1955.

Habenstein, Robert W., and William M. Lamers. *The History of American Funeral Directing.* Rev. ed. Milwaukee: National Funeral Directors Association, 1962.

Halporn, Roberta. *New York Is a Rubber's Paradise: A Guide to Historical Cemeteries in the Five Boroughs.* Brooklyn, N.Y.: Center for Thanatology Research and Education, 1999.

Hansen, James L. "Research in Newspapers," in *The Source: A Guidebook of American Genealogy.* Rev. ed. Edited by Loretto Dennis Szucs and Sandra Hargreaves Luebking. Salt Lake City: Ancestry, 1997.

Hatcher, Patricia Law. *Abstract of Graves of Revolutionary Patriots.* 4 vols. Dallas, Tex.: Pioneer Heritage Press, 1987.

Helge, Janice, "Managing a Cemetery Project." Federation of Genealogical Societies' *Forum* 13 (Summer 2001): 11–14.

Hogg, Anne M., ed. *Virginia Cemeteries: A Guide to Resources.* Charlottesville: University Press of Virginia, 1994.

Holt, Dean W. *American Military Cemeteries: A Comprehensive Illustrated Guide to the Hallowed Grounds of the United States, Including Cemeteries Overseas.* Jefferson, N.C.: McFarland and Co., 1992.

Horton, Loren N. "Messages in Stone: Symbolism on Victorian Grave Markers." *The Palimpsest* 70 (Summer 1989): 62–72.

Howard, Jerry. "The Garden of Earthly Remains." *Horticulture* (September 1987): 46–56.

Howarth, Glennys, and Peter Jupp, eds. *The Changing Face of Death: Historical Accounts of Death and Disposal*. New York: St. Martin's Press, 1997.

Huber, Leonard V. *Clasped Hands: Symbolism in New Orleans Cemeteries*. University of Southwestern Louisiana, 1982.

Iserson, Kenneth V. *Death to Dust: What Happens to Dead Bodies?* Tucson, Ariz.: Galen Press, 1994.

Jackson, Kenneth T., and Camilo José Vergara. *Silent Cities: The Evolution of the American Cemetery*. New York: Princeton Architectural Press, 1989.

Jacobs, G. Walker. *Stranger, Stop and Cast an Eye: A Guide to Gravestones and Gravestone Rubbing*. Brattleboro, Vt.: Stephen Greene Press, 1973.

Jalland, Patricia. *Death in the Victorian Family*. New York: Oxford University Press, 1996.

Jarboe, Betty M. *Obituaries: A Guide to Sources*. 2d ed. Boston: G.K. Hall, 1989.

Jerger, Jeanette L. *A Medical Miscellany for Genealogists*. Bowie, Md.: Heritage Books, 1995.

Jones, Constance. *R.I.P.: The Complete Book of Death and Dying*. New York: HarperCollins, 1997.

Jones, Mary-Ellen. "Photographing Tombstones: Equipment and Techniques." Technical Leaflet 92. Nashville: American Association for State and Local History, 1977.

Jordon, Terry G. *Texas Graveyards: A Cultural Legacy*. Austin: University of Texas Press, 1982.

Kaufman, Martin, and Leslie L. Hanawalt. "Body Snatching in the Midwest." *Michigan History* 55 (1): 23–40.

Keister, Douglas, and Xavier A. Cronin. *Going Out in Style: The Architecture of Eternity*. New York: Facts on File, 1997.

Knapp, Michael G., and Constance Potter. "Here Rests in Honored Glory: World War I Graves Registration," *Prologue* 23 (Summer 1991): 190–193.

Kot, Elizabeth G., and James D. Kot. *United States Cemetery Address Book*. Vallejo, Calif.: Indices Publishing, 1994.

Kramer, Gloria J. *A Walking Guide to the Virginia City Cemeteries*. Reno, Nev.: the author, 1987.

Kraut, Alan M. *Silent Travelers: Germs, Genes, and the "Immigrant Menace."* New York: BasicBooks, 1994.

Kull, Andrew. *New England Cemeteries: A Collector's Guide*. Brattleboro, Vt.: The Stephen Greene Press, 1975.

Laderman, Gary. *The Sacred Remains: American Attitudes Toward Death, 1799–1883*. New Haven: Yale University Press, 1996.

Library of Congress. *Newspapers in Microform: Foreign Countries*. Washington, D.C.: Library of Congress, 1948 and supplements.

Library of Congress. *Newspapers in Microform: United States*, Washington,

D.C.: Library of Congress, Catalog Publications Divisions, 1948 and supplements.

Linden, Blanche M.G. "The Willow Tree and Urn Motif: Changing Ideas About Death and Nature." *Markers* I (1980): 149–155.

Ludwig, Allan I. *Graven Images: New England Stonecarving and Its Symbols, 1650–1815.* Middletown, Conn.: Wesleyan University Press, 1966, reprint 2000.

McGeer, William J.A. *Reproducing Relief Surfaces: A Complete Handbook of Rubbing, Dabbing, Casting, and Daubing.* Concord, Mass.: Minuteman Press, 1972.

Melnyk, Marcia. *The Genealogist's Question & Answer Book.* Cincinnati: Betterway Books, 2002.

Merrill, Kay R., ed. *Colorado Cemetery Directory.* Denver: Colorado Council of Genealogical Societies, 1985.

———. *Copying Cemeteries.* 2d ed. rev. Englewood, Colo.: 1982.

Meyer, Richard E., ed. *Cemeteries and Gravemarkers: Voices of American Culture.* Ann Arbor, Mich.: UMI Research Press, 1989.

———. *Ethnicity and the American Cemetery.* Bowling Green, Ohio: Popular Press, 1993.

Mills, Terry. "Interpreting Memorial Art." *Copper State Bulletin* 18 (Arizona State Genealogical Society) Spring 1983: 14–18.

Mitford, Jessica. *The American Way of Death Revisited.* New York: Alfred A. Knopf, 1998.

Moore, Lanny, and Jerry Oldshue. *Cemeteries and Local History: A Manual and Guide.* Tuscaloosa: The University of Alabama, n.d.

Murphy, Edwin. *After the Funeral: The Posthumous Adventures of Famous Corpses.* Secaucus, N.J.: Carol Publishing Group, 1995.

*The National Yellow Book of Funeral Directors.* Youngstown, Ohio: Nomis Publications, annual.

Newman, John J. "Cemetery Transcribing: Preparations and Procedures." Technical leaflet no. 9. Nashville: American Association for State and Local History (AASLH), 1971. Also published in the AASLH's *History News* 26 (May 1971): [97–108].

The *New York Times Index.* 1851–present. Published annually since 1913.

The *New York Times Obituaries Index,* 1858–1968; suppl. 1969–1978.

Nishiura, Elizabeth, ed. *American Battle Monuments: A Guide to Military Cemeteries and Monuments Maintained by the American Battle Monuments Commission.* Detroit, Mich.: Omnigraphics, 1989.

Nolan, Ann, and Keith A. Buckley. *Indiana Stonecarver: The Story of Thomas R. Reding.* Indianapolis: Indiana Historical Society, 1984.

Nutty, Coleen Lou. *Cemetery Symbolism of Prairie Pioneers: Gravestone Art and Social Change in Story County, Iowa.* Ames: Iowa State University, 1978.

Olderr, Steven. *Symbolism: A Comprehensive Dictionary.* Jefferson, N.C.: McFarland and Co., 1986.

*Personal Name Index to The New York Times Index*, 1851–1974; suppl. 1974–1993.

Pike, Martha, and Janice Gray Armstrong. *A Time to Mourn: Expressions of Grief in Nineteenth Century America.* Stony Brook, N.Y.: The Museums at Stony Brook, 1980.

Potter, Constance. "World War I Gold Star Mothers Pilgrimages." 2 parts. *Prologue* 31 (Summer 1999): 140–145, (Fall 1999): 210–215.

Powell, J.H. *Bring Out Your Dead: The Great Plague of Yellow Fever in Philadelphia in 1793.* New York: Time Life Books, 1949.

Prechtel-Kluskens, Claire. "Headstones of Union Civil War Veterans." Federation of Genealogical Societies *Forum* 11 (Spring 1999): 1, 27.

———. "Looking for the Gravestone of a Union Civil War Veteran?" *NGS Newsletter* 24 (May/June 1998): 226.

Quigley, Christine. *The Corpse: A History.* Jefferson, N.C.: McFarland and Co., 1996.

Ragon, Michel. *The Space of Death: A Study of Funerary Architecture, Decoration, and Urbanism.* Charlottesville: University Press of Virginia, 1983.

Ramsland, Katherine. *Cemetery Stories: Haunted Graveyards, Embalming Secrets, and the Life of a Corpse After Death.* New York: HarperEntertainment, 2001.

Reamy, Martha, and William Reamy. *Index to the Roll of Honor, With a Foreword and an Index to Burial Sites Compiled by Mark Hughes.* Baltimore: Genealogical Publishing Co., 1995.

Rees, Nigel. *Epitaphs: A Dictionary of Grave Epigrams and Memorial Eloquence.* New York: Carroll and Graf, 1994.

Regan-Dinius, Jeannie. "Preserving the Past for the Future: Indiana's Statewide Cemetery Registry." *The Hoosier Genealogist* 41 (June 2001): 78–83.

Ridlen, Susanne S. *Tree-Stump Tombstones: A Field Guide to Rustic Funerary Art in Indiana.* Kokomo, Ind.: Old Richardville Publications, 1999.

Rinhart, Floyd, and Marion Rinhart. *The American Daguerreotype.* Athens: The University of Georgia Press, 1981.

Roach, Marilynne K. *Gallows and Graves: The Search to Locate the Death and Burial Sites of the People Executed for Witchcraft in 1692.* Watertown, Mass.: Sassafras Grove Press, 1997.

Robinson, David, and Dean R. Koontz. *Beautiful Death: Art of the Cemetery.* New York: Penguin, 1996.

Rosenberg, Charles. *The Cholera Years: The United States in 1832, 1849, and 1866.* Chicago: University of Chicago Press, 1962.

Rothman, Sheila M. *Living in the Shadow of Death: Tuberculosis and the Social Experience of Illness in American History.* New York: BasicBooks, 1994.

Ruby, Jay. *Secure the Shadow: Death and Photography in America.* Cambridge: MIT Press, 2000.

Saxbe, William B. Jr. "Nineteenth-Century Death Records: How Dependable Are They?" *National Genealogical Society Quarterly* 87 (March 1999): 43–54.

———. "Non-Population Schedules, 1850–1880," *[Ohio Genealogical Society] Report* 24 (Spring 1984): 1–2.

Schafer, Louis S. *Best of Gravestone Humor.* New York: Sterling Publishing Co., 1990.

———. *Tombstones of Your Ancestors.* Bowie, Md.: Heritage Books, 1991.

Schmidt, Alvin J. *Fraternal Organizations.* Westport, Conn.: Greenwood Press, 1980.

Schorsch, Anita. *Mourning Becomes America: Mourning Art in the New Nation.* Clinton, N.J.: Main Street Press, 1976.

Scott, Ken. "Needlework Samplers and Mourning Pictures as Genealogical Evidence." *National Genealogical Society Quarterly* 67 (September 1979): 167–174.

Scott, Kenneth, abstracter. *Coroner's Reports, New York City, 1823–1842.* New York: The New York Genealogical and Biographical Society, 1989.

———. *Coroner's Reports, New York City, 1843–1849.* New York: The New York Genealogical and Biographical Society, 1991.

———. "Early New York City Coroner's Reports," *The New York Genealogical and Biographical Record* 119 (April 1988): 76–79; continued (July 1988): 145–150; (October 1988): 217–219; vol. 120 (January 1989): 18–20; (April 1989): 88–92.

Shultz, Suzanne M. *Body Snatching: The Robbing of Graves for the Education of Physicians in Early Nineteenth Century America.* Jefferson, N.C.: McFarland and Co., 1992.

Shushan, E.R. *Grave Matters.* New York: Ballantine Books, 1990.

Sloane, David Charles. *The Last Great Necessity: Cemeteries in American History.* Baltimore: Johns Hopkins University Press, 1991.

Smith, Elmer L. *Early American Grave Stone Designs.* Witmer, Penn.: Applied Arts, 1968.

Smith, Ronald G.E. *The Death Care Industries in the United States.* Jefferson, N.C.: McFarland and Co., 1996.

Spencer, Thomas E. *Where They're Buried: A Directory Containing More Than Twenty Thousand Names of Notable Persons Buried in American Cemeteries.* Baltimore: Clearfield Co., 1999.

Stannard, David E. *The Puritan Way of Death: A Study in Religion, Culture, and Social Change.* New York: Oxford University Press, 1977.

Strangstad, Lynette. *A Graveyard Preservation Primer.* Nashville: American Association for State and Local History, 1988.

Swan, Robert J. "Prelude and Aftermath of the Doctors' Riot of 1788: A Religious Interpretation of White and Black Reaction to Grave Robbing." *New York History* 81 (October 2000): 417–456.

Tashjian, Dickran, and Ann Tashjian. *Memorials for Children of Change: The Art of Early New England Stonecarving.* Middletown, Conn.: Wesleyan University Press, 1974.

U.S. Quartermaster's Department. *Roll of Honor: Names of Soldiers Who Died in Defence of the American Union, Interred in the National Cemeteries.*

Washington, D.C.: Government Printing Office, 1866–1868; reprinted in 10 vols. Baltimore: Genealogical Publishing Co., Baltimore, 1994.

Wallis, Charles L. *Stories on Stone*. New York: Oxford University Press, 1954.

Wasserman, Tamara E. *Gravestone Designs: Rubbings and Photographs From Early New York and New Jersey*. New York: Dover, 1972.

Watters, David H. *"With Bodilie Eyes": Eschatological Themes in Puritan Literature and Gravestone Art*. Ann Arbor, Mich.: UMI Research Press, 1981.

Weitzman, David. *Underfoot: An Everyday Guide to Exploring the American Past*. New York: Charles Scribner's Sons, 1976.

Wilkins, Robert. *Death: A History of Man's Obsessions and Fears*. New York: Barnes and Noble, 1990.

Williams, Melvin G. *The Last Word: The Lure and Lore of Early New England Graveyards*. Boston: Oldstone Enterprises, 1973.

Wilson, John S. "Purchase Delay, Pricing Factors, and Attribution Elements in Gravestones From the Shop of Ithamar Spauldin." *Markers* IX (1992): 105–131.

## Do You Have an Unusual Cemetery Story or Tombstone Photograph?

If you would like to share your cemetery stories or tombstone photographs for possible inclusion in the next edition of this book, please contact Sharon through her Web site at <www.sharoncarmack.com>.

# Index

# Explore your family history with Betterway Books!

*The Genealogist's Computer Companion*—Master the basics of online research and turn your computer into an efficient, versatile research tool. Respected genealogist Rhonda McClure shows you how, providing guidelines and advice that enable you to find new information, verify existing research, and save time. She also provides an invaluable glossary of genealogical and technical terms. *ISBN 1-55870-591-0, paperback, 192 pages, #70529-K*

*A Genealogist's Guide to Discovering Your Immigrant & Ethnic Ancestors*— Learn research techniques specific to your own ancestors' national and regional backgrounds. Sharon Carmack helps you to determine when your ancestors arrived in America, where they most likely settled, and what resources are available for further research. Includes plenty of friendly, authoritative advice to get you started and keep you on the right track. *ISBN 1-55870-524-4, paperback, 272 pages, #70462-K*

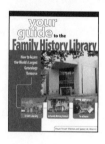

*Your Guide to the Family History Library*—The Family History Library in Salt Lake City is the largest collection of genealogy and family history materials in the world. No other repository compares for both quantity and quality of research materials. Written for beginning and intermediate genealogists, *Your Guide to the Family History Library* will help you use the library's resources effectively, both on site and online. *ISBN 1-55870-578-3, paperback, 272 pages, #70513-K*

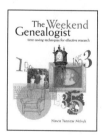

*The Weekend Genealogist*—Maximize your family research efficiency! With this guide, you can focus your efforts in searching for family documents while still gaining the best results. Organization and research techniques are presented in a clear, easy-to-follow format perfect for advanced researchers *and* beginners. You'll learn how to work more efficiently using family history facilities, the Internet—even the postal service. *ISBN 1-55870-546-5, paperback, 144 pages, #70496-K*

*These and other fine titles from Betterway Books are available from your local bookstore, online supplier or by calling (800) 448-0915.*